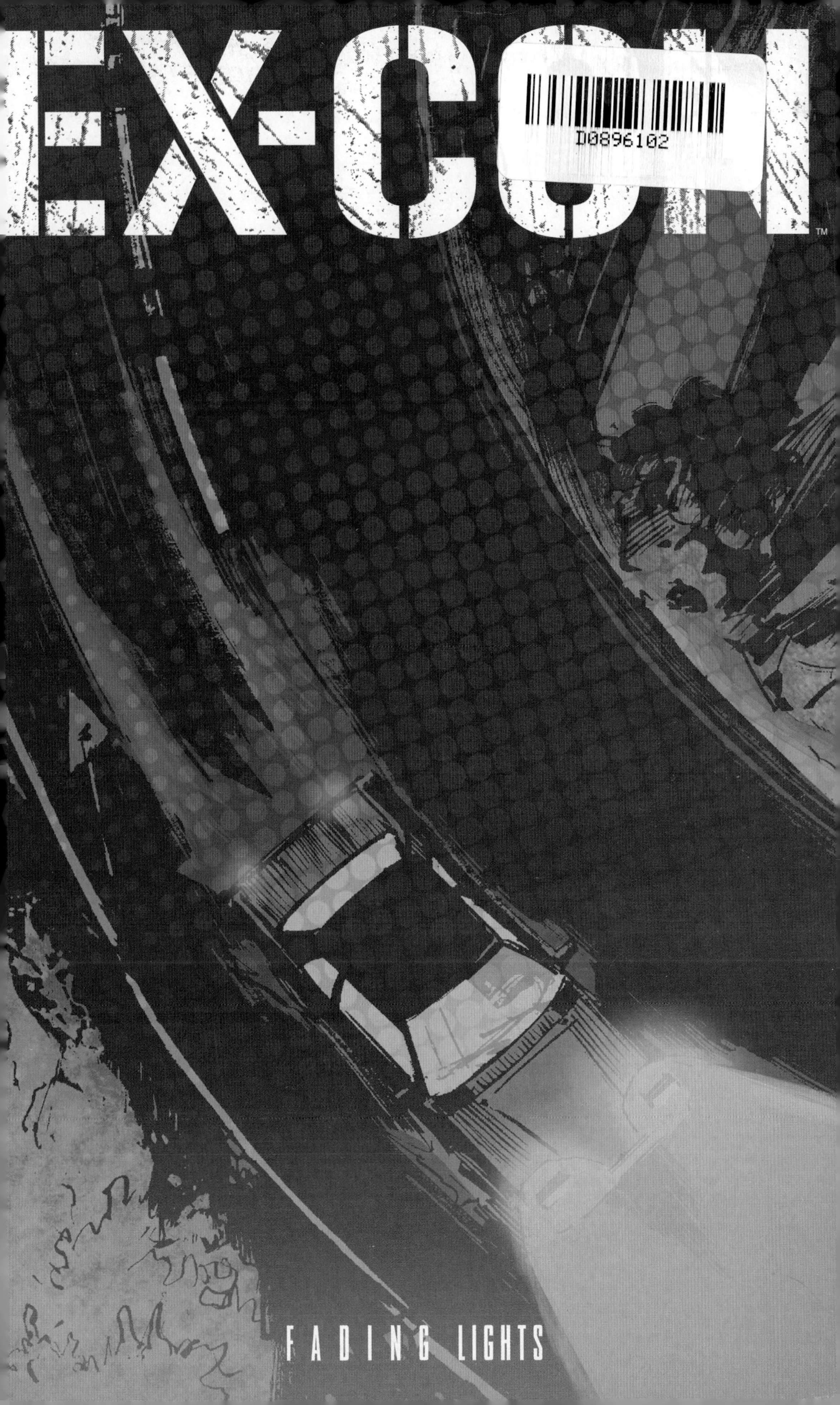
EX-CON™
FADING LIGHTS

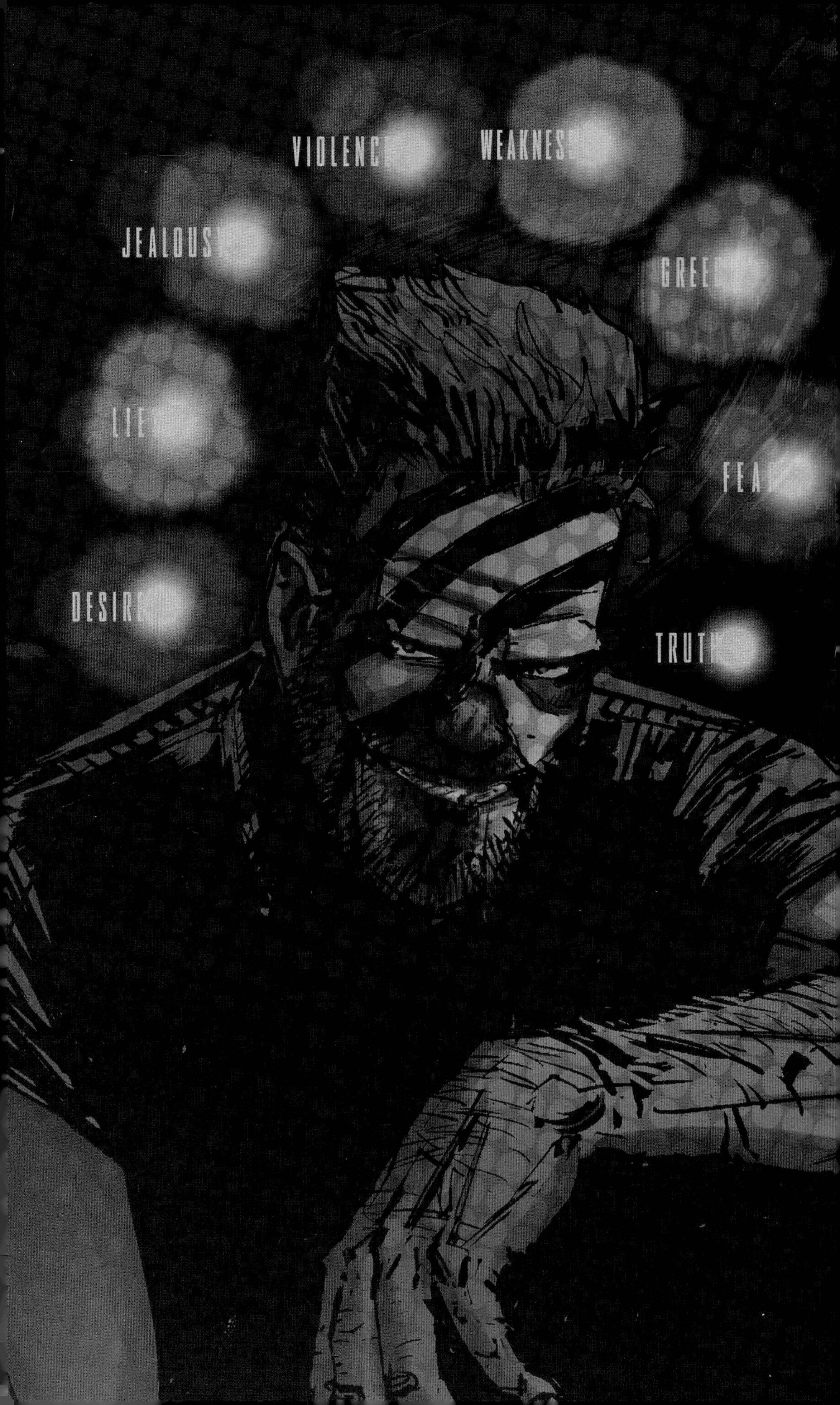
VIOLENC
WEAKNES
JEALOUS
GREE
LIE
FEA
DESIR
TRUT

EX-CON

FADING LIGHTS

WRITTEN BY
DUANE SWIERCZYNSKI

ILLUSTRATED BY
KEITH BURNS

COLORED BY
AIKAU OLIVA

LETTERED BY
ROB STEEN

COVER ART BY
TIM BRADSTREET

COLLECTION DESIGN BY
GEOFF HARKINS

DYNAMITE®

Nick Barrucci, CEO / Publisher
Juan Collado, President / COO

Joe Rybandt, Senior Editor
Hannah Elder, Associate Editor
Molly Mahan, Associate Editor

Jason Ullmeyer, Design Director
Katie Hidalgo, Graphic Designer
Chris Caniano, Digital Associate
Rachel Kilbury, Digital Assistant

Rich Young, Director Business Development
Keith Davidsen, Marketing Manager
Kevin Pearl, Sales Associate

Online at www.**DYNAMITE**.com
On Twitter @**dynamitecomics**
On Facebook **/Dynamitecomics**
On YouTube **/Dynamitecomics**
On Tumblr **dynamitecomics.tumblr.com**

ISBN-1-60690-695-X
ISBN-978-1-60690-695-8
First Printing
10 9 8 7 6 5 4 3 2 1

ONE

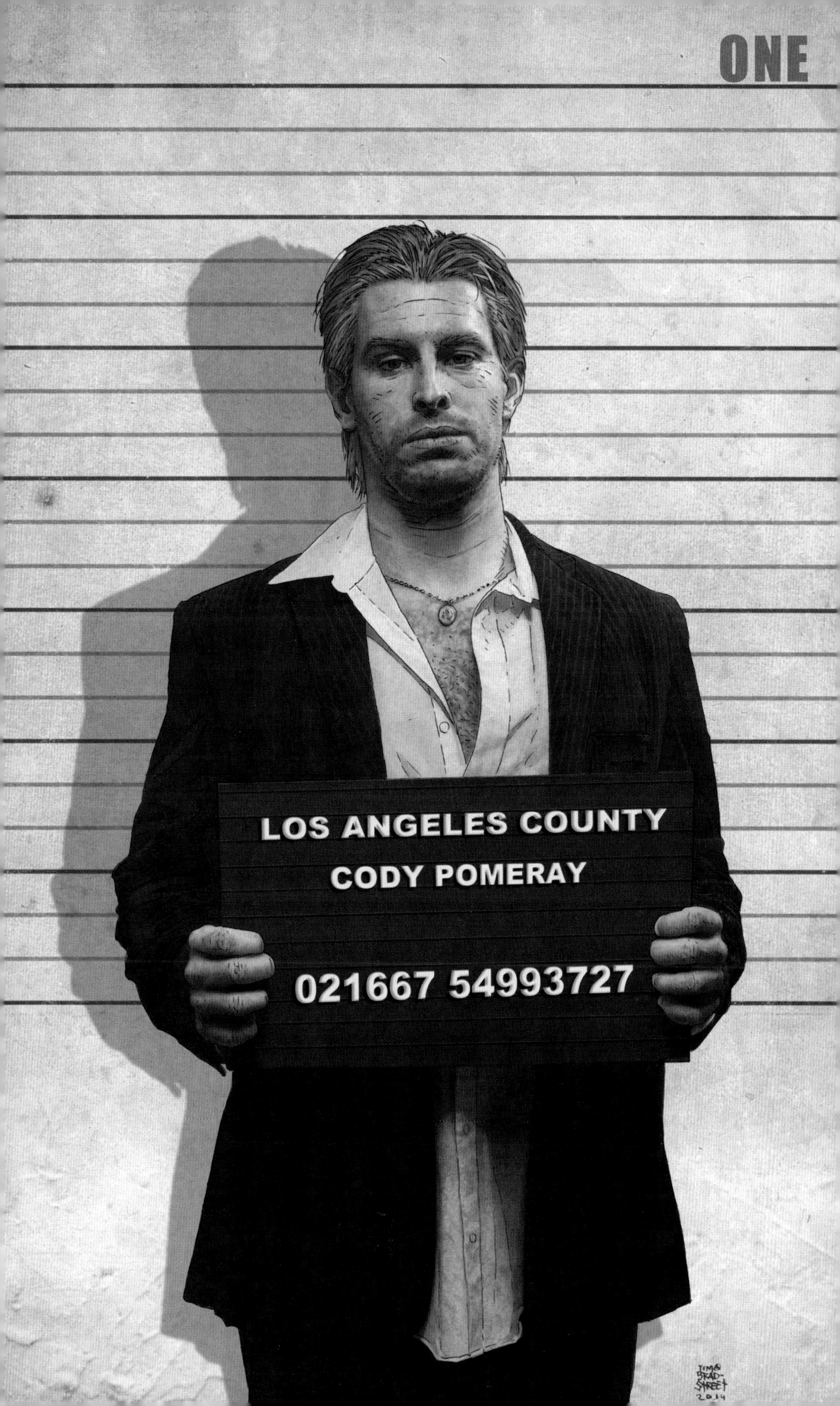
LOS ANGELES COUNTY
CODY POMERAY
021667 54993727
TIM BRADSTREET 2014

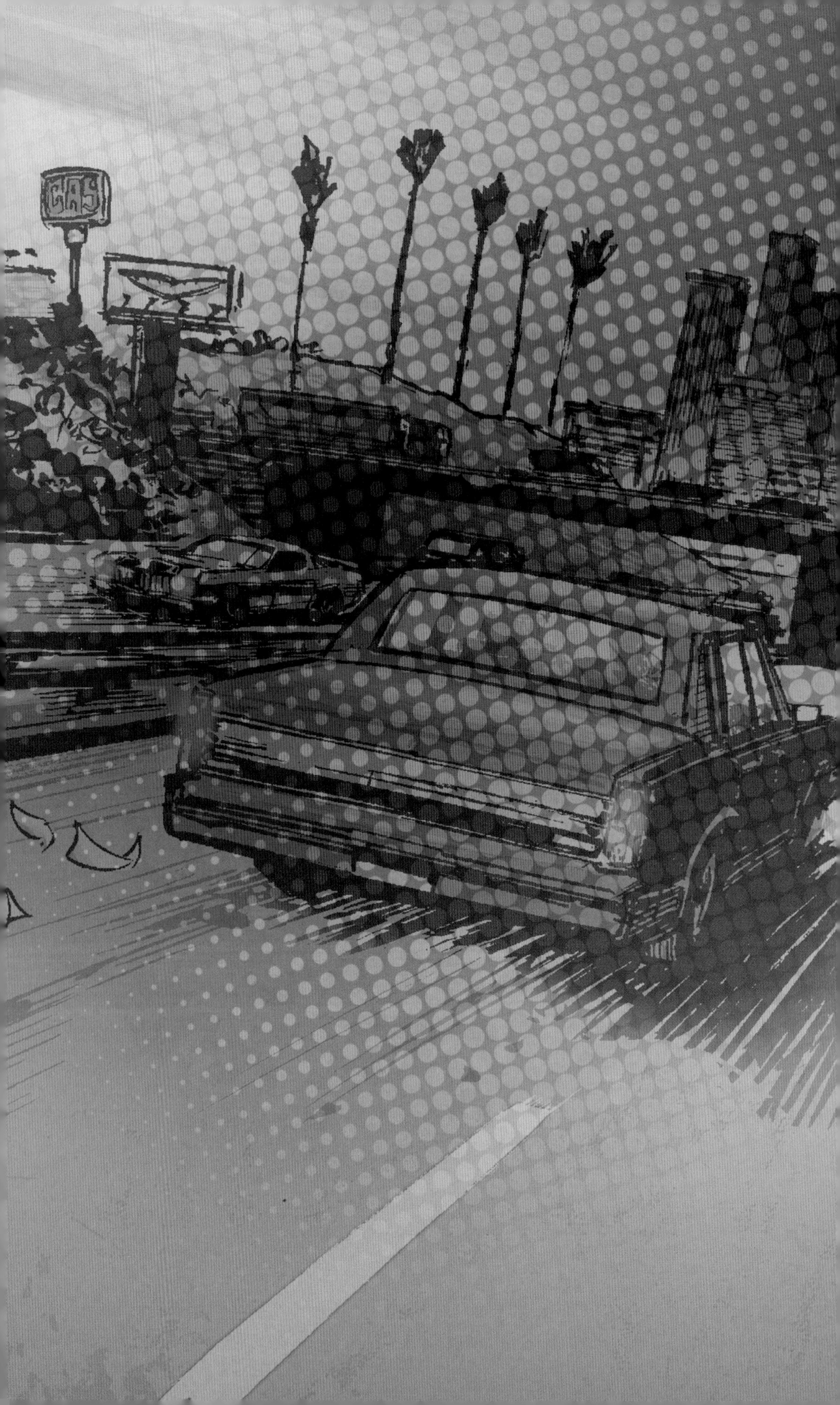
GAS

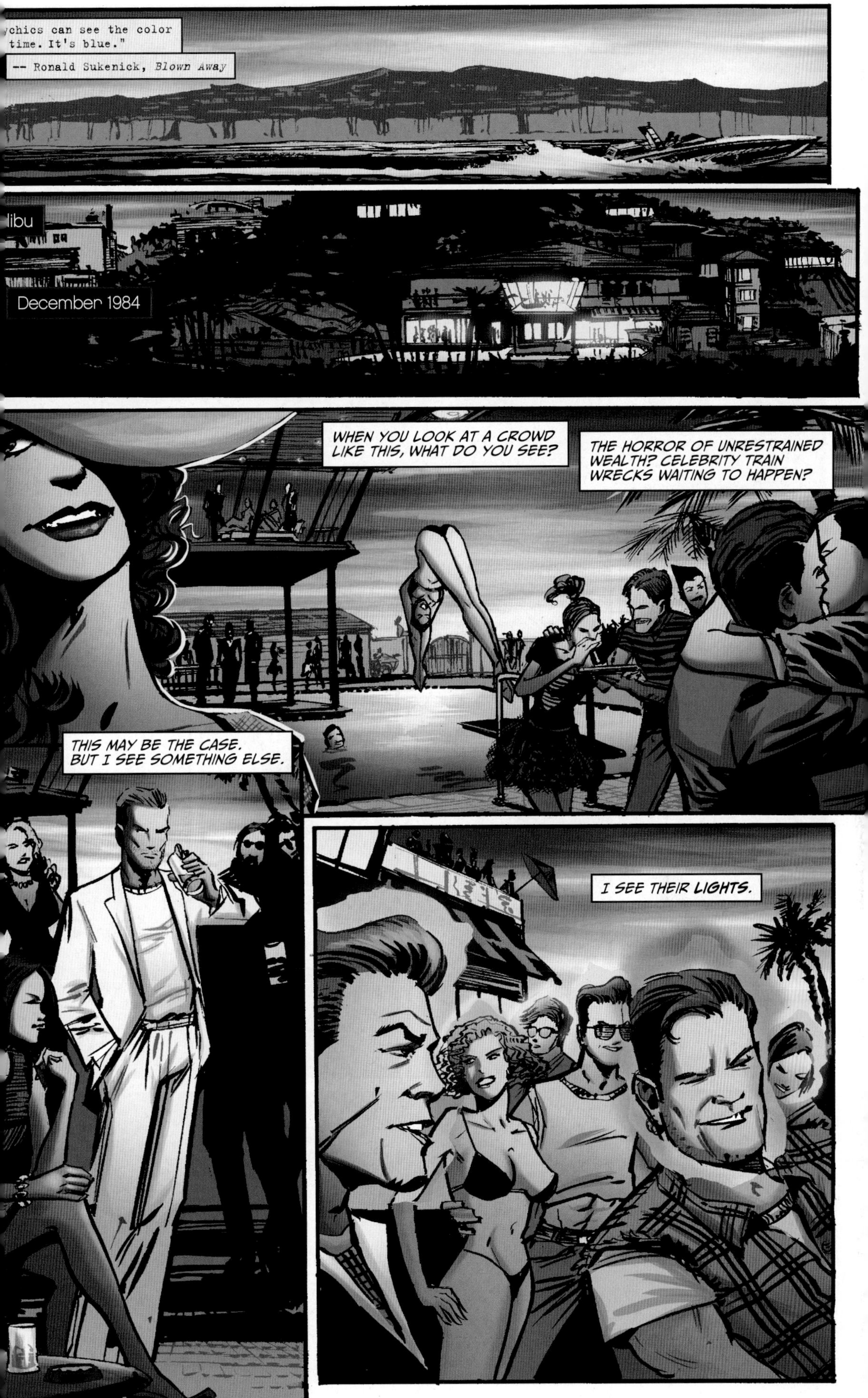
ychics can see the color
time. It's blue."
-- Ronald Sukenick, *Blown Away*
libu
December 1984
WHEN YOU LOOK AT A CROWD LIKE THIS, WHAT DO YOU SEE?
THE HORROR OF UNRESTRAINED WEALTH? CELEBRITY TRAIN WRECKS WAITING TO HAPPEN?
THIS MAY BE THE CASE. BUT I SEE SOMETHING ELSE.
I SEE THEIR **LIGHTS**.

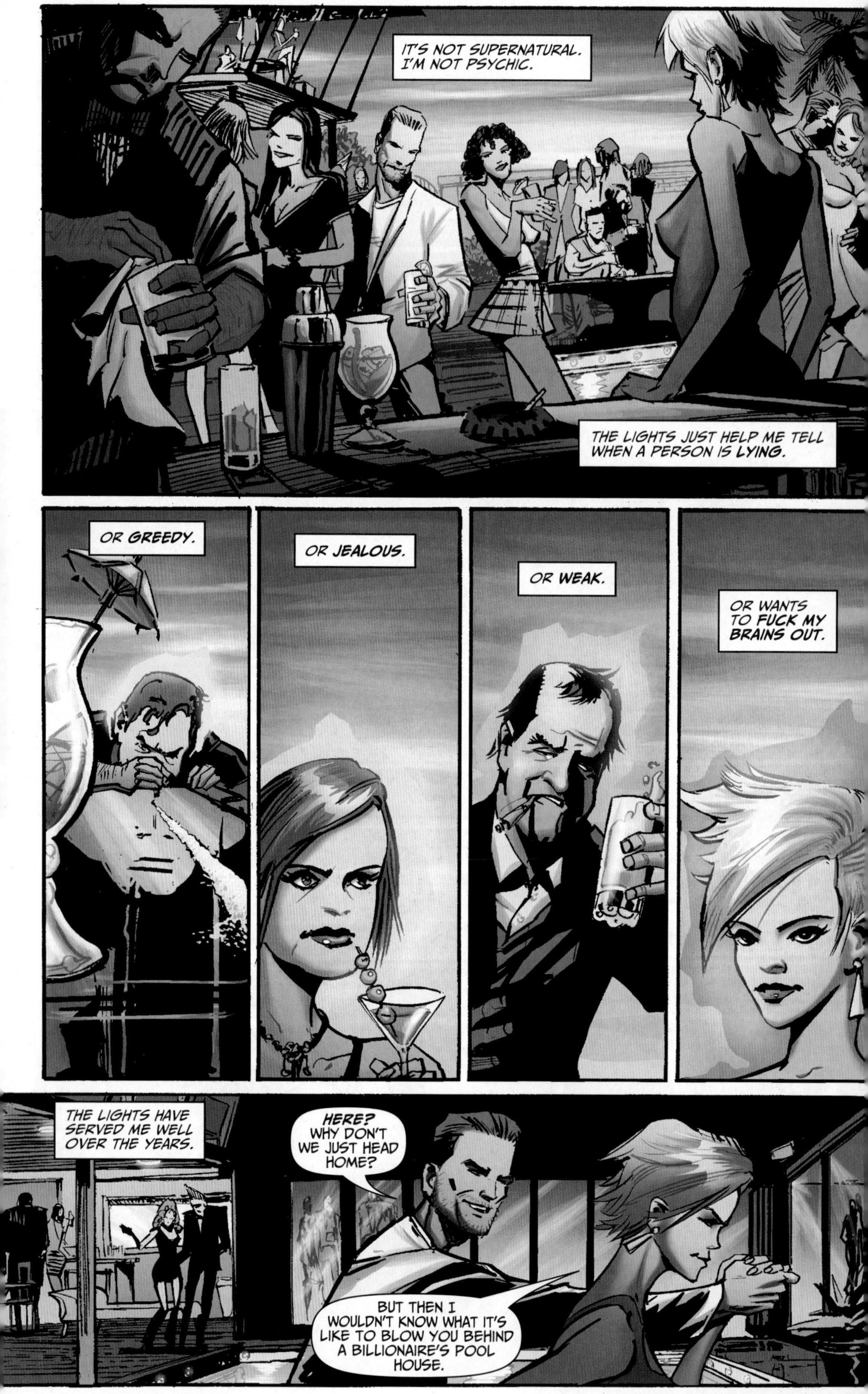
IT'S NOT SUPERNATURAL. I'M NOT PSYCHIC.
THE LIGHTS JUST HELP ME TELL WHEN A PERSON IS LYING.
OR GREEDY.
OR JEALOUS.
OR WEAK.
OR WANTS TO FUCK MY BRAINS OUT.
THE LIGHTS HAVE SERVED ME WELL OVER THE YEARS.
HERE? WHY DON'T WE JUST HEAD HOME?
BUT THEN I WOULDN'T KNOW WHAT IT'S LIKE TO BLOW YOU BEHIND A BILLIONAIRE'S POOL HOUSE.

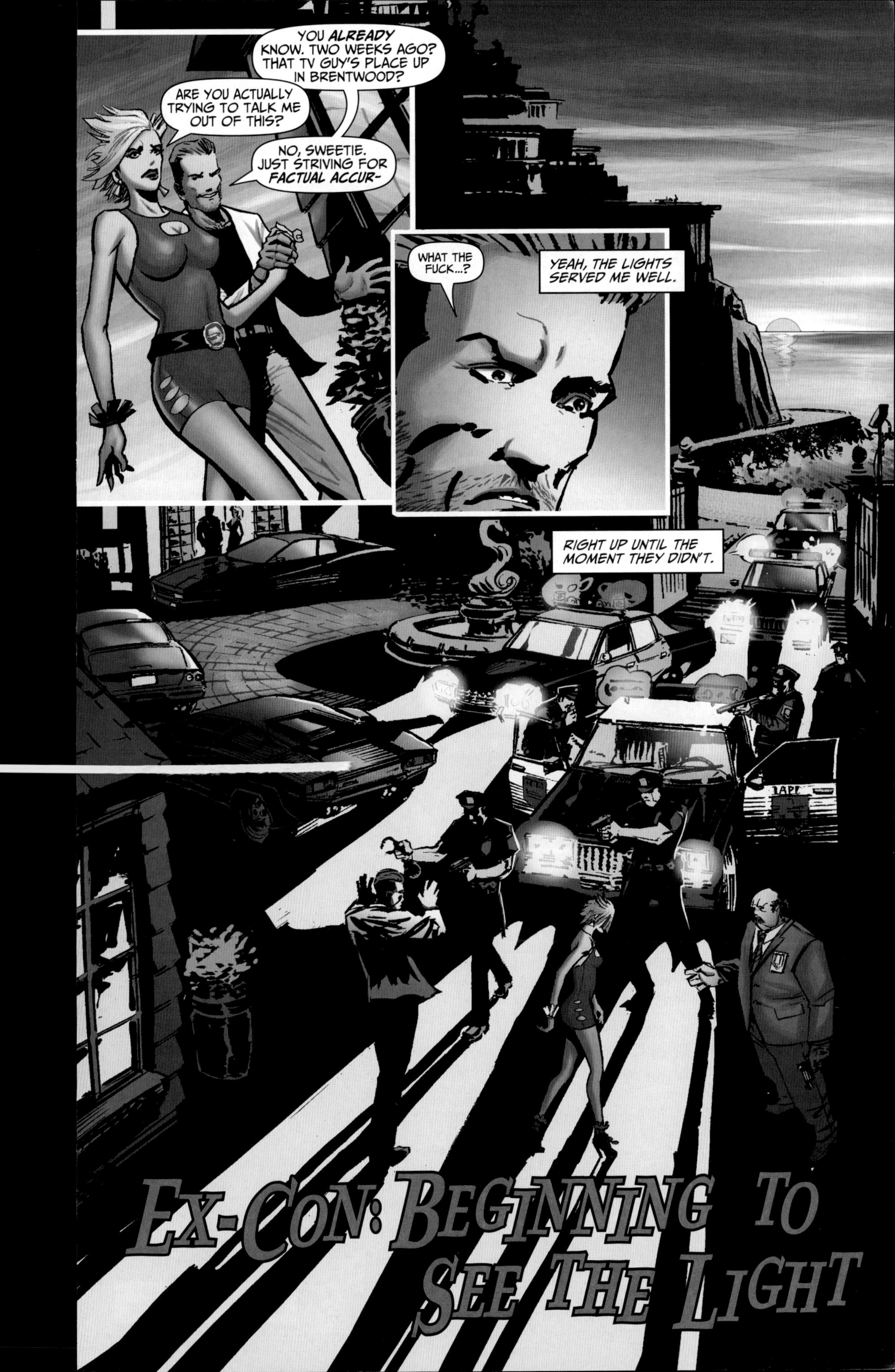

ARE YOU ACTUALLY TRYING TO TALK ME OUT OF THIS?
YOU ALREADY KNOW. TWO WEEKS AGO? THAT TV GUY'S PLACE UP IN BRENTWOOD?
NO, SWEETIE. JUST STRIVING FOR FACTUAL ACCUR-
WHAT THE FUCK...?
YEAH, THE LIGHTS SERVED ME WELL.
RIGHT UP UNTIL THE MOMENT THEY DIDN'T.
LAPD
EX-CON: BEGINNING TO SEE THE LIGHT

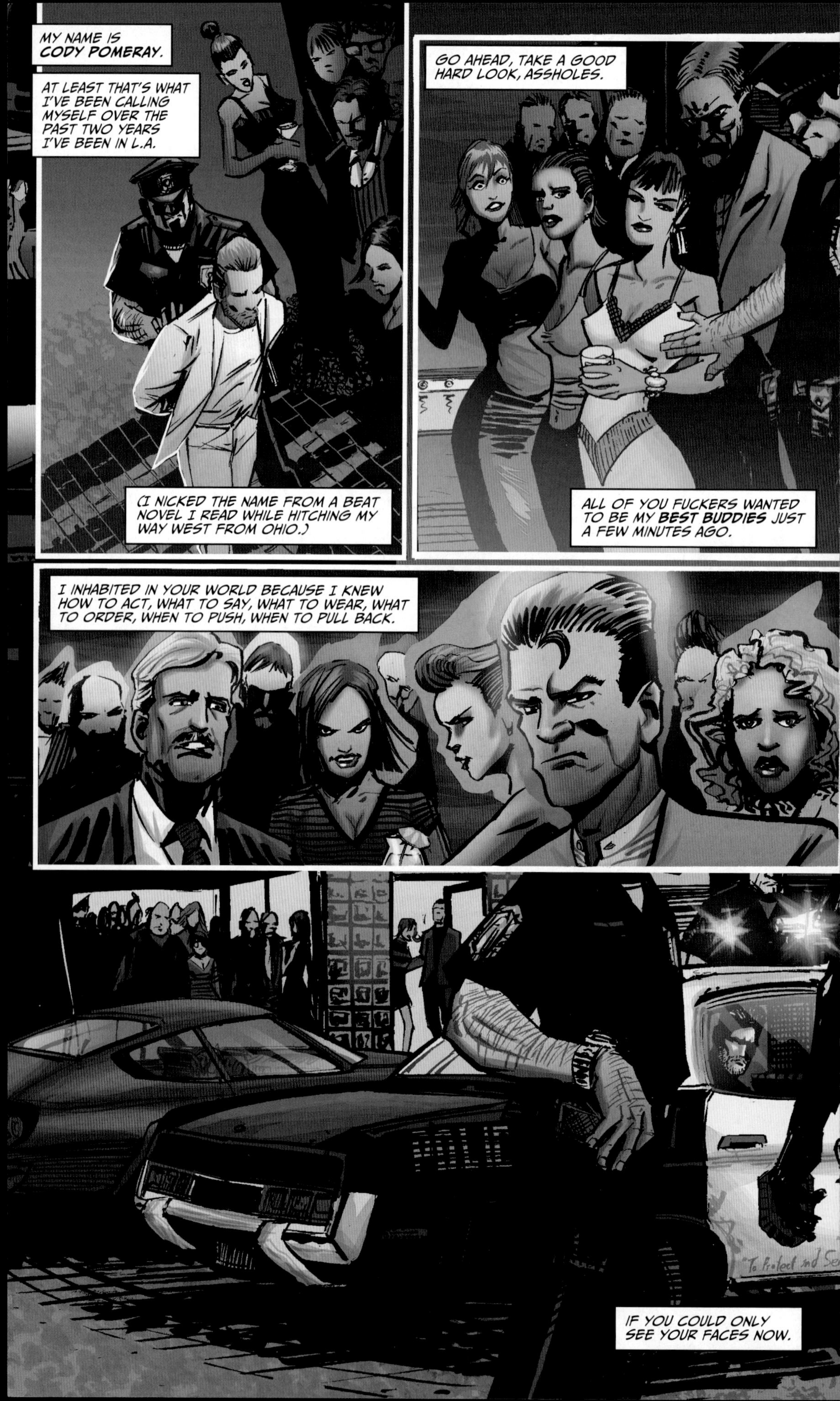
MY NAME IS **CODY POMERAY.**
AT LEAST THAT'S WHAT I'VE BEEN CALLING MYSELF OVER THE PAST TWO YEARS I'VE BEEN IN L.A.
(I NICKED THE NAME FROM A BEAT NOVEL I READ WHILE HITCHING MY WAY WEST FROM OHIO.)
GO AHEAD, TAKE A GOOD HARD LOOK, ASSHOLES.
ALL OF YOU FUCKERS WANTED TO BE MY **BEST BUDDIES** JUST A FEW MINUTES AGO.
I INHABITED IN YOUR WORLD BECAUSE I KNEW HOW TO ACT, WHAT TO SAY, WHAT TO WEAR, WHAT TO ORDER, WHEN TO PUSH, WHEN TO PULL BACK.
IF YOU COULD ONLY SEE YOUR FACES NOW.

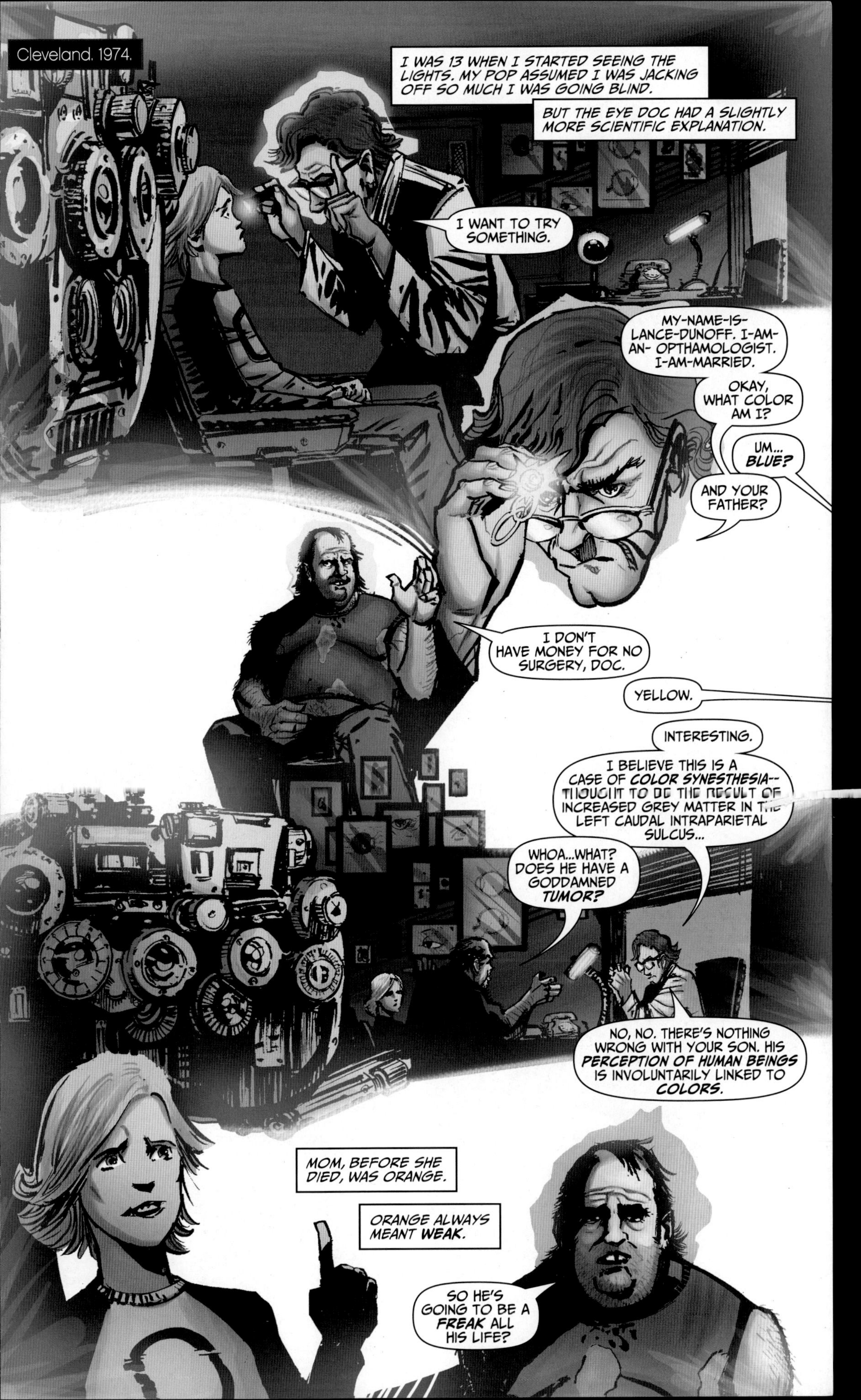

Cleveland. 1974.
I WAS 13 WHEN I STARTED SEEING THE LIGHTS. MY POP ASSUMED I WAS JACKING OFF SO MUCH I WAS GOING BLIND.
BUT THE EYE DOC HAD A SLIGHTLY MORE SCIENTIFIC EXPLANATION.
I WANT TO TRY SOMETHING.
MY-NAME-IS-LANCE-DUNOFF. I-AM-AN- OPTHAMOLOGIST. I-AM-MARRIED.
OKAY, WHAT COLOR AM I?
UM... BLUE?
AND YOUR FATHER?
I DON'T HAVE MONEY FOR NO SURGERY, DOC.
YELLOW.
INTERESTING.
I BELIEVE THIS IS A CASE OF COLOR SYNESTHESIA-- THOUGHT TO BE THE RESULT OF INCREASED GREY MATTER IN THE LEFT CAUDAL INTRAPARIETAL SULCUS...
WHOA...WHAT? DOES HE HAVE A GODDAMNED TUMOR?
NO, NO. THERE'S NOTHING WRONG WITH YOUR SON. HIS PERCEPTION OF HUMAN BEINGS IS INVOLUNTARILY LINKED TO COLORS.
MOM, BEFORE SHE DIED, WAS ORANGE.
ORANGE ALWAYS MEANT WEAK.
SO HE'S GOING TO BE A FREAK ALL HIS LIFE?

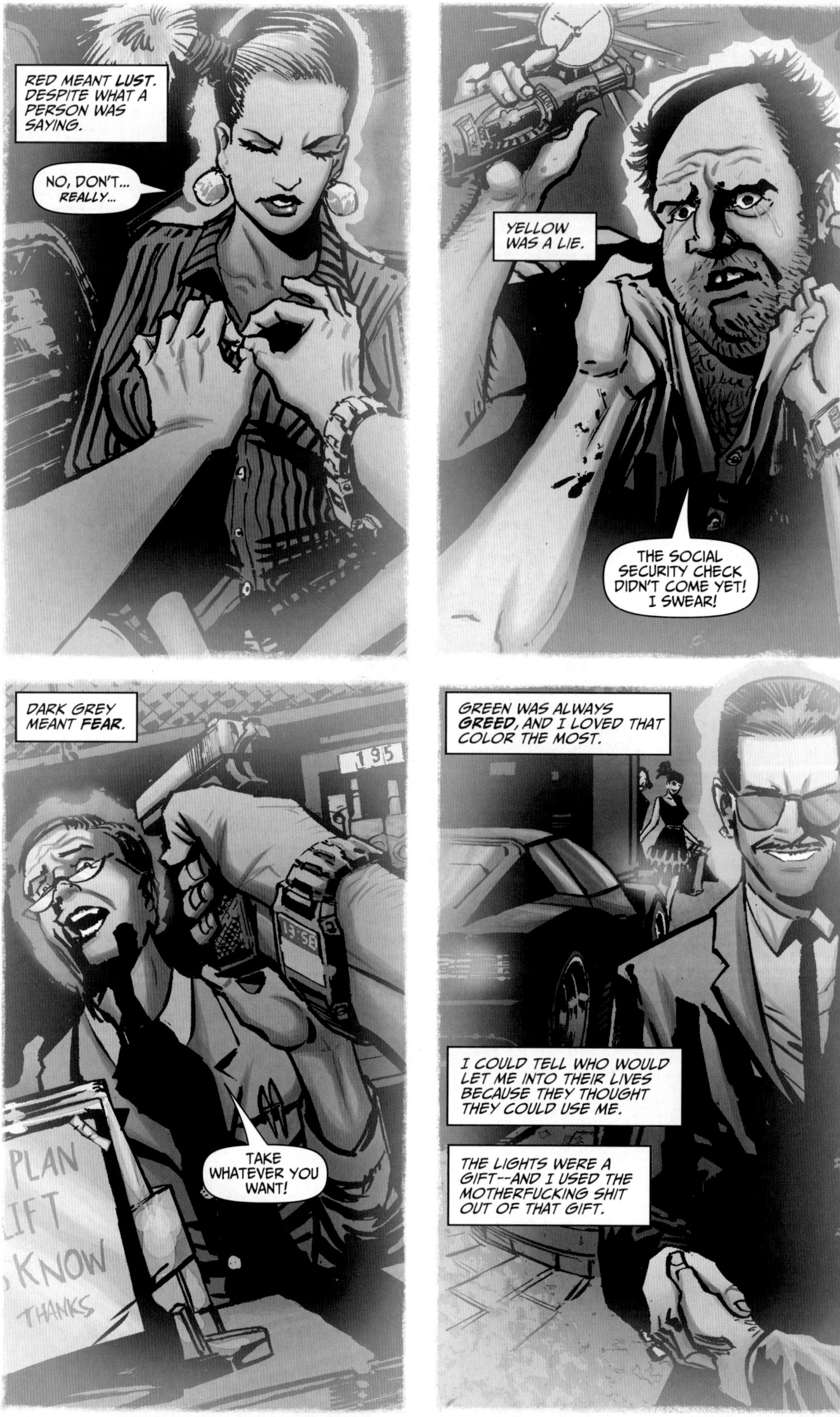
RED MEANT LUST. DESPITE WHAT A PERSON WAS SAYING.
NO, DON'T... REALLY...
YELLOW WAS A LIE.
THE SOCIAL SECURITY CHECK DIDN'T COME YET! I SWEAR!
DARK GREY MEANT FEAR.
135
13:58
TAKE WHATEVER YOU WANT!
PLAN
LIFT
KNOW
THANKS
GREEN WAS ALWAYS GREED, AND I LOVED THAT COLOR THE MOST.
I COULD TELL WHO WOULD LET ME INTO THEIR LIVES BECAUSE THEY THOUGHT THEY COULD USE ME.
THE LIGHTS WERE A GIFT--AND I USED THE MOTHERFUCKING SHIT OUT OF THAT GIFT.

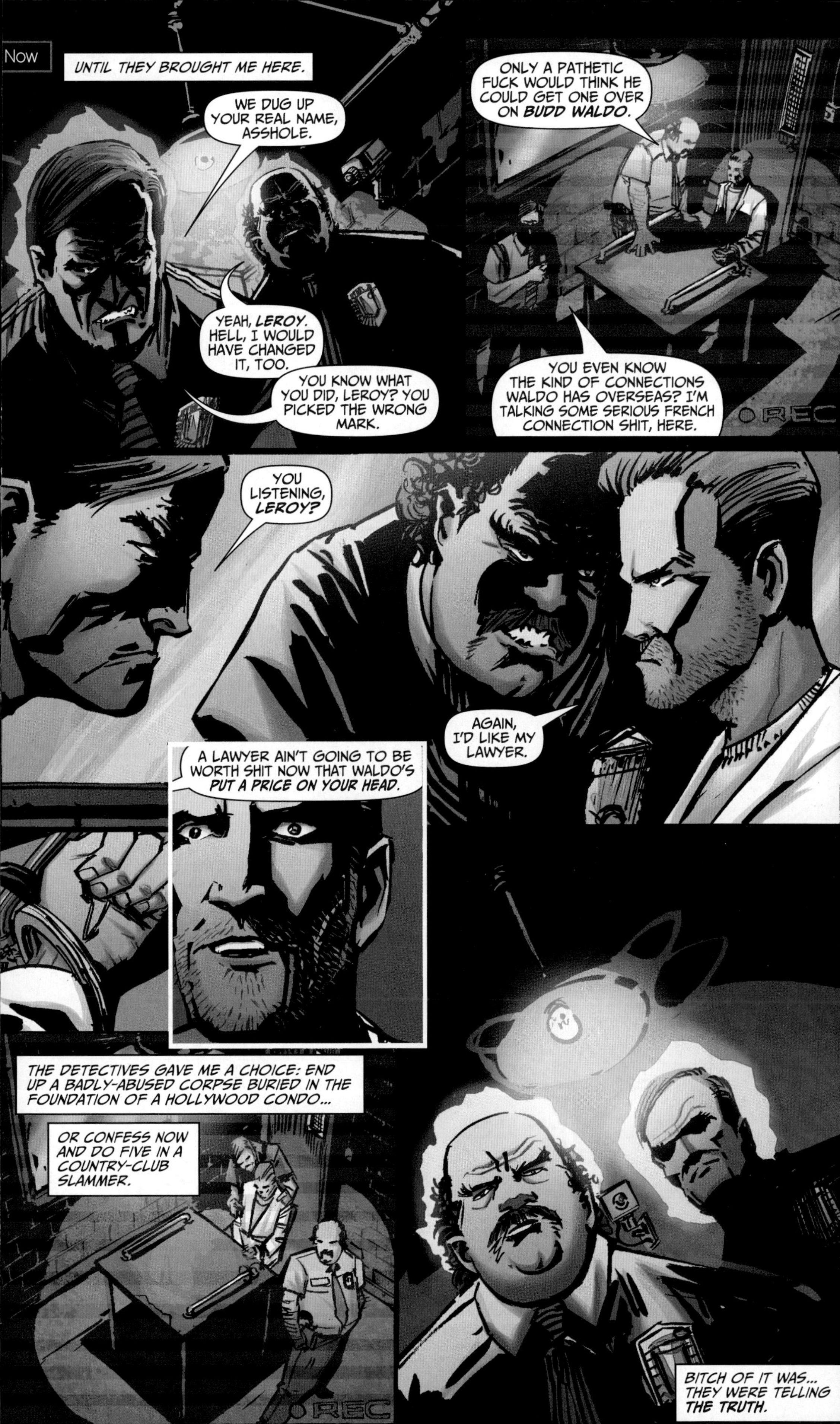

Now
UNTIL THEY BROUGHT ME HERE.
WE DUG UP YOUR REAL NAME, ASSHOLE.
YEAH, LEROY. HELL, I WOULD HAVE CHANGED IT, TOO.
YOU KNOW WHAT YOU DID, LEROY? YOU PICKED THE WRONG MARK.
ONLY A PATHETIC FUCK WOULD THINK HE COULD GET ONE OVER ON BUDD WALDO.
YOU EVEN KNOW THE KIND OF CONNECTIONS WALDO HAS OVERSEAS? I'M TALKING SOME SERIOUS FRENCH CONNECTION SHIT, HERE.
REC
YOU LISTENING, LEROY?
AGAIN, I'D LIKE MY LAWYER.
A LAWYER AIN'T GOING TO BE WORTH SHIT NOW THAT WALDO'S PUT A PRICE ON YOUR HEAD.
THE DETECTIVES GAVE ME A CHOICE: END UP A BADLY-ABUSED CORPSE BURIED IN THE FOUNDATION OF A HOLLYWOOD CONDO...
OR CONFESS NOW AND DO FIVE IN A COUNTRY-CLUB SLAMMER.
REC
BITCH OF IT WAS... THEY WERE TELLING THE TRUTH.

UP TO A POINT.

...HEREBY REMAND YOU TO NO LESS THAN *FIVE YEARS* AT SAN QUENTIN...

SAN QUENTIN!? WHAT THE FUCK, RESNICK? YOU TOLD ME I'D BE GETTING *FIVE YEARS* AT CMC!

CMC: THE CALIFORNIA MEN'S COLONY, NEAR SAN LUIS OBISPO. KNOWN AS THE "COUNTRY CLUB OF CALIFORNIA PRISONS."

I'LL TAKE CARE OF THIS, CODY.

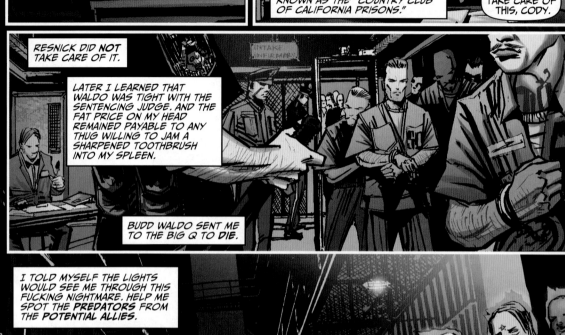

RESNICK DID *NOT* TAKE CARE OF IT.

LATER I LEARNED THAT WALDO WAS TIGHT WITH THE SENTENCING JUDGE. AND THE FAT PRICE ON MY HEAD REMAINED PAYABLE TO ANY THUG WILLING TO JAM A SHARPENED TOOTHBRUSH INTO MY SPLEEN.

BUDD WALDO SENT ME TO THE BIG Q TO *DIE*.

I TOLD MYSELF THE LIGHTS WOULD SEE ME THROUGH THIS FUCKING NIGHTMARE. HELP ME SPOT THE *PREDATORS* FROM THE *POTENTIAL ALLIES*.

JUST LIKE ALWAYS.

I WAS WRONG ABOUT THAT, TOO.

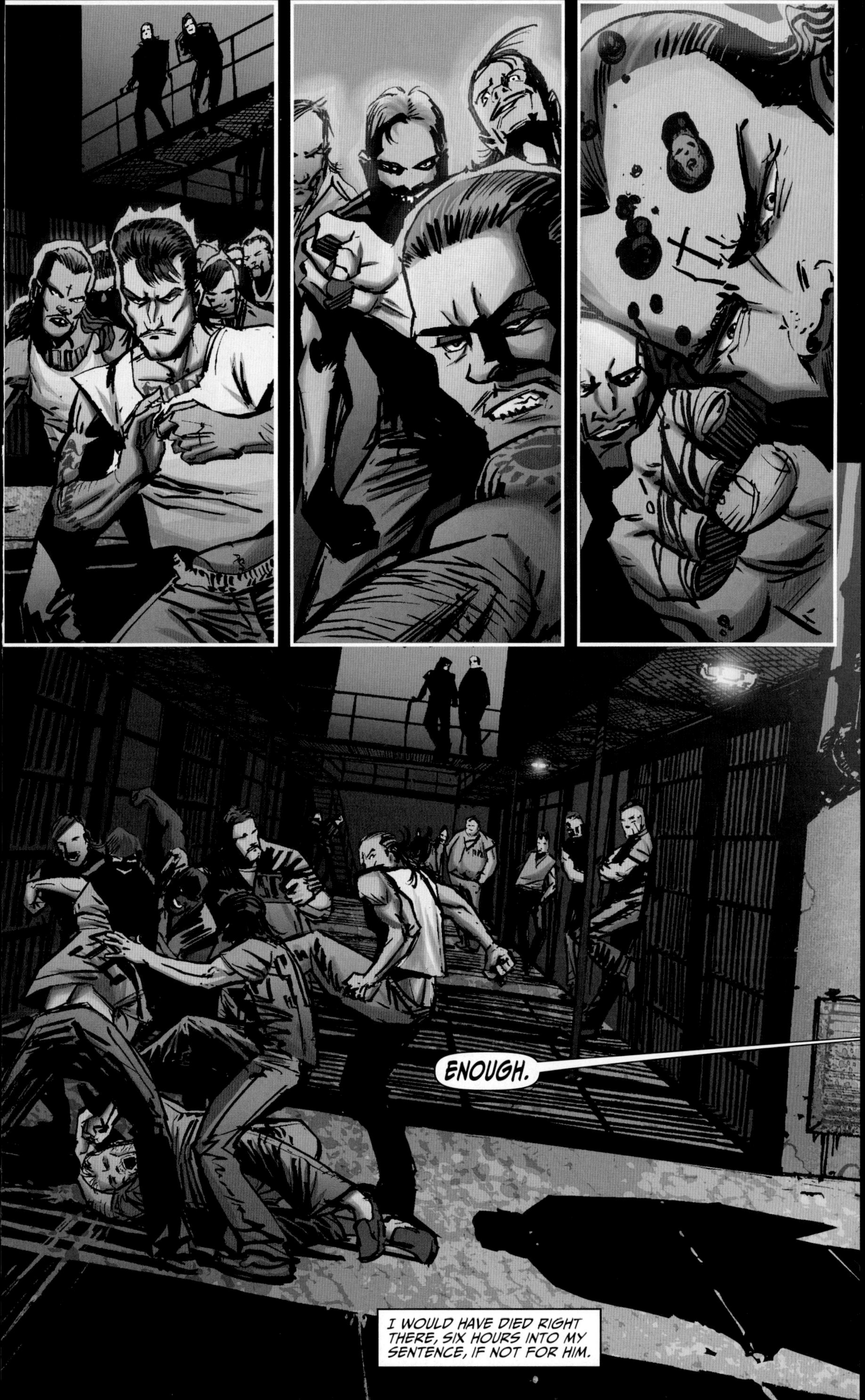
ENOUGH.
I WOULD HAVE DIED RIGHT THERE, SIX HOURS INTO MY SENTENCE, IF NOT FOR HIM.

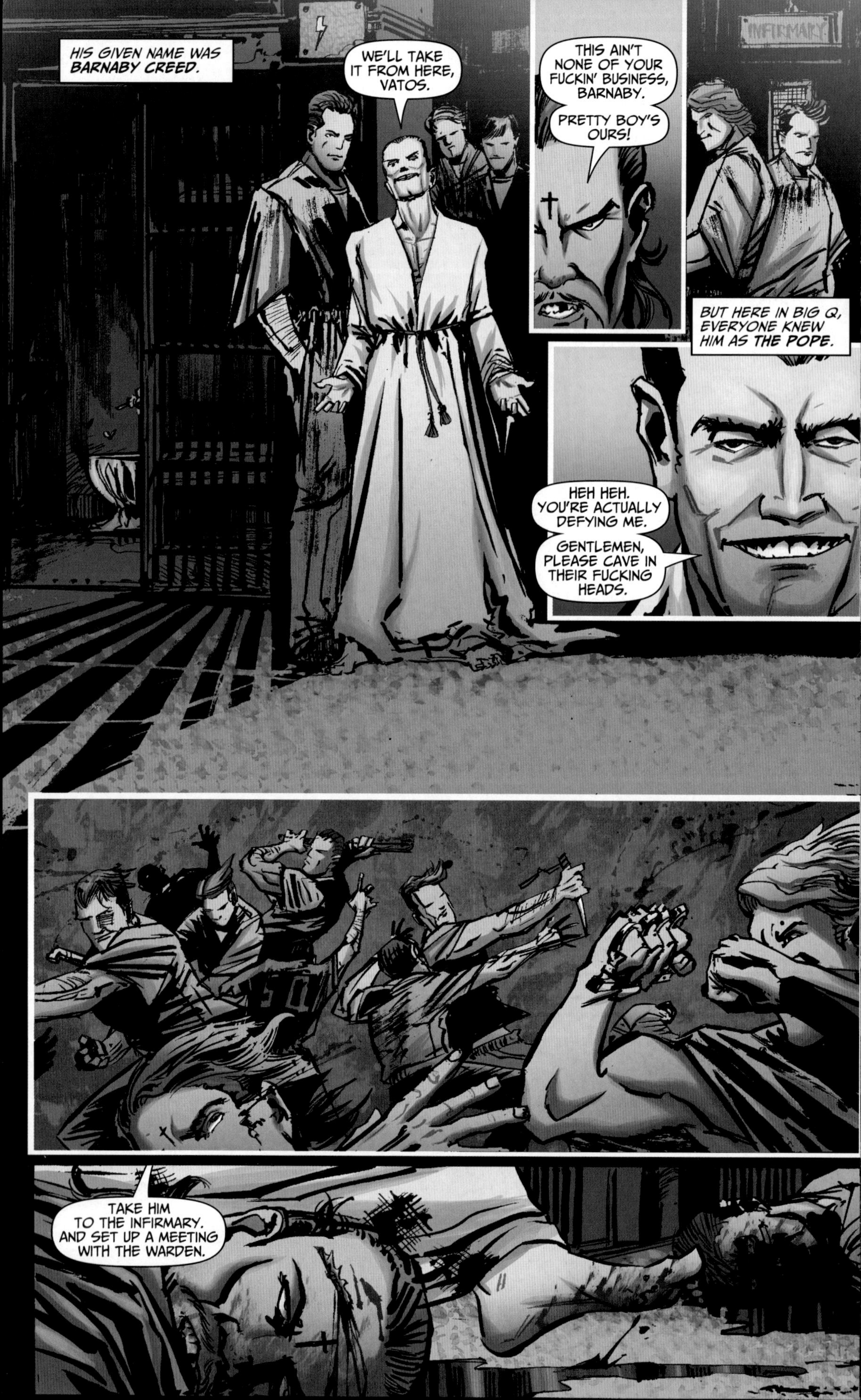

INFIRMARY
HIS GIVEN NAME WAS BARNABY CREED.
WE'LL TAKE IT FROM HERE, VATOS.
THIS AIN'T NONE OF YOUR FUCKIN' BUSINESS, BARNABY.
PRETTY BOY'S OURS!
BUT HERE IN BIG Q, EVERYONE KNEW HIM AS THE POPE.
HEH HEH. YOU'RE ACTUALLY DEFYING ME.
GENTLEMEN, PLEASE CAVE IN THEIR FUCKING HEADS.
TAKE HIM TO THE INFIRMARY. AND SET UP A MEETING WITH THE WARDEN.

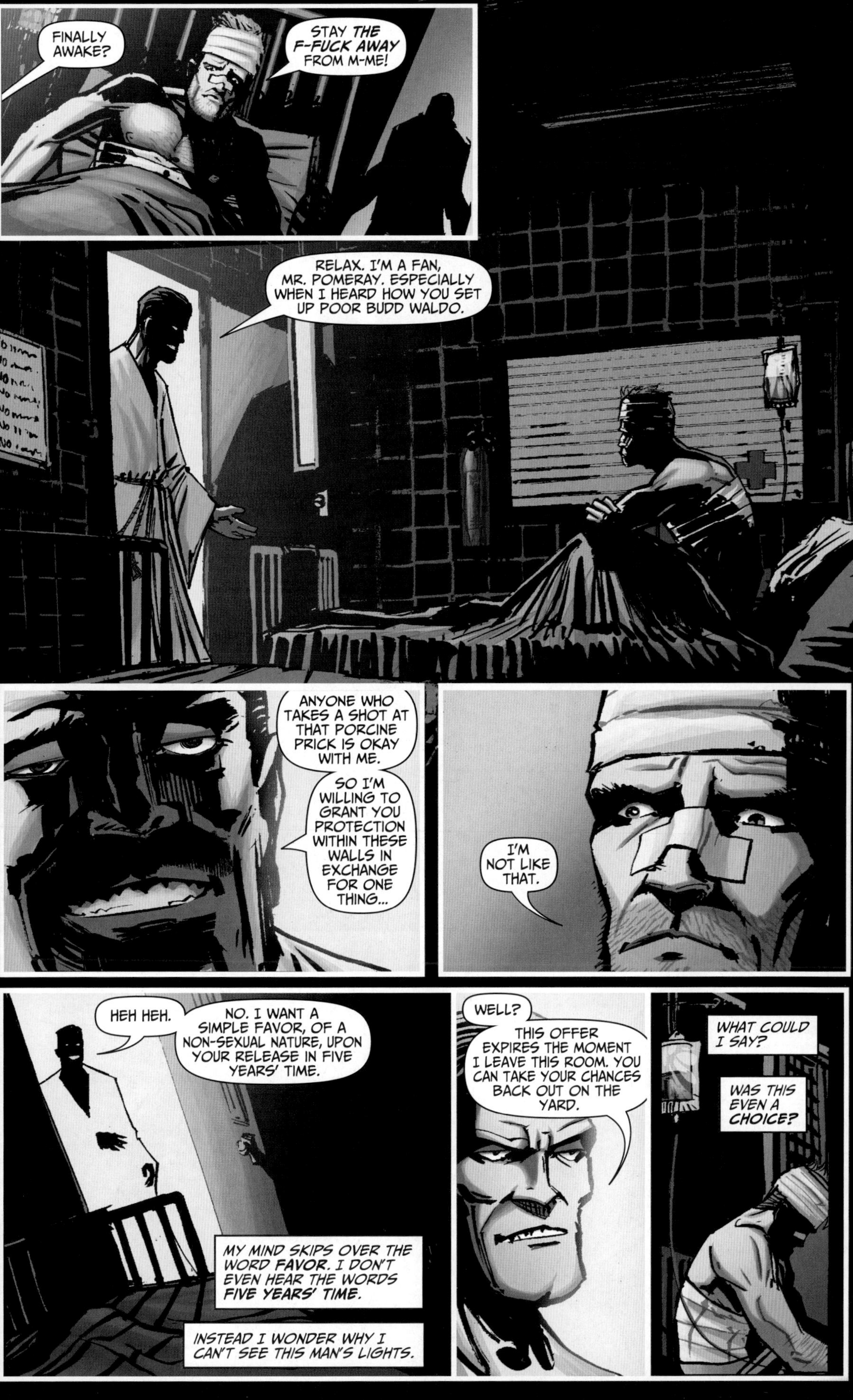

FINALLY AWAKE?
STAY THE F-FUCK AWAY FROM M-ME!
RELAX. I'M A FAN, MR. POMERAY. ESPECIALLY WHEN I HEARD HOW YOU SET UP POOR BUDD WALDO.
ANYONE WHO TAKES A SHOT AT THAT PORCINE PRICK IS OKAY WITH ME.
SO I'M WILLING TO GRANT YOU PROTECTION WITHIN THESE WALLS IN EXCHANGE FOR ONE THING...
I'M NOT LIKE THAT.
HEH HEH.
NO. I WANT A SIMPLE FAVOR, OF A NON-SEXUAL NATURE, UPON YOUR RELEASE IN FIVE YEARS' TIME.
MY MIND SKIPS OVER THE WORD FAVOR. I DON'T EVEN HEAR THE WORDS FIVE YEARS' TIME.
INSTEAD I WONDER WHY I CAN'T SEE THIS MAN'S LIGHTS.
WELL?
THIS OFFER EXPIRES THE MOMENT I LEAVE THIS ROOM. YOU CAN TAKE YOUR CHANCES BACK OUT ON THE YARD.
WHAT COULD I SAY?
WAS THIS EVEN A CHOICE?

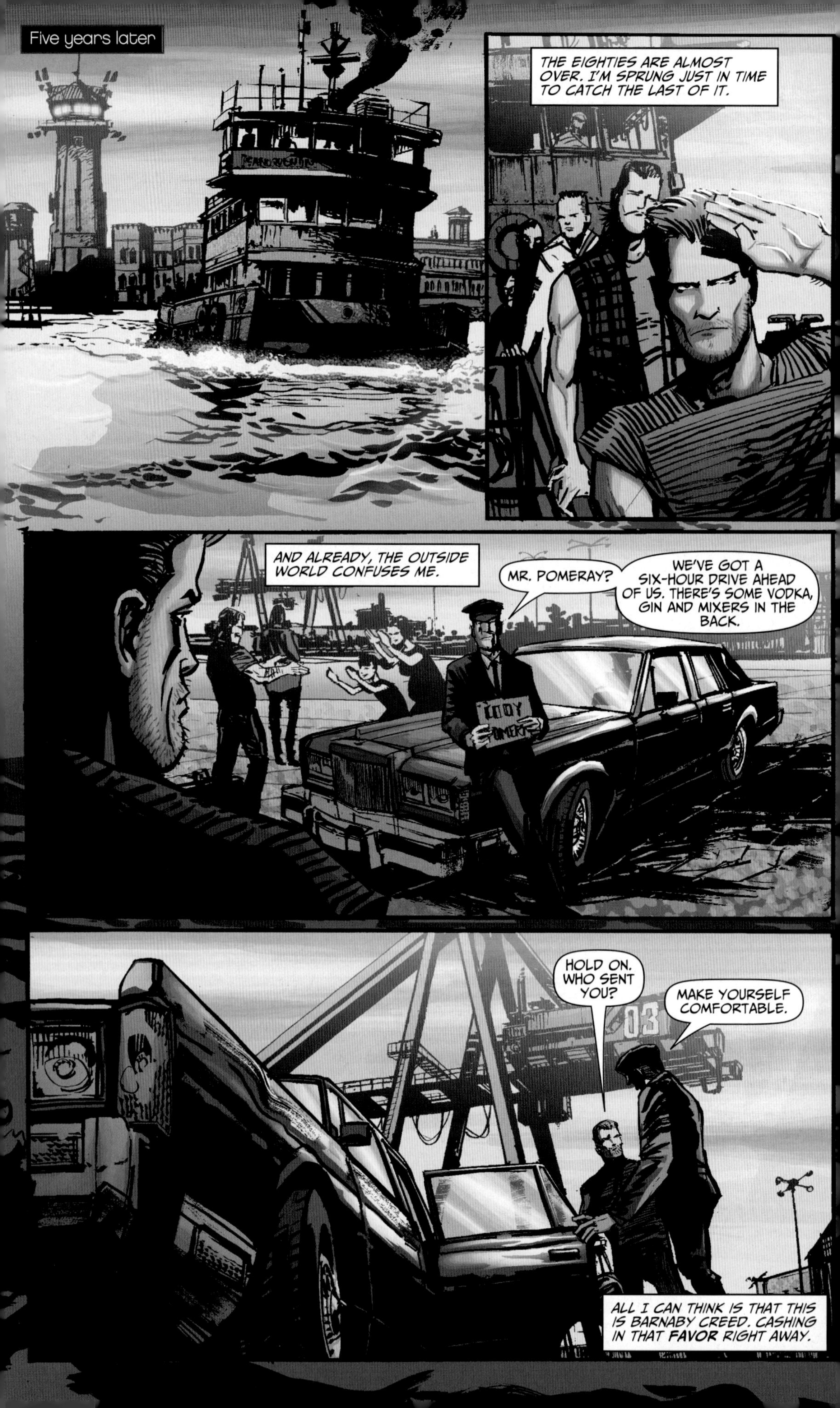
Five years later
THE EIGHTIES ARE ALMOST OVER. I'M SPRUNG JUST IN TIME TO CATCH THE LAST OF IT.
AND ALREADY, THE OUTSIDE WORLD CONFUSES ME.
MR. POMERAY?
WE'VE GOT A SIX-HOUR DRIVE AHEAD OF US. THERE'S SOME VODKA, GIN AND MIXERS IN THE BACK.
HOLD ON. WHO SENT YOU?
MAKE YOURSELF COMFORTABLE.
ALL I CAN THINK IS THAT THIS IS BARNABY CREED. CASHING IN THAT FAVOR RIGHT AWAY.

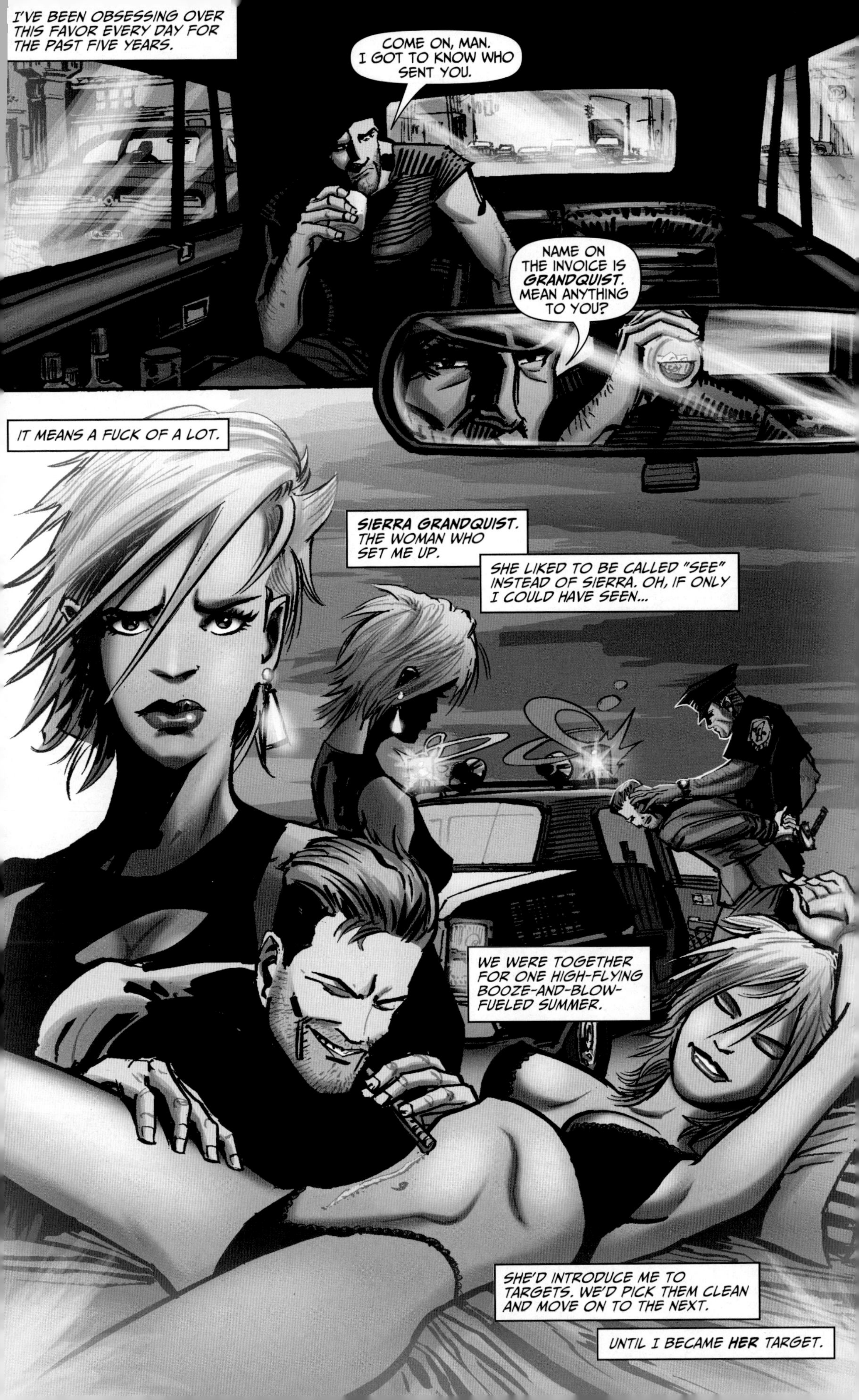

I'VE BEEN OBSESSING OVER THIS FAVOR EVERY DAY FOR THE PAST FIVE YEARS.
COME ON, MAN. I GOT TO KNOW WHO SENT YOU.
NAME ON THE INVOICE IS GRANDQUIST. MEAN ANYTHING TO YOU?
IT MEANS A FUCK OF A LOT.
SIERRA GRANDQUIST. THE WOMAN WHO SET ME UP.
SHE LIKED TO BE CALLED "SEE" INSTEAD OF SIERRA. OH, IF ONLY I COULD HAVE SEEN...
WE WERE TOGETHER FOR ONE HIGH-FLYING BOOZE-AND-BLOW-FUELED SUMMER.
SHE'D INTRODUCE ME TO TARGETS. WE'D PICK THEM CLEAN AND MOVE ON TO THE NEXT.
UNTIL I BECAME HER TARGET.

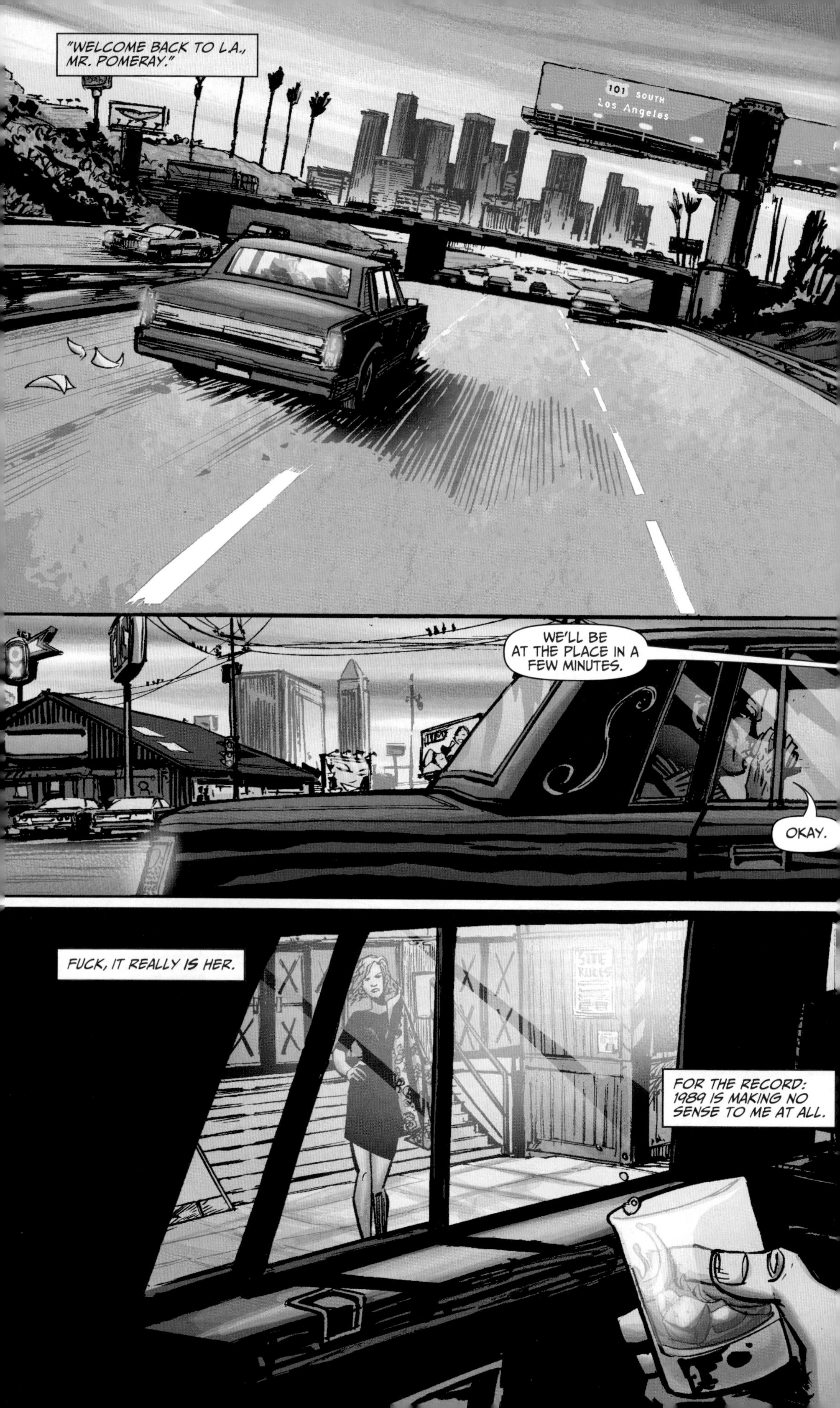
"WELCOME BACK TO L.A., MR. POMERAY."
101 SOUTH
Los Angeles
WE'LL BE AT THE PLACE IN A FEW MINUTES.
OKAY.
FUCK, IT REALLY IS HER.
SITE RULES
FOR THE RECORD: 1989 IS MAKING NO SENSE TO ME AT ALL.

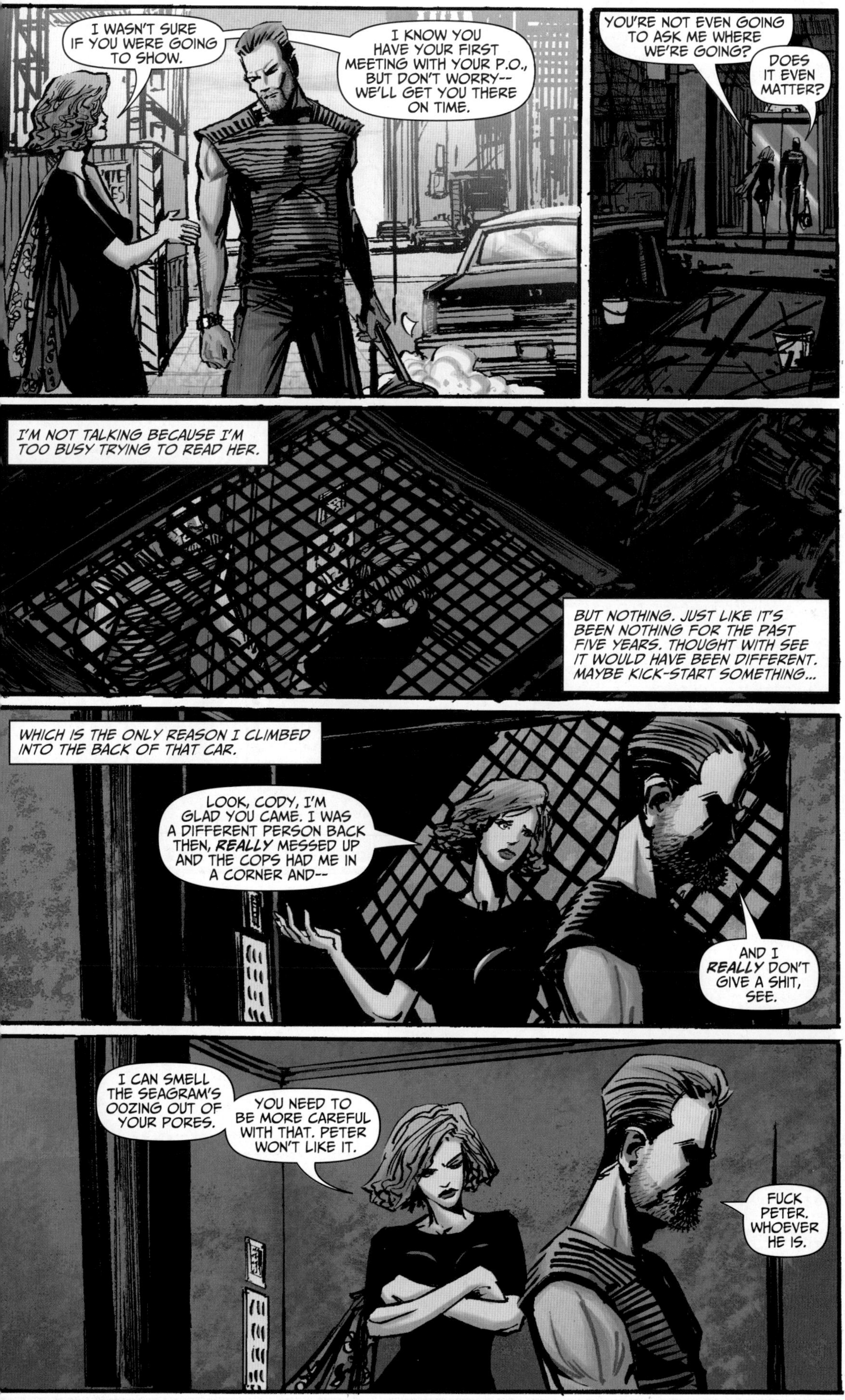

I WASN'T SURE IF YOU WERE GOING TO SHOW.
I KNOW YOU HAVE YOUR FIRST MEETING WITH YOUR P.O., BUT DON'T WORRY-- WE'LL GET YOU THERE ON TIME.
YOU'RE NOT EVEN GOING TO ASK ME WHERE WE'RE GOING?
DOES IT EVEN MATTER?
I'M NOT TALKING BECAUSE I'M TOO BUSY TRYING TO READ HER.
BUT NOTHING. JUST LIKE IT'S BEEN NOTHING FOR THE PAST FIVE YEARS. THOUGHT WITH SEE IT WOULD HAVE BEEN DIFFERENT. MAYBE KICK-START SOMETHING...
WHICH IS THE ONLY REASON I CLIMBED INTO THE BACK OF THAT CAR.
LOOK, CODY, I'M GLAD YOU CAME. I WAS A DIFFERENT PERSON BACK THEN, REALLY MESSED UP AND THE COPS HAD ME IN A CORNER AND--
AND I REALLY DON'T GIVE A SHIT, SEE.
I CAN SMELL THE SEAGRAM'S OOZING OUT OF YOUR PORES.
YOU NEED TO BE MORE CAREFUL WITH THAT. PETER WON'T LIKE IT.
FUCK PETER. WHOEVER HE IS.

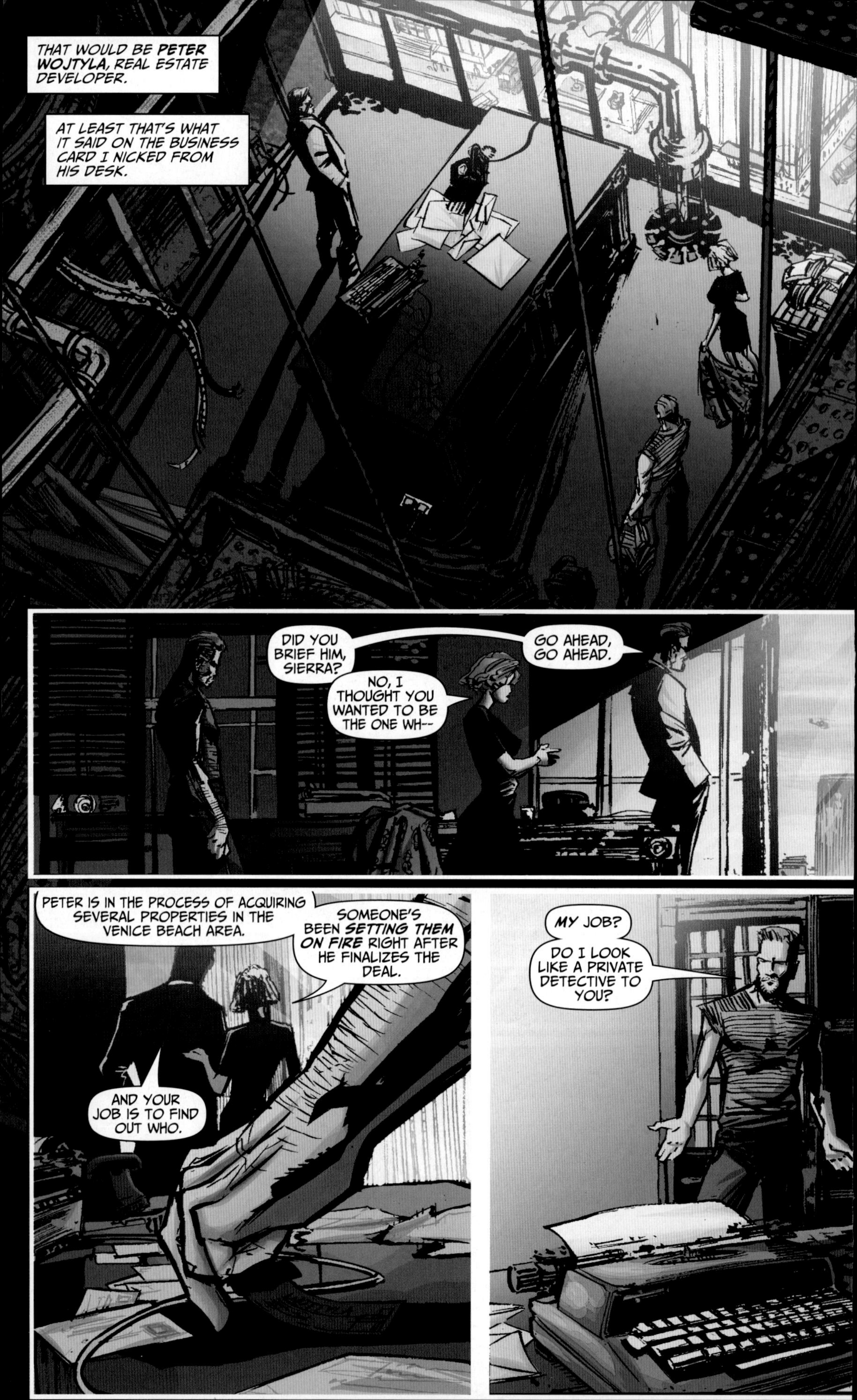
THAT WOULD BE PETER WOJTYLA, REAL ESTATE DEVELOPER.
AT LEAST THAT'S WHAT IT SAID ON THE BUSINESS CARD I NICKED FROM HIS DESK.
DID YOU BRIEF HIM, SIERRA?
NO, I THOUGHT YOU WANTED TO BE THE ONE WH--
GO AHEAD, GO AHEAD.
PETER IS IN THE PROCESS OF ACQUIRING SEVERAL PROPERTIES IN THE VENICE BEACH AREA.
SOMEONE'S BEEN SETTING THEM ON FIRE RIGHT AFTER HE FINALIZES THE DEAL.
AND YOUR JOB IS TO FIND OUT WHO.
MY JOB?
DO I LOOK LIKE A PRIVATE DETECTIVE TO YOU?

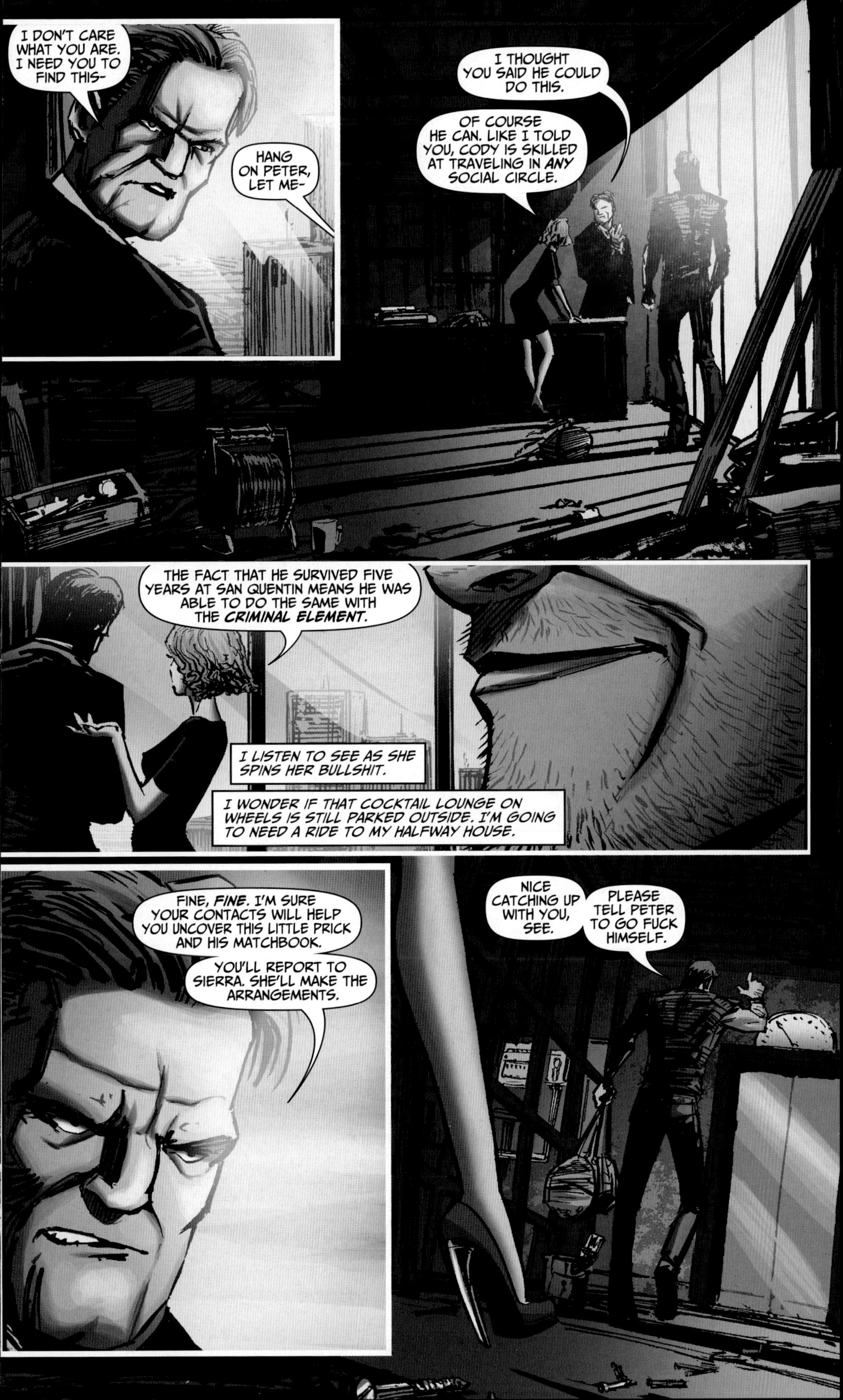
I DON'T CARE WHAT YOU ARE. I NEED YOU TO FIND THIS-
HANG ON PETER, LET ME-
I THOUGHT YOU SAID HE COULD DO THIS.
OF COURSE HE CAN. LIKE I TOLD YOU, CODY IS SKILLED AT TRAVELING IN *ANY* SOCIAL CIRCLE.
THE FACT THAT HE SURVIVED FIVE YEARS AT SAN QUENTIN MEANS HE WAS ABLE TO DO THE SAME WITH THE *CRIMINAL ELEMENT*.
I LISTEN TO SEE AS SHE SPINS HER BULLSHIT.
I WONDER IF THAT COCKTAIL LOUNGE ON WHEELS IS STILL PARKED OUTSIDE. I'M GOING TO NEED A RIDE TO MY HALFWAY HOUSE.
FINE, *FINE*. I'M SURE YOUR CONTACTS WILL HELP YOU UNCOVER THIS LITTLE PRICK AND HIS MATCHBOOK.
YOU'LL REPORT TO SIERRA. SHE'LL MAKE THE ARRANGEMENTS.
NICE CATCHING UP WITH YOU, SEE.
PLEASE TELL PETER TO GO FUCK HIMSELF.

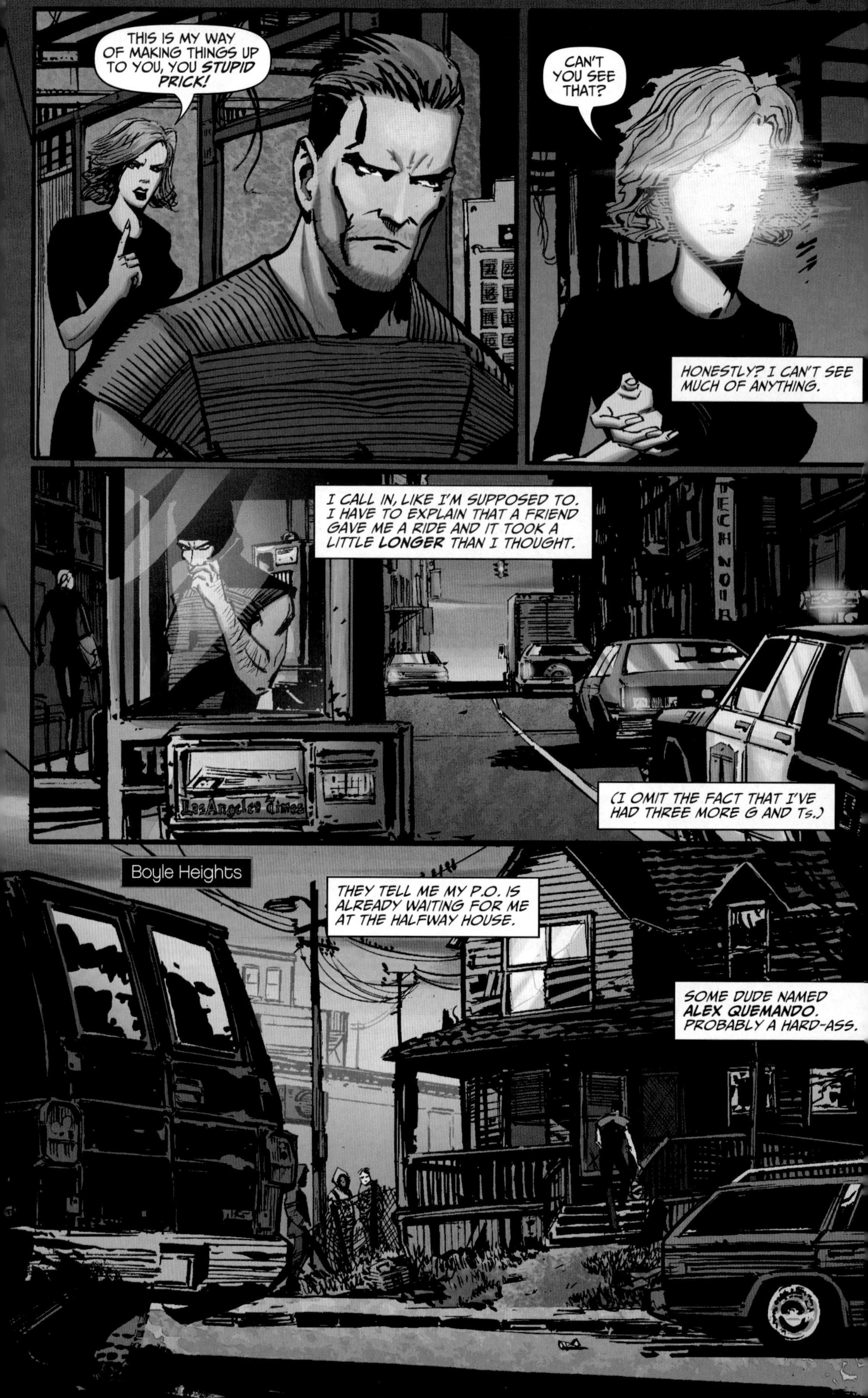

THIS IS MY WAY OF MAKING THINGS UP TO YOU, YOU STUPID PRICK!
CAN'T YOU SEE THAT?
HONESTLY? I CAN'T SEE MUCH OF ANYTHING.
I CALL IN, LIKE I'M SUPPOSED TO. I HAVE TO EXPLAIN THAT A FRIEND GAVE ME A RIDE AND IT TOOK A LITTLE LONGER THAN I THOUGHT.
Los Angeles Times
(I OMIT THE FACT THAT I'VE HAD THREE MORE G AND Ts.)
Boyle Heights
THEY TELL ME MY P.O. IS ALREADY WAITING FOR ME AT THE HALFWAY HOUSE.
SOME DUDE NAMED ALEX QUEMANDO. PROBABLY A HARD-ASS.

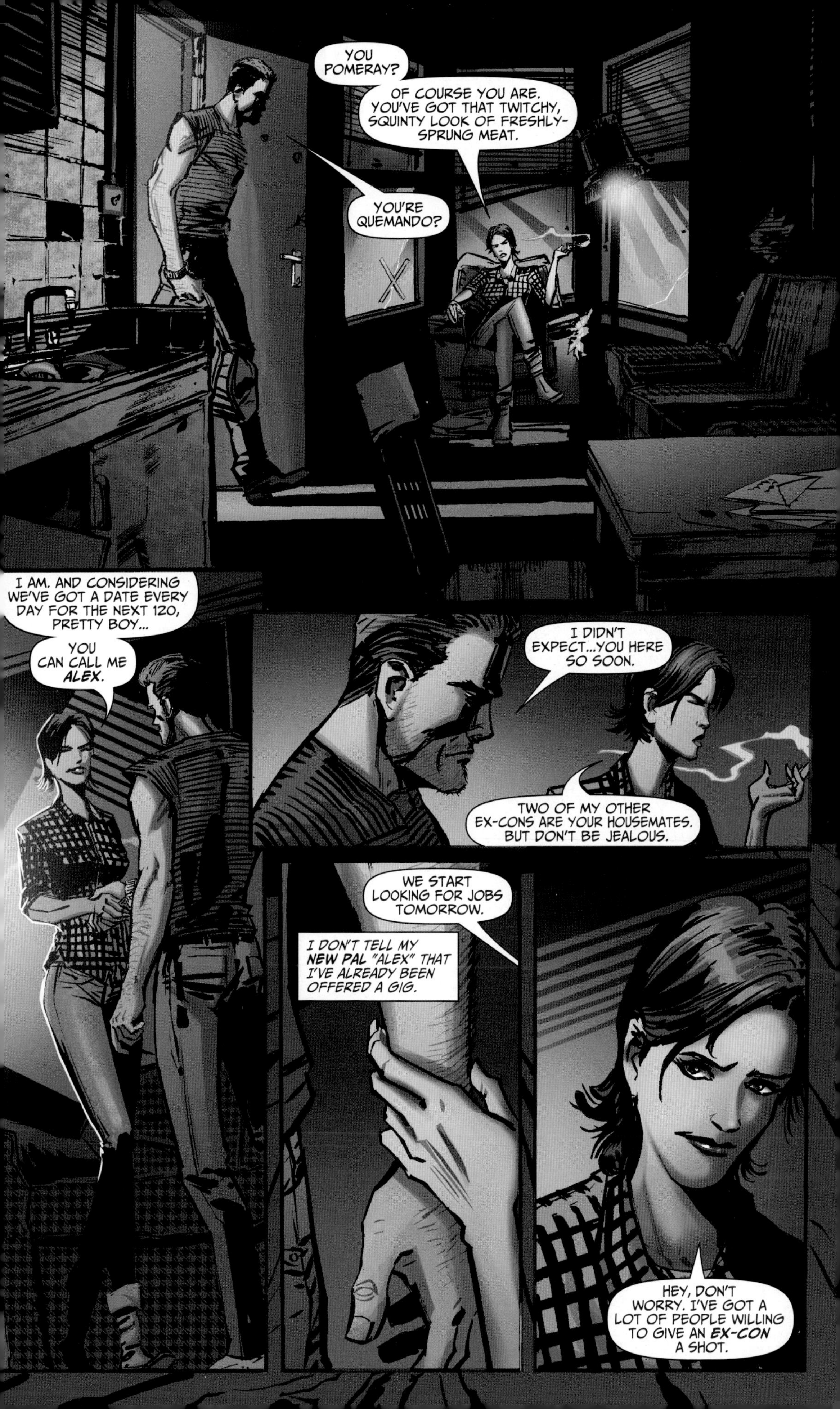
YOU POMERAY?
OF COURSE YOU ARE. YOU'VE GOT THAT TWITCHY, SQUINTY LOOK OF FRESHLY-SPRUNG MEAT.
YOU'RE QUEMANDO?
I AM. AND CONSIDERING WE'VE GOT A DATE EVERY DAY FOR THE NEXT 120, PRETTY BOY...
YOU CAN CALL ME ALEX.
I DIDN'T EXPECT...YOU HERE SO SOON.
TWO OF MY OTHER EX-CONS ARE YOUR HOUSEMATES. BUT DON'T BE JEALOUS.
WE START LOOKING FOR JOBS TOMORROW.
I DON'T TELL MY NEW PAL "ALEX" THAT I'VE ALREADY BEEN OFFERED A GIG.
HEY, DON'T WORRY. I'VE GOT A LOT OF PEOPLE WILLING TO GIVE AN EX-CON A SHOT.

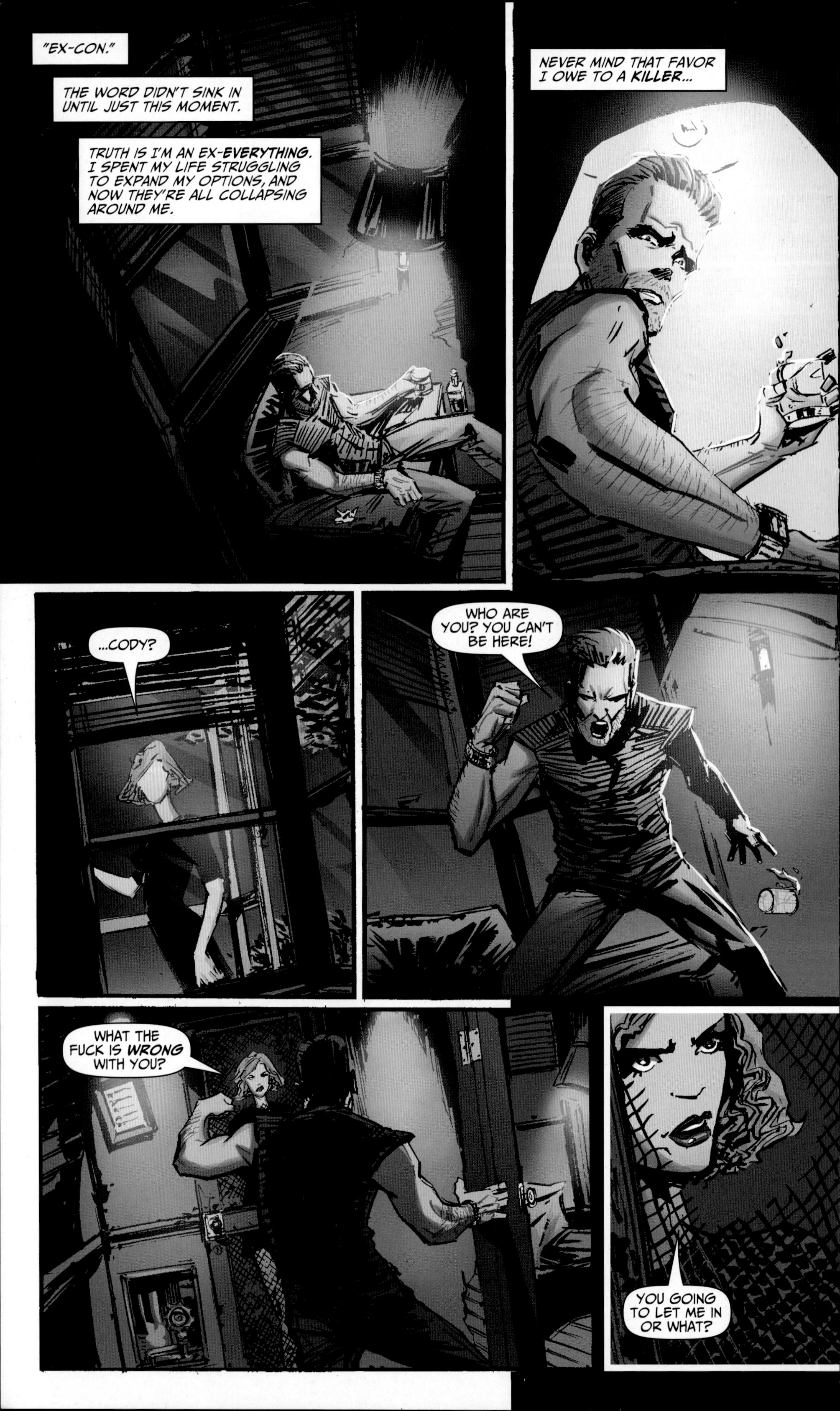
"EX-CON."
THE WORD DIDN'T SINK IN UNTIL JUST THIS MOMENT.
TRUTH IS I'M AN EX-**EVERYTHING**. I SPENT MY LIFE STRUGGLING TO EXPAND MY OPTIONS, AND NOW THEY'RE ALL COLLAPSING AROUND ME.
NEVER MIND THAT FAVOR I OWE TO A **KILLER**...
...CODY?
WHO ARE YOU? YOU CAN'T BE HERE!
WHAT THE FUCK IS **WRONG** WITH YOU?
YOU GOING TO LET ME IN OR WHAT?

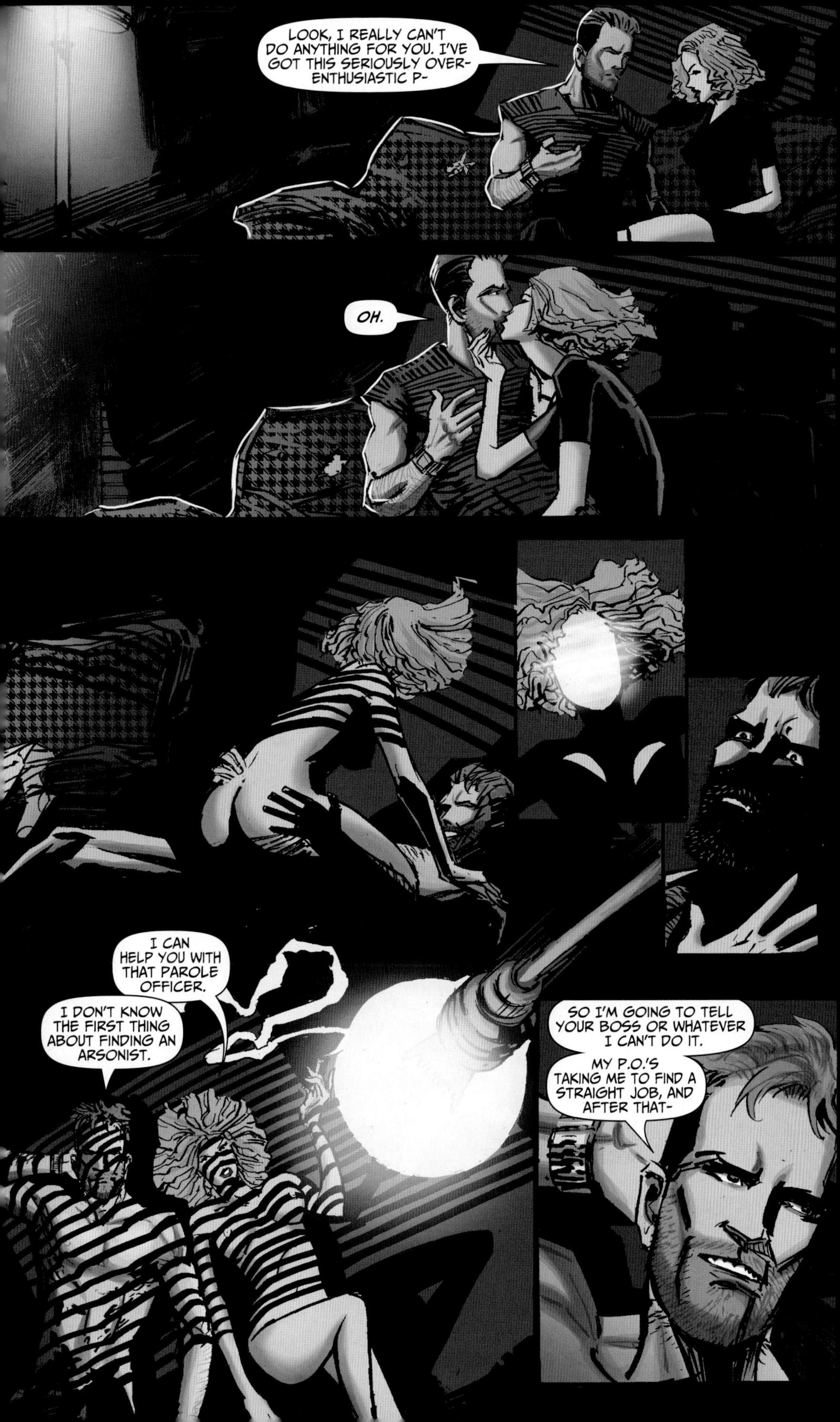
LOOK, I REALLY CAN'T DO ANYTHING FOR YOU. I'VE GOT THIS SERIOUSLY OVER-ENTHUSIASTIC P-
OH.
I CAN HELP YOU WITH THAT PAROLE OFFICER.
I DON'T KNOW THE FIRST THING ABOUT FINDING AN ARSONIST.
SO I'M GOING TO TELL YOUR BOSS OR WHATEVER I CAN'T DO IT.
MY P.O.'S TAKING ME TO FIND A STRAIGHT JOB, AND AFTER THAT-

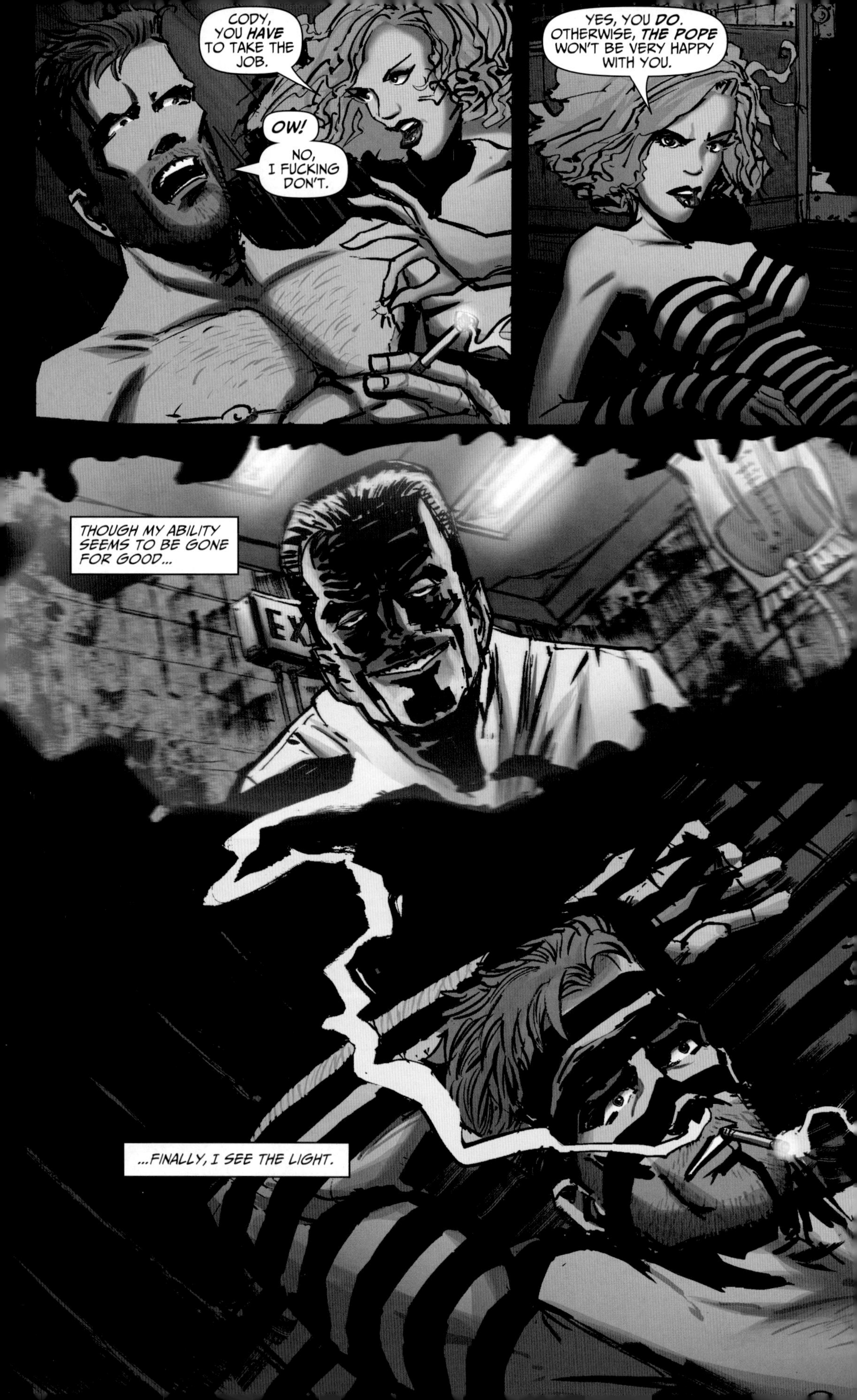
CODY, YOU HAVE TO TAKE THE JOB.
OW!
NO, I FUCKING DON'T.
YES, YOU DO. OTHERWISE, THE POPE WON'T BE VERY HAPPY WITH YOU.
THOUGH MY ABILITY SEEMS TO BE GONE FOR GOOD...
...FINALLY, I SEE THE LIGHT.

TWO

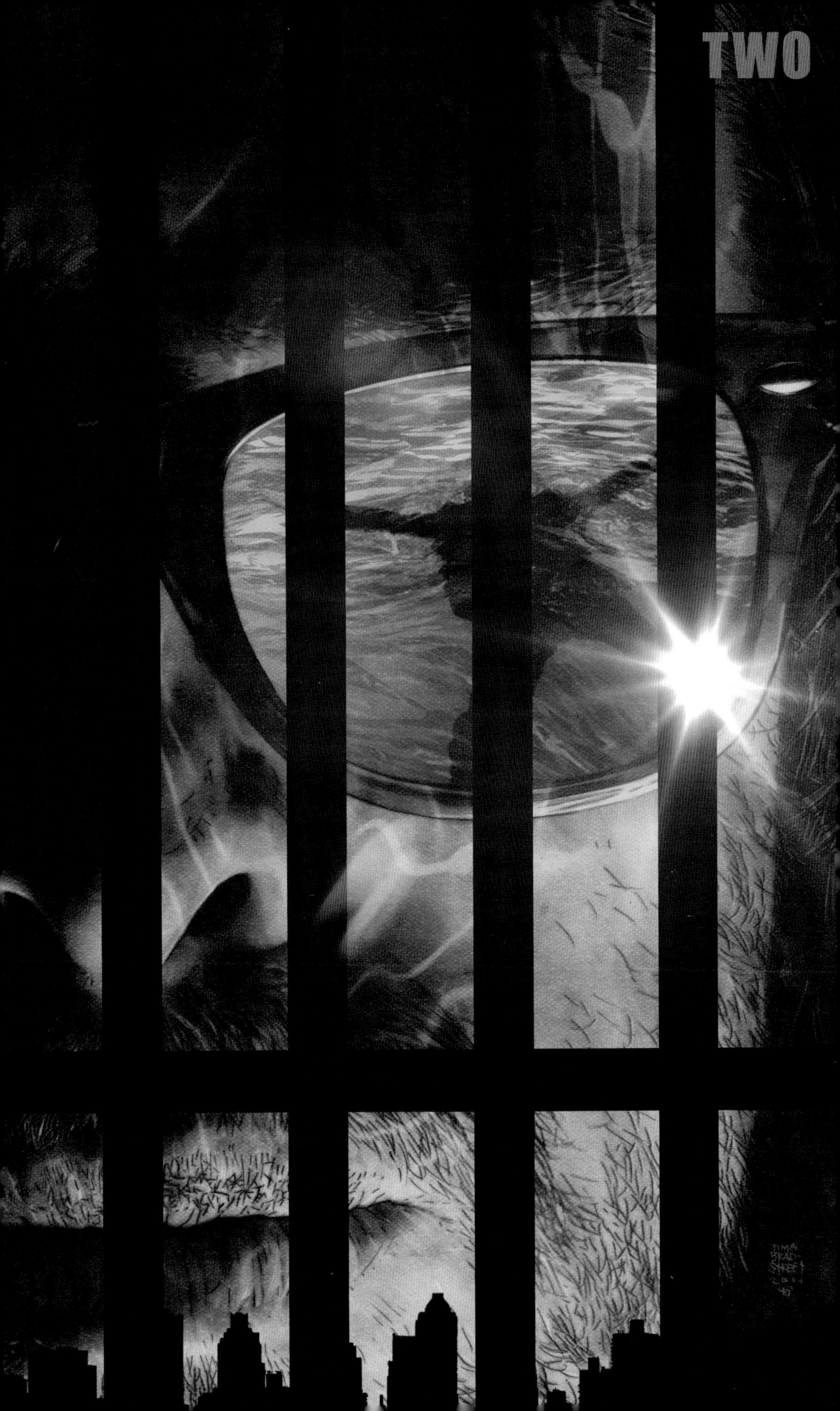

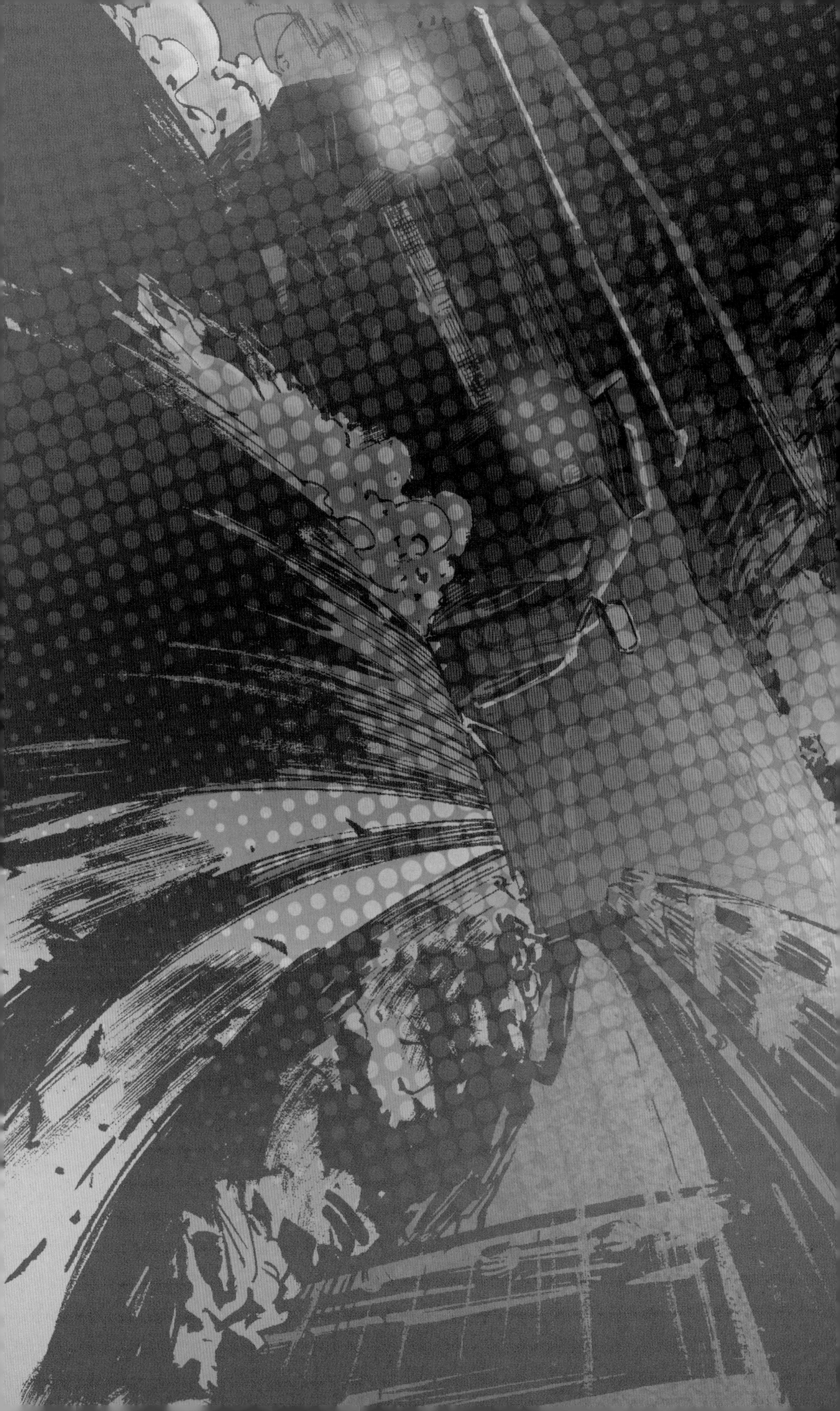

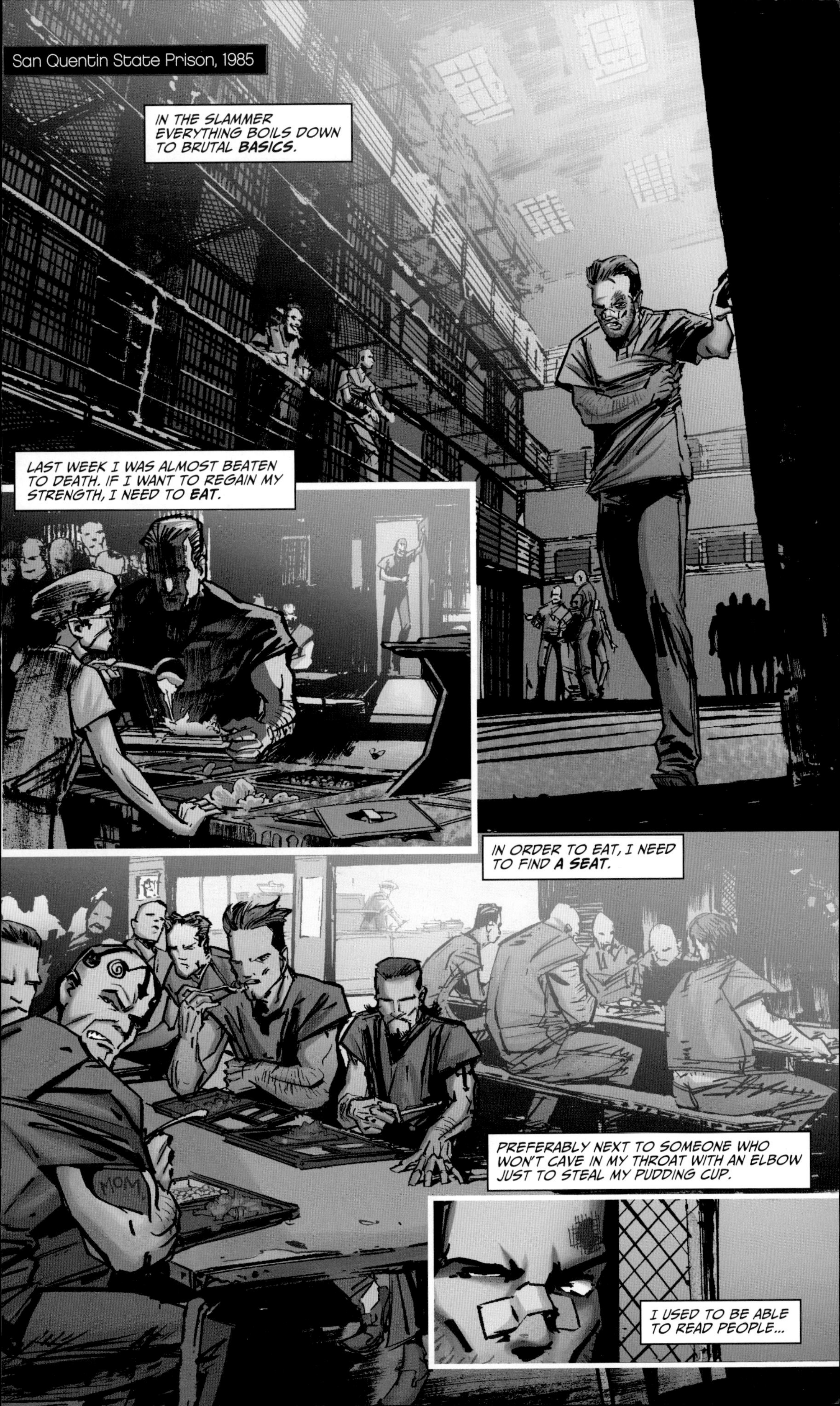
San Quentin State Prison, 1985
IN THE SLAMMER EVERYTHING BOILS DOWN TO BRUTAL BASICS.
LAST WEEK I WAS ALMOST BEATEN TO DEATH. IF I WANT TO REGAIN MY STRENGTH, I NEED TO EAT.
IN ORDER TO EAT, I NEED TO FIND A SEAT.
MOM
PREFERABLY NEXT TO SOMEONE WHO WON'T CAVE IN MY THROAT WITH AN ELBOW JUST TO STEAL MY PUDDING CUP.
I USED TO BE ABLE TO READ PEOPLE...

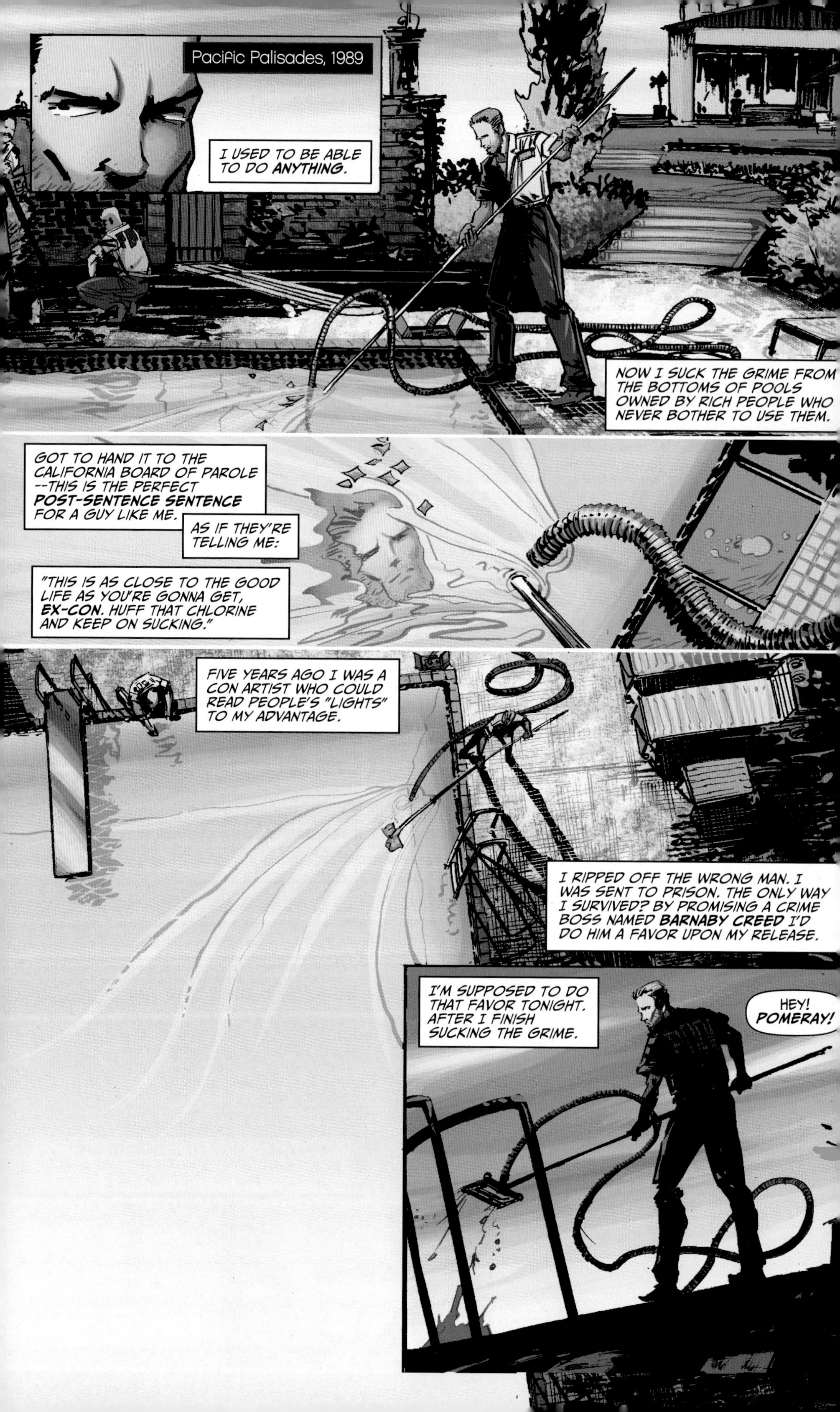

Pacific Palisades, 1989
I USED TO BE ABLE TO DO ANYTHING.
NOW I SUCK THE GRIME FROM THE BOTTOMS OF POOLS OWNED BY RICH PEOPLE WHO NEVER BOTHER TO USE THEM.
GOT TO HAND IT TO THE CALIFORNIA BOARD OF PAROLE --THIS IS THE PERFECT POST-SENTENCE SENTENCE FOR A GUY LIKE ME.
AS IF THEY'RE TELLING ME:
"THIS IS AS CLOSE TO THE GOOD LIFE AS YOU'RE GONNA GET, EX-CON. HUFF THAT CHLORINE AND KEEP ON SUCKING."
FIVE YEARS AGO I WAS A CON ARTIST WHO COULD READ PEOPLE'S "LIGHTS" TO MY ADVANTAGE.
I RIPPED OFF THE WRONG MAN. I WAS SENT TO PRISON. THE ONLY WAY I SURVIVED? BY PROMISING A CRIME BOSS NAMED BARNABY CREED I'D DO HIM A FAVOR UPON MY RELEASE.
I'M SUPPOSED TO DO THAT FAVOR TONIGHT. AFTER I FINISH SUCKING THE GRIME.
HEY! POMERAY!

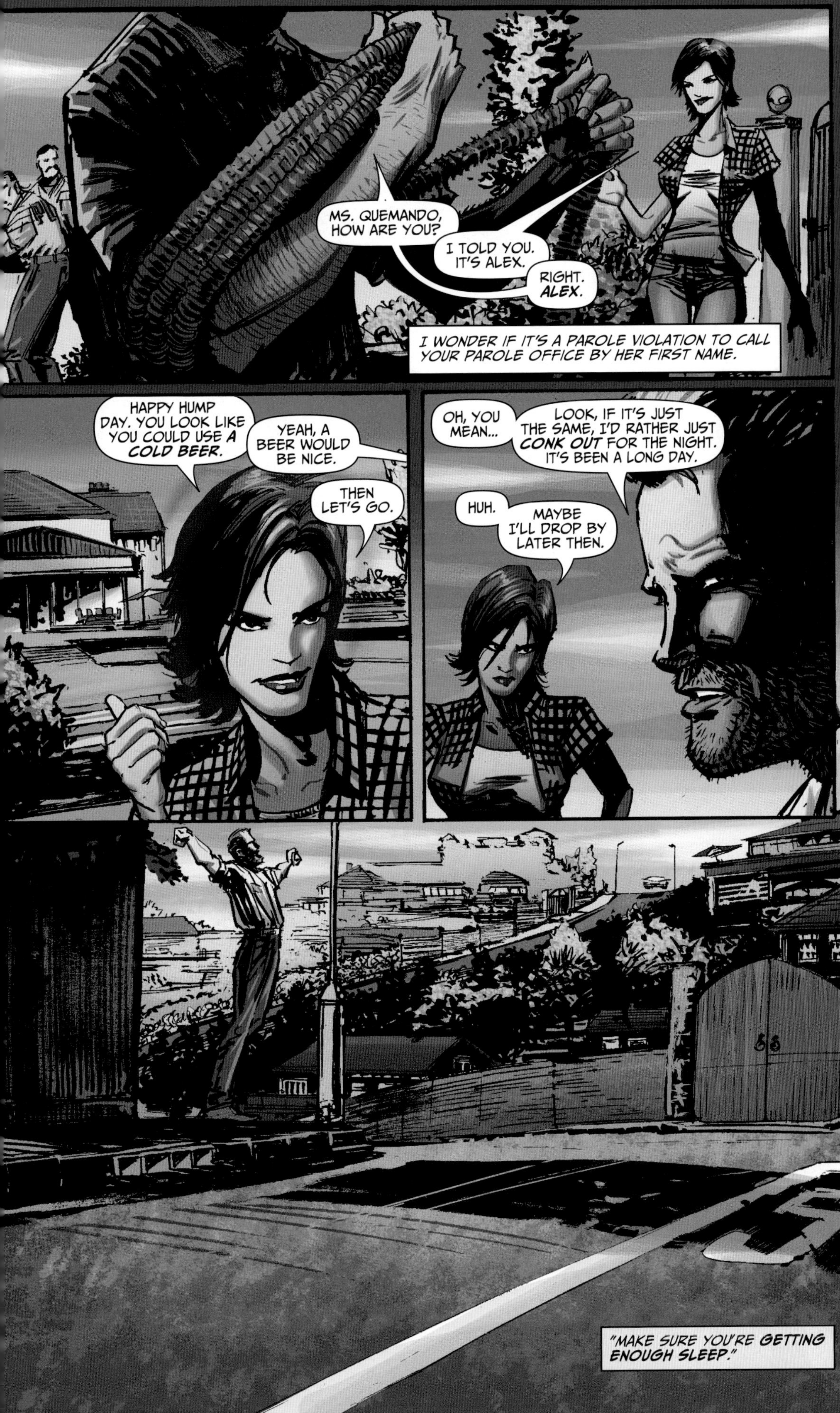

MS. QUEMANDO, HOW ARE YOU?
I TOLD YOU. IT'S ALEX.
RIGHT. **ALEX**.
I WONDER IF IT'S A PAROLE VIOLATION TO CALL YOUR PAROLE OFFICE BY HER FIRST NAME.
HAPPY HUMP DAY. YOU LOOK LIKE YOU COULD USE **A COLD BEER**.
YEAH, A BEER WOULD BE NICE.
THEN LET'S GO.
OH, YOU MEAN...
LOOK, IF IT'S JUST THE SAME, I'D RATHER JUST **CONK OUT** FOR THE NIGHT. IT'S BEEN A LONG DAY.
HUH.
MAYBE I'LL DROP BY LATER THEN.
*"MAKE SURE YOU'RE **GETTING ENOUGH SLEEP**."*

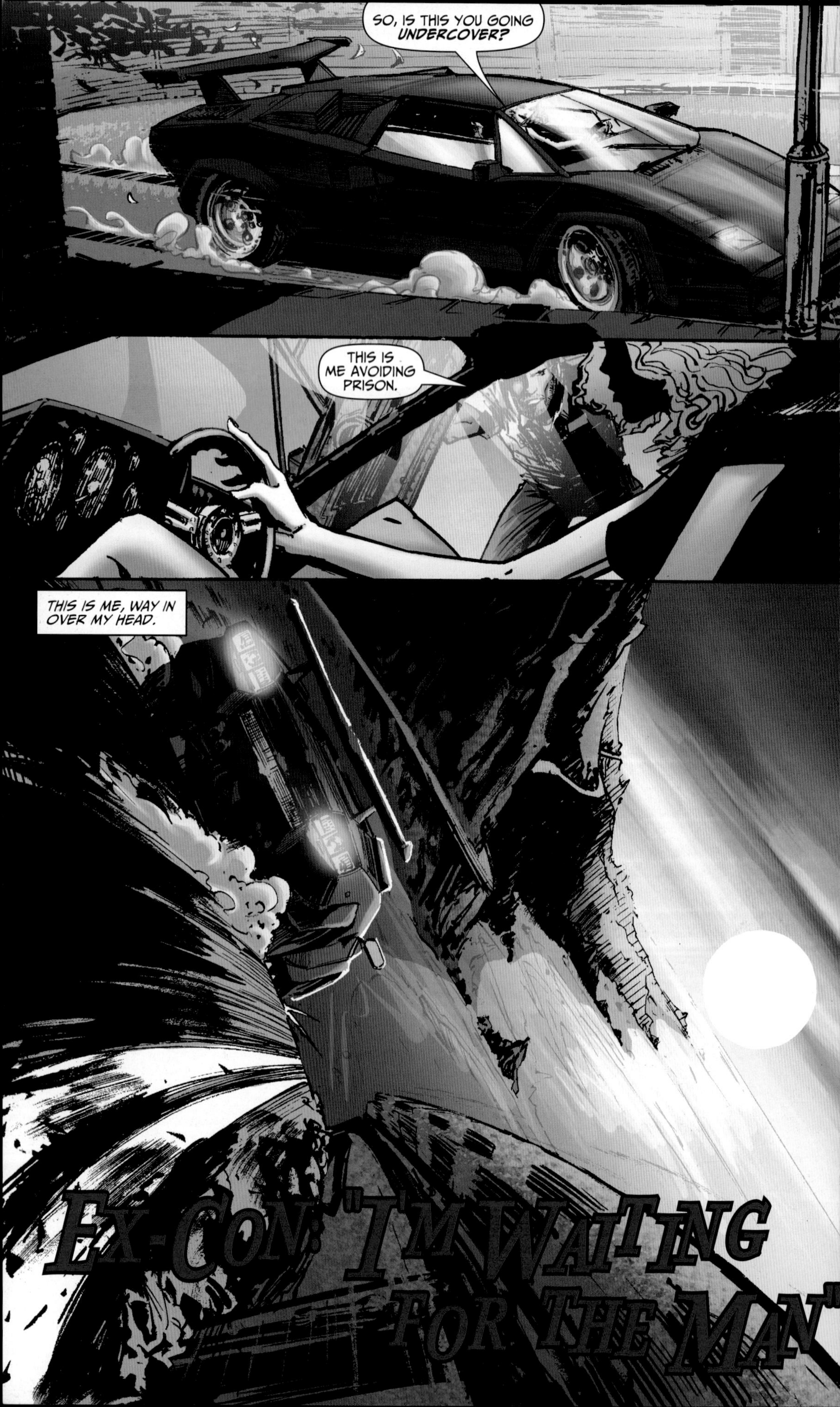
SO, IS THIS YOU GOING UNDERCOVER?
THIS IS ME AVOIDING PRISON.
THIS IS ME, WAY IN OVER MY HEAD.
EX-CON: "I'M WAITING FOR THE MAN"

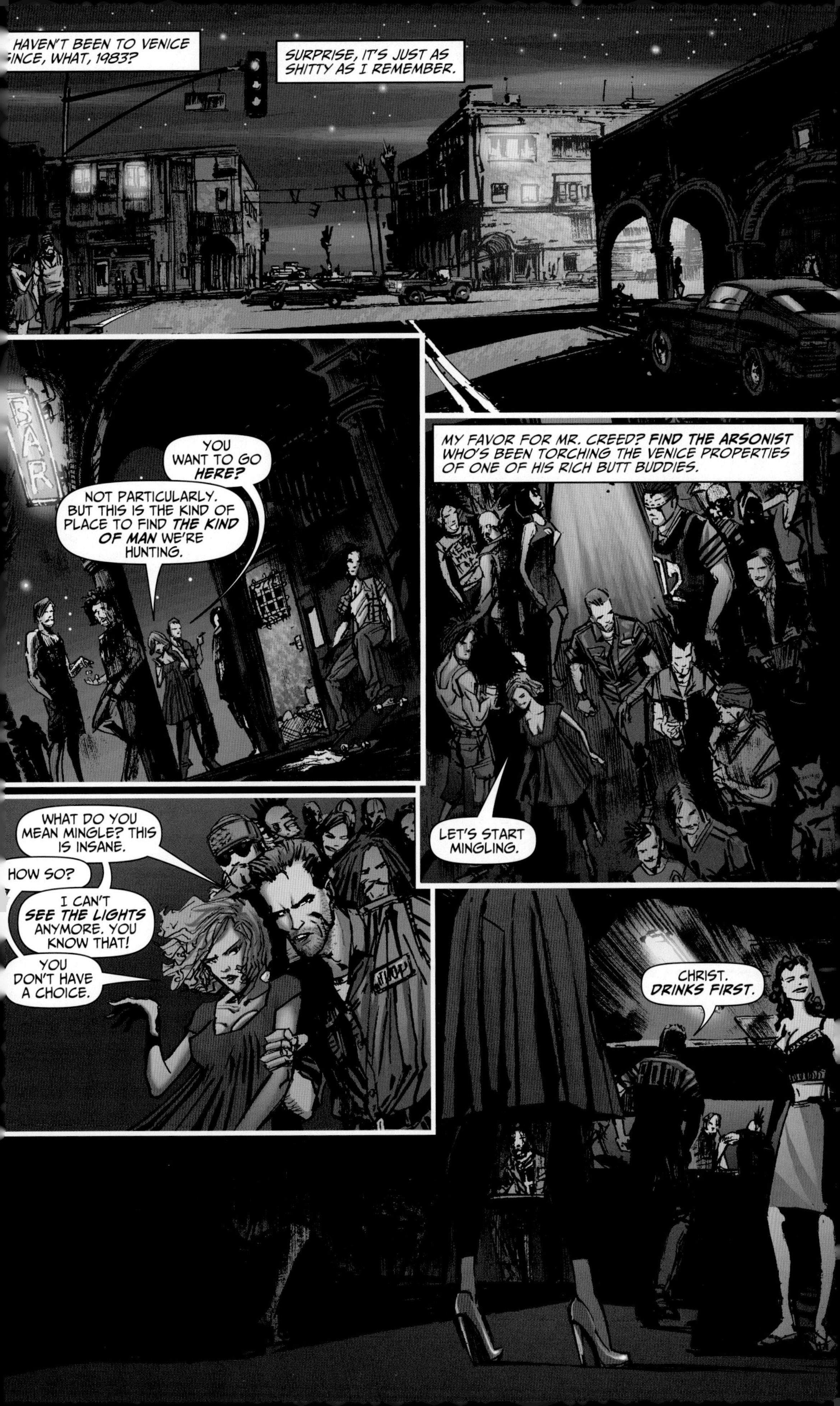
HAVEN'T BEEN TO VENICE SINCE, WHAT, 1983?
SURPRISE, IT'S JUST AS SHITTY AS I REMEMBER.
BAR
YOU WANT TO GO HERE?
NOT PARTICULARLY. BUT THIS IS THE KIND OF PLACE TO FIND THE KIND OF MAN WE'RE HUNTING.
MY FAVOR FOR MR. CREED? FIND THE ARSONIST WHO'S BEEN TORCHING THE VENICE PROPERTIES OF ONE OF HIS RICH BUTT BUDDIES.
LET'S START MINGLING.
WHAT DO YOU MEAN MINGLE? THIS IS INSANE.
HOW SO?
I CAN'T SEE THE LIGHTS ANYMORE. YOU KNOW THAT!
YOU DON'T HAVE A CHOICE.
CHRIST. DRINKS FIRST.

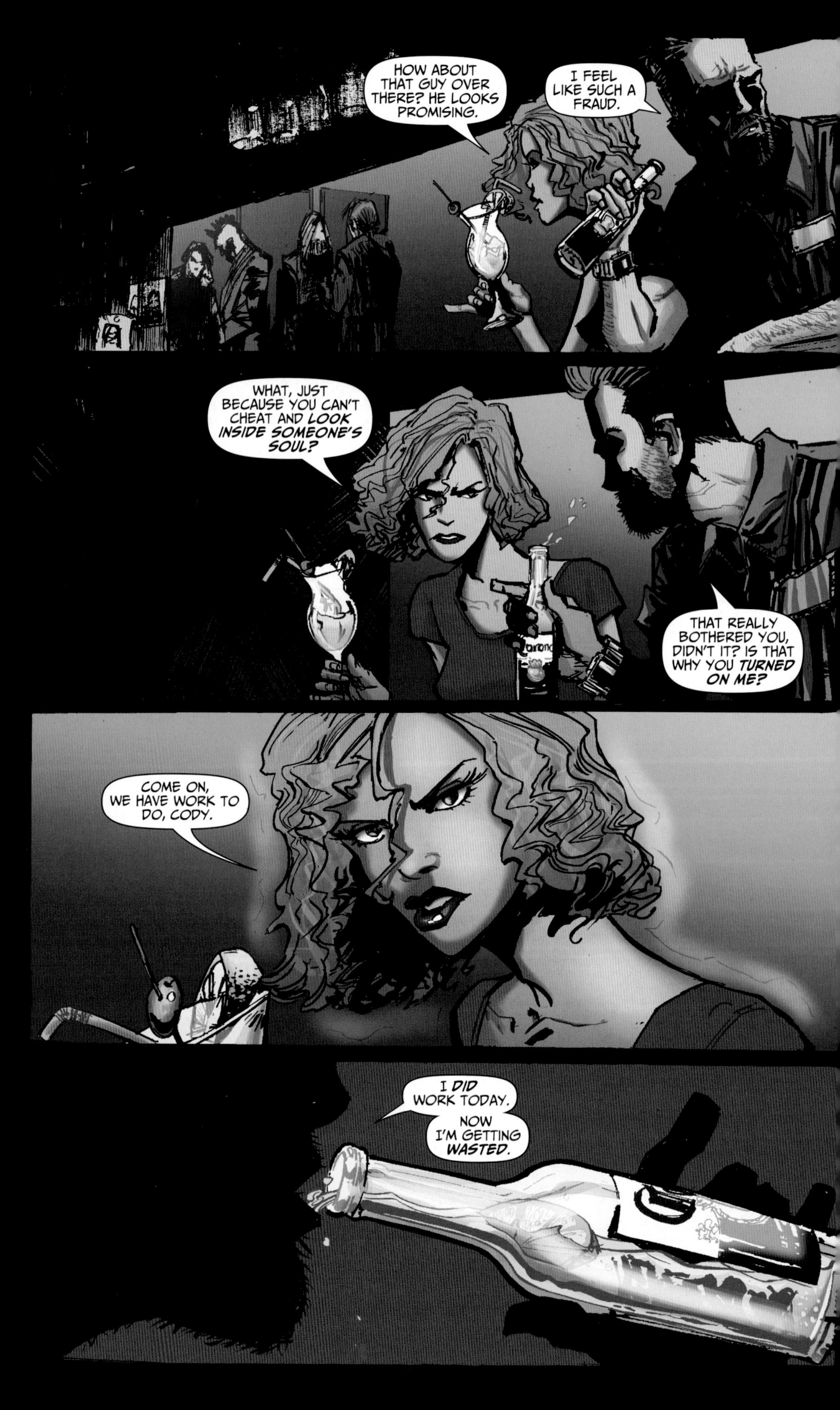
HOW ABOUT THAT GUY OVER THERE? HE LOOKS PROMISING.
I FEEL LIKE SUCH A FRAUD.
WHAT, JUST BECAUSE YOU CAN'T CHEAT AND *LOOK INSIDE SOMEONE'S SOUL?*
THAT REALLY BOTHERED YOU, DIDN'T IT? IS THAT WHY YOU *TURNED ON ME?*
COME ON, WE HAVE WORK TO DO, CODY.
I *DID* WORK TODAY.
NOW I'M GETTING *WASTED.*

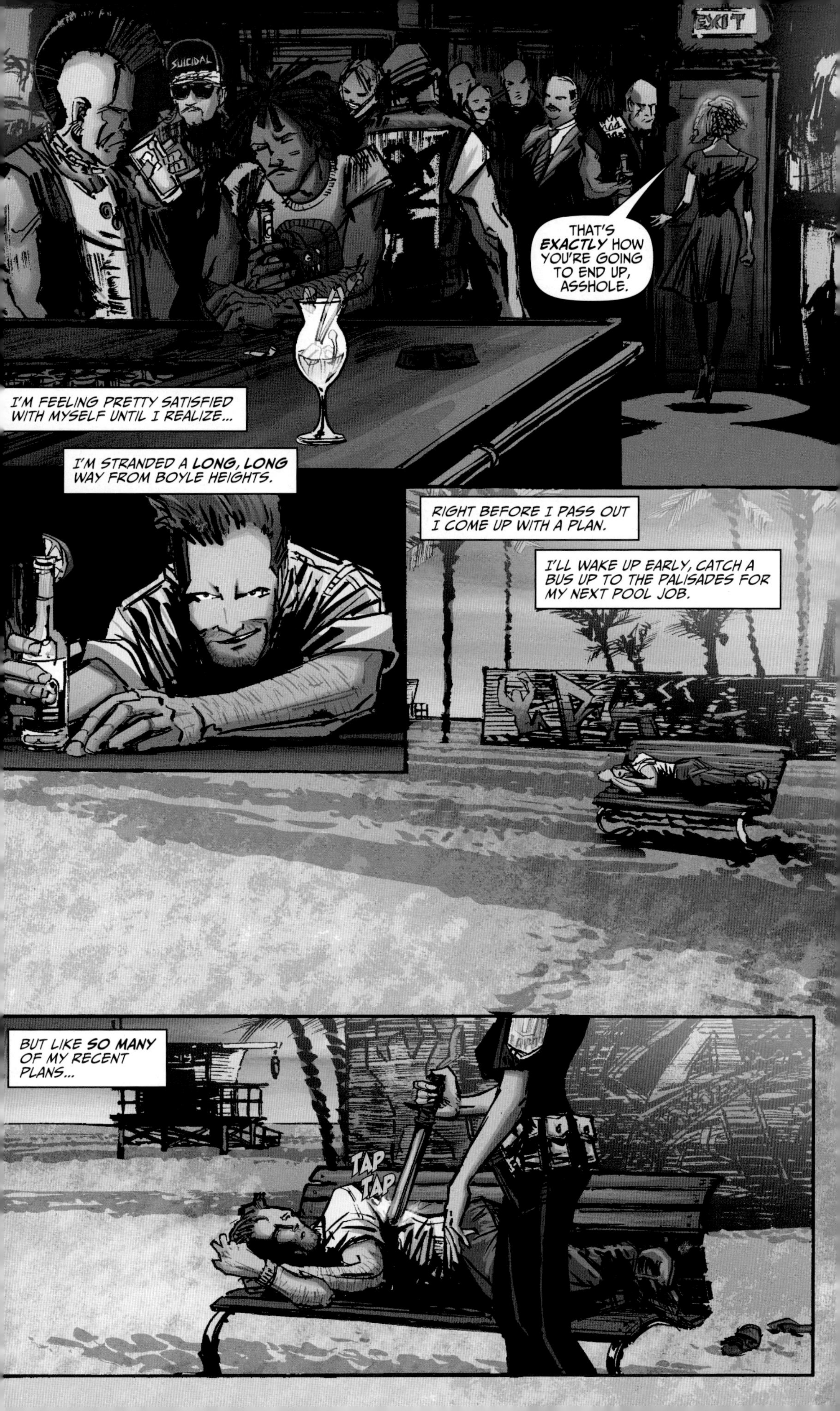
SUICIDAL
EXIT
THAT'S EXACTLY HOW YOU'RE GOING TO END UP, ASSHOLE.
I'M FEELING PRETTY SATISFIED WITH MYSELF UNTIL I REALIZE...
I'M STRANDED A LONG, LONG WAY FROM BOYLE HEIGHTS.
RIGHT BEFORE I PASS OUT I COME UP WITH A PLAN.
I'LL WAKE UP EARLY, CATCH A BUS UP TO THE PALISADES FOR MY NEXT POOL JOB.
BUT LIKE SO MANY OF MY RECENT PLANS...
TAP TAP

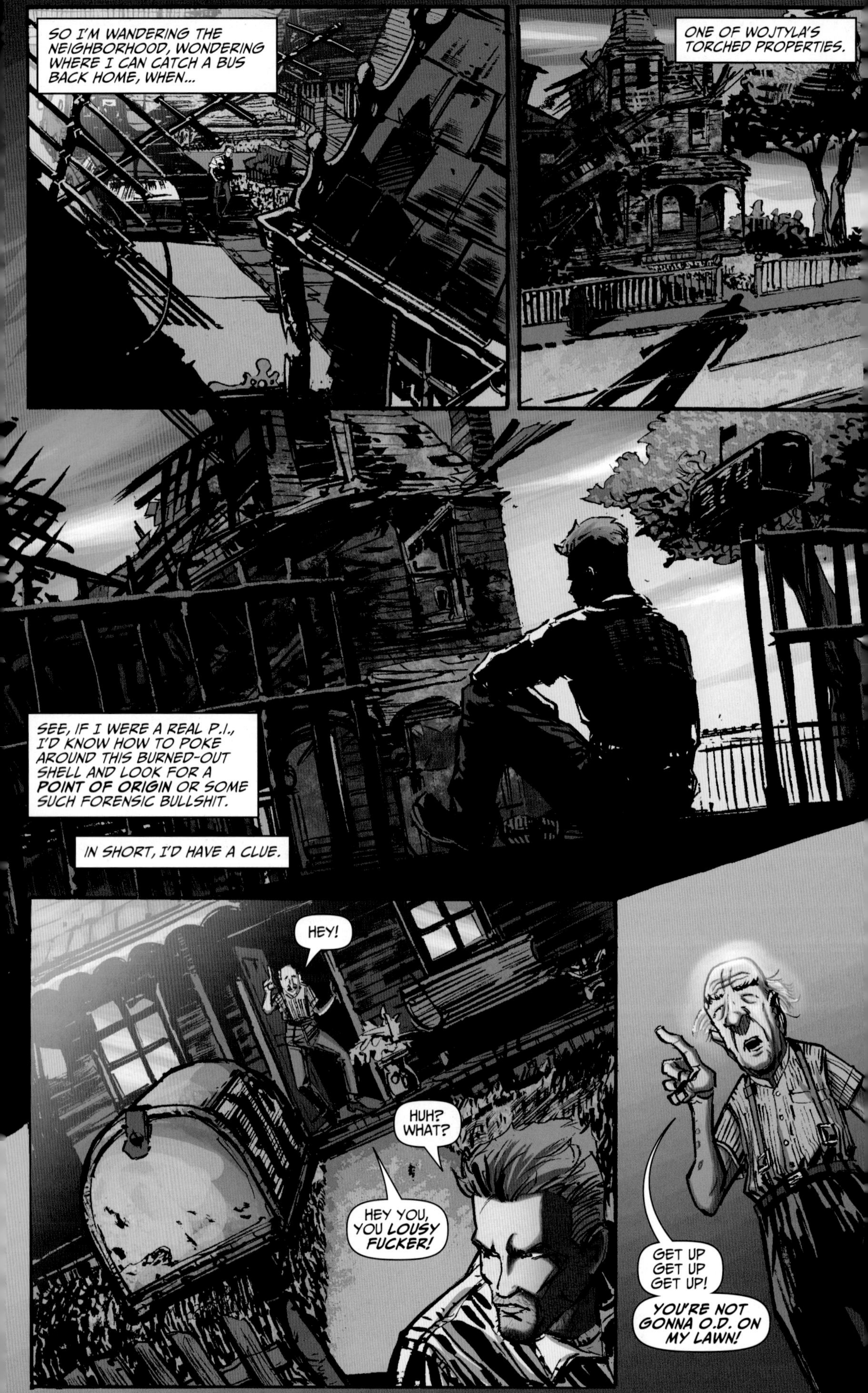
SO I'M WANDERING THE NEIGHBORHOOD, WONDERING WHERE I CAN CATCH A BUS BACK HOME, WHEN...
ONE OF WOJTYLA'S TORCHED PROPERTIES.
SEE, IF I WERE A REAL P.I., I'D KNOW HOW TO POKE AROUND THIS BURNED-OUT SHELL AND LOOK FOR A POINT OF ORIGIN OR SOME SUCH FORENSIC BULLSHIT.
IN SHORT, I'D HAVE A CLUE.
HEY!
HUH? WHAT?
HEY YOU, YOU LOUSY FUCKER!
GET UP GET UP GET UP!
YOU'RE NOT GONNA O.D. ON MY LAWN!

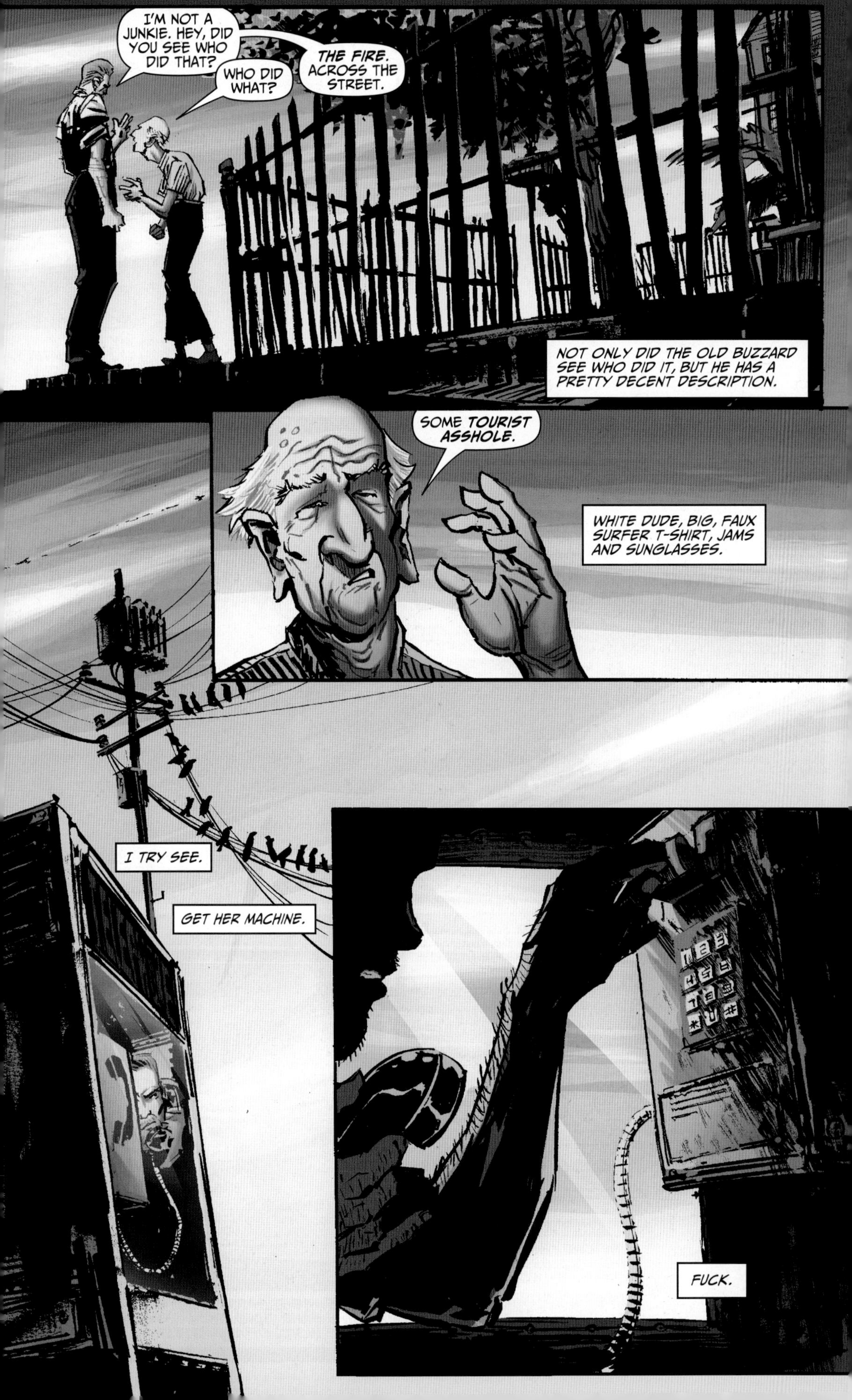
I'M NOT A JUNKIE. HEY, DID YOU SEE WHO DID THAT?
WHO DID WHAT?
THE FIRE. ACROSS THE STREET.
NOT ONLY DID THE OLD BUZZARD SEE WHO DID IT, BUT HE HAS A PRETTY DECENT DESCRIPTION.
SOME TOURIST ASSHOLE.
WHITE DUDE, BIG, FAUX SURFER T-SHIRT, JAMS AND SUNGLASSES.
I TRY SEE.
GET HER MACHINE.
FUCK.

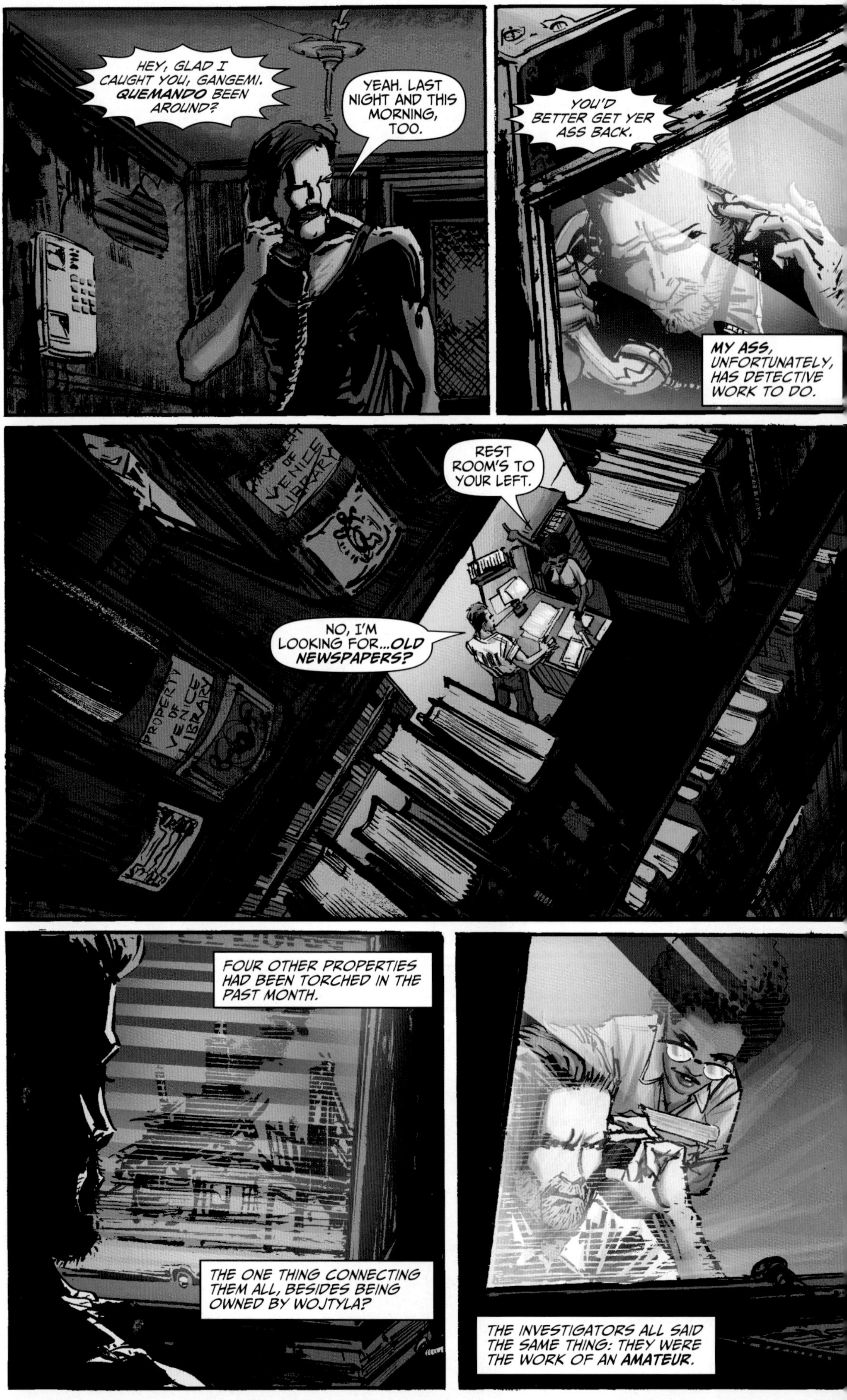
HEY, GLAD I CAUGHT YOU, GANGEMI. QUEMANDO BEEN AROUND?
YEAH. LAST NIGHT AND THIS MORNING, TOO.
YOU'D BETTER GET YER ASS BACK.
MY ASS, UNFORTUNATELY, HAS DETECTIVE WORK TO DO.
PROPERTY OF VENICE LIBRARY
REST ROOM'S TO YOUR LEFT.
NO, I'M LOOKING FOR...OLD NEWSPAPERS?
PROPERTY OF VENICE LIBRARY
FOUR OTHER PROPERTIES HAD BEEN TORCHED IN THE PAST MONTH.
THE ONE THING CONNECTING THEM ALL, BESIDES BEING OWNED BY WOJTYLA?
THE INVESTIGATORS ALL SAID THE SAME THING: THEY WERE THE WORK OF AN AMATEUR.

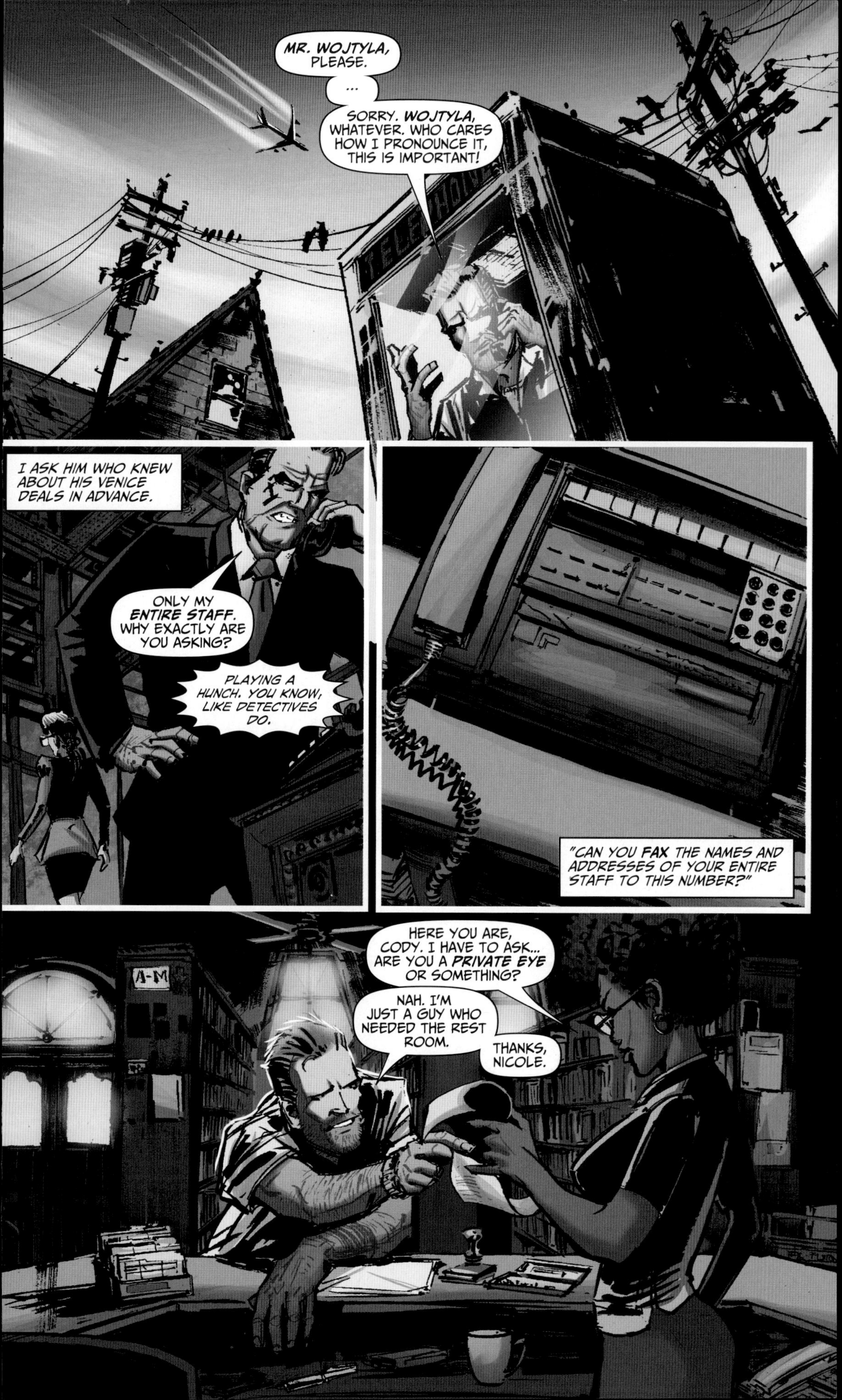

MR. WOJTYLA, PLEASE.
...
SORRY. WOJTYLA, WHATEVER. WHO CARES HOW I PRONOUNCE IT, THIS IS IMPORTANT!
I ASK HIM WHO KNEW ABOUT HIS VENICE DEALS IN ADVANCE.
ONLY MY ENTIRE STAFF. WHY EXACTLY ARE YOU ASKING?
PLAYING A HUNCH. YOU KNOW, LIKE DETECTIVES DO.
"CAN YOU FAX THE NAMES AND ADDRESSES OF YOUR ENTIRE STAFF TO THIS NUMBER?"
HERE YOU ARE, CODY. I HAVE TO ASK... ARE YOU A PRIVATE EYE OR SOMETHING?
NAH. I'M JUST A GUY WHO NEEDED THE REST ROOM.
THANKS, NICOLE.
A-M

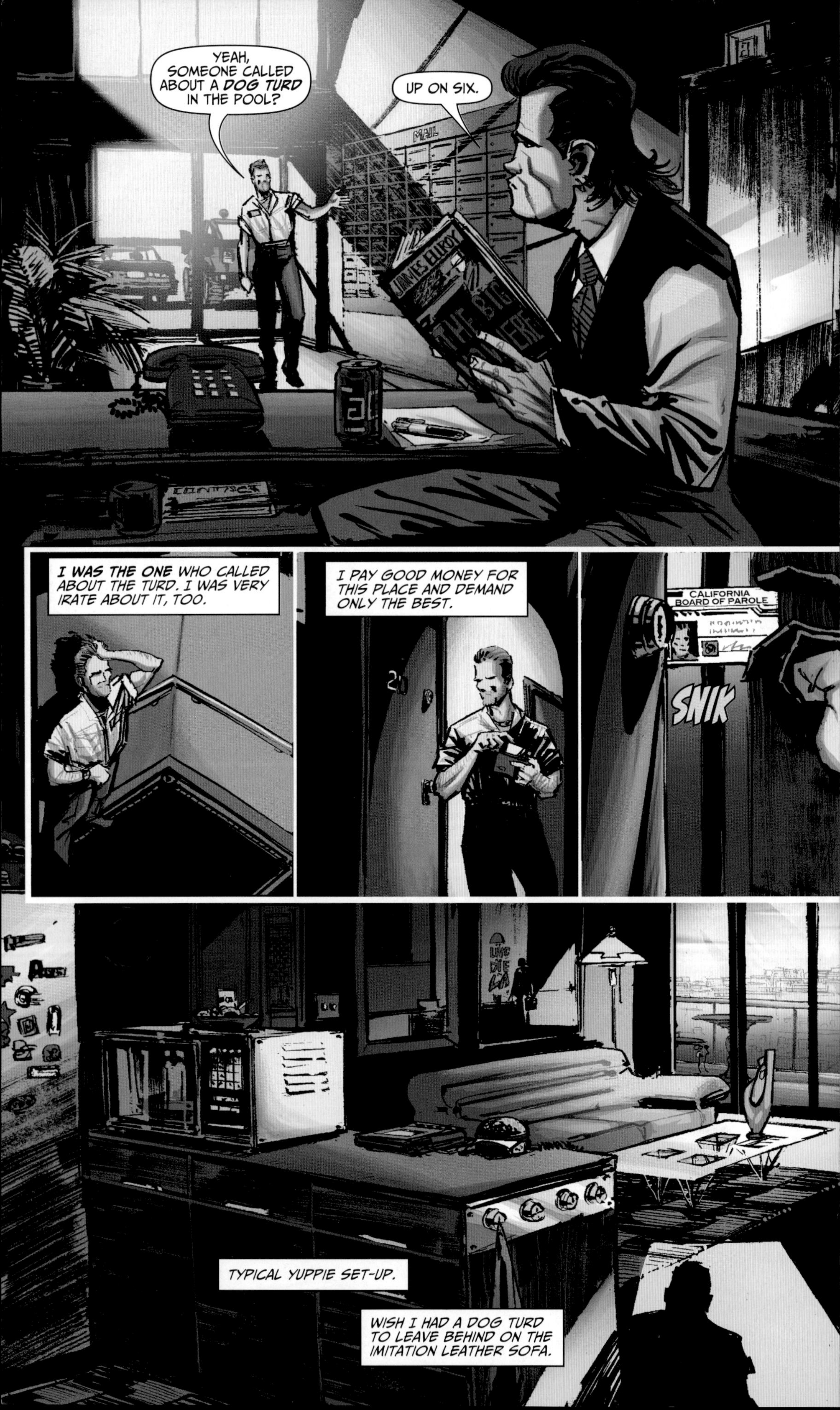

YEAH, SOMEONE CALLED ABOUT A DOG TURD IN THE POOL?
UP ON SIX.
MAIL
JAMES ELLROY
I WAS THE ONE WHO CALLED ABOUT THE TURD. I WAS VERY IRATE ABOUT IT, TOO.
I PAY GOOD MONEY FOR THIS PLACE AND DEMAND ONLY THE BEST.
CALIFORNIA BOARD OF PAROLE
SNIK
TYPICAL YUPPIE SET-UP.
WISH I HAD A DOG TURD TO LEAVE BEHIND ON THE IMITATION LEATHER SOFA.

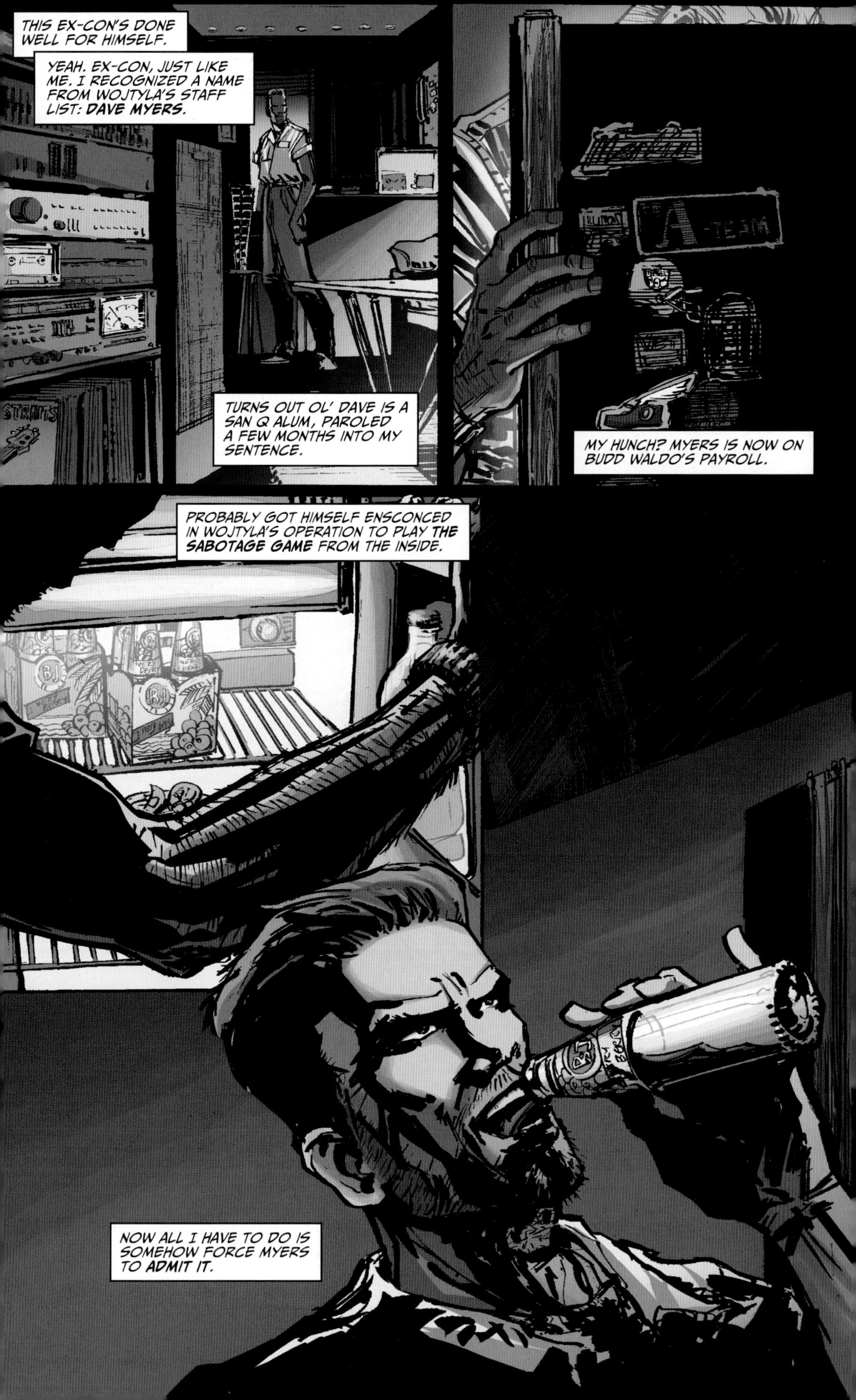
THIS EX-CON'S DONE WELL FOR HIMSELF.
YEAH. EX-CON, JUST LIKE ME. I RECOGNIZED A NAME FROM WOJTYLA'S STAFF LIST: **DAVE MYERS.**
TURNS OUT OL' DAVE IS A SAN Q ALUM, PAROLED A FEW MONTHS INTO MY SENTENCE.
A-TEAM
MY HUNCH? MYERS IS NOW ON BUDD WALDO'S PAYROLL.
PROBABLY GOT HIMSELF ENSCONCED IN WOJTYLA'S OPERATION TO PLAY **THE SABOTAGE GAME** FROM THE INSIDE.
NOW ALL I HAVE TO DO IS SOMEHOW FORCE MYERS TO **ADMIT** IT.

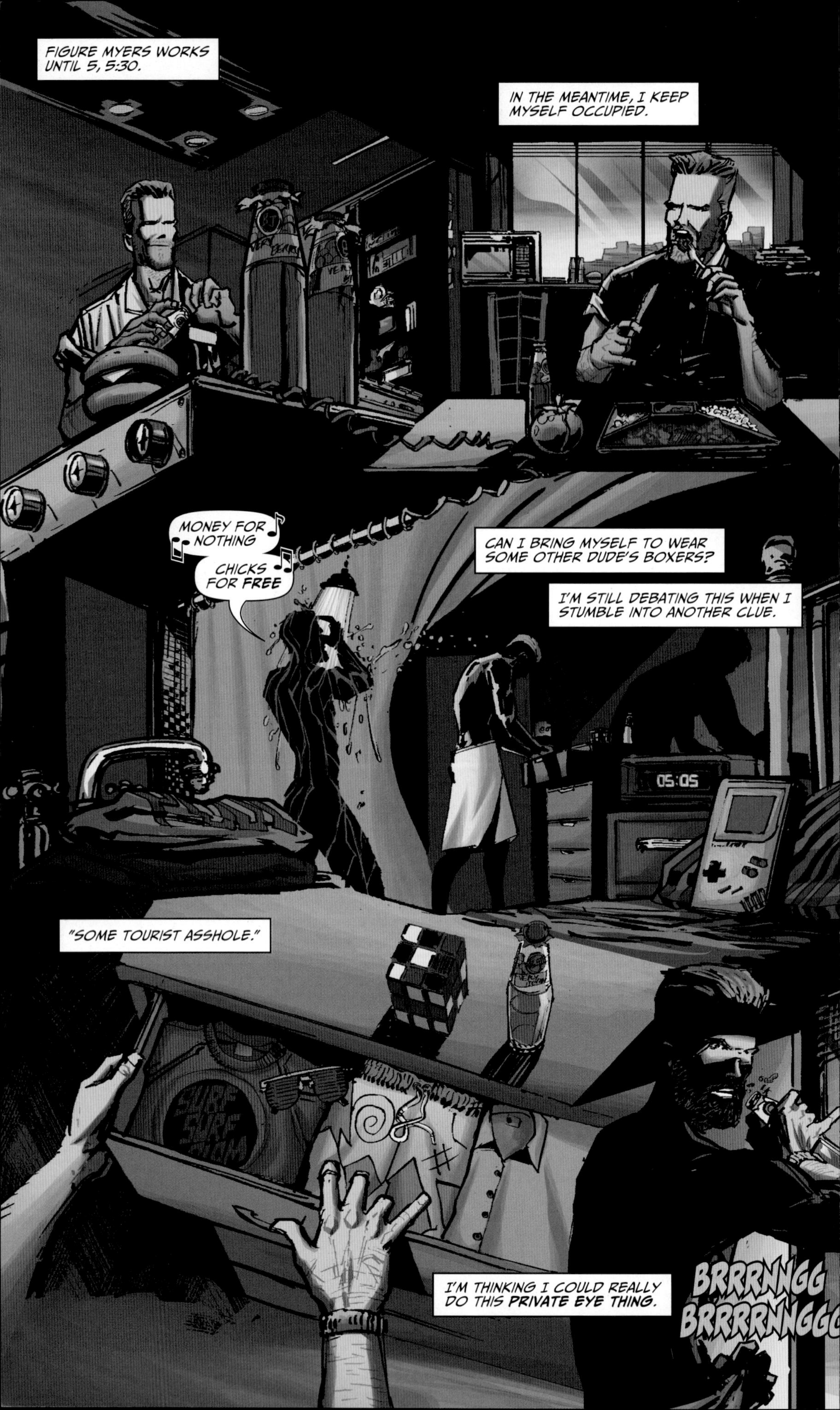
FIGURE MYERS WORKS UNTIL 5, 5:30.
IN THE MEANTIME, I KEEP MYSELF OCCUPIED.
MONEY FOR NOTHING
CHICKS FOR FREE
CAN I BRING MYSELF TO WEAR SOME OTHER DUDE'S BOXERS?
I'M STILL DEBATING THIS WHEN I STUMBLE INTO ANOTHER CLUE.
05:05
"SOME TOURIST ASSHOLE."
I'M THINKING I COULD REALLY DO THIS PRIVATE EYE THING.
BRRRNNGG
BRRRRNNGG

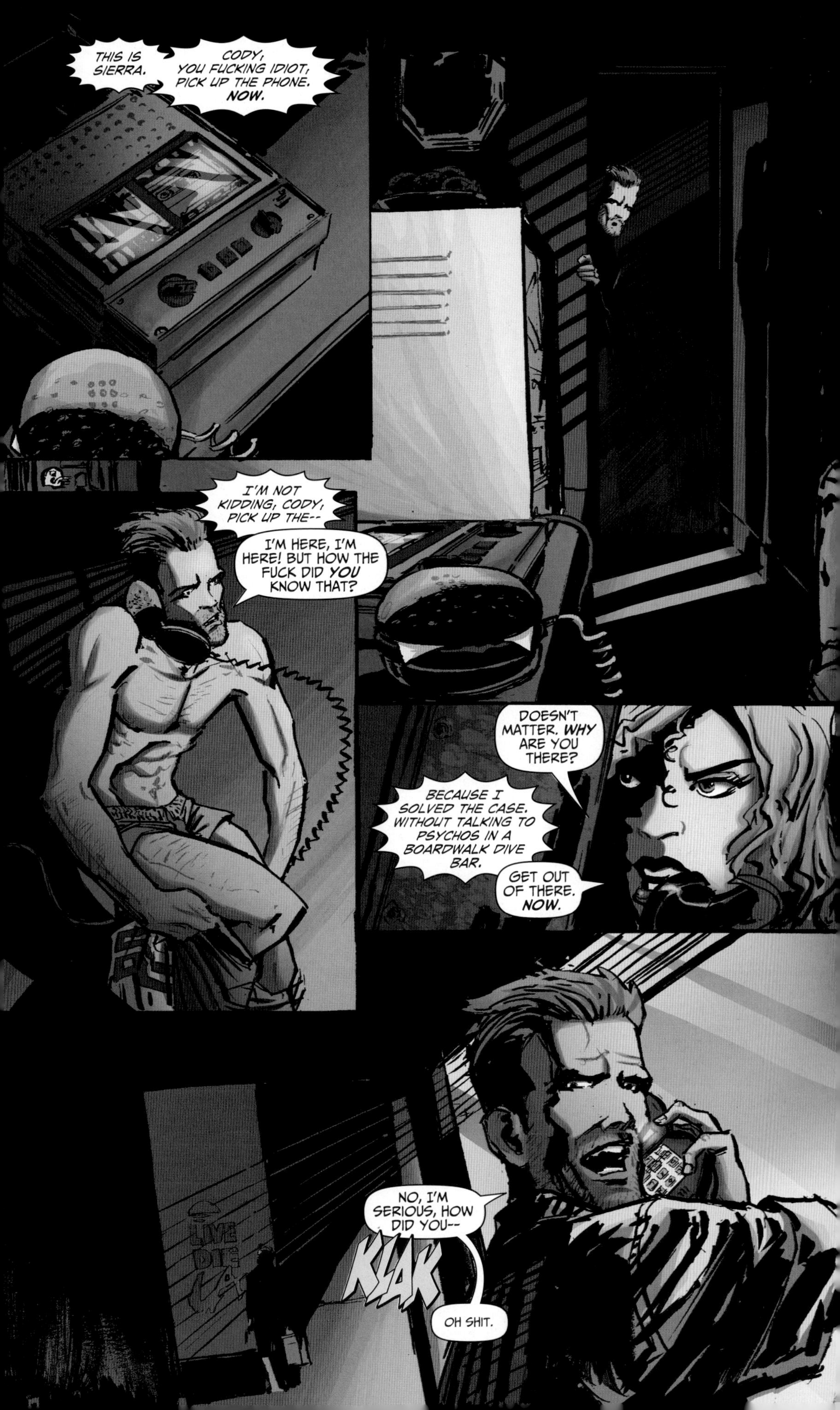
THIS IS SIERRA.
CODY, YOU FUCKING IDIOT, PICK UP THE PHONE. NOW.
I'M NOT KIDDING, CODY, PICK UP THE--
I'M HERE, I'M HERE! BUT HOW THE FUCK DID YOU KNOW THAT?
DOESN'T MATTER. WHY ARE YOU THERE?
BECAUSE I SOLVED THE CASE. WITHOUT TALKING TO PSYCHOS IN A BOARDWALK DIVE BAR.
GET OUT OF THERE. NOW.
NO, I'M SERIOUS, HOW DID YOU--
KLAK
OH SHIT.

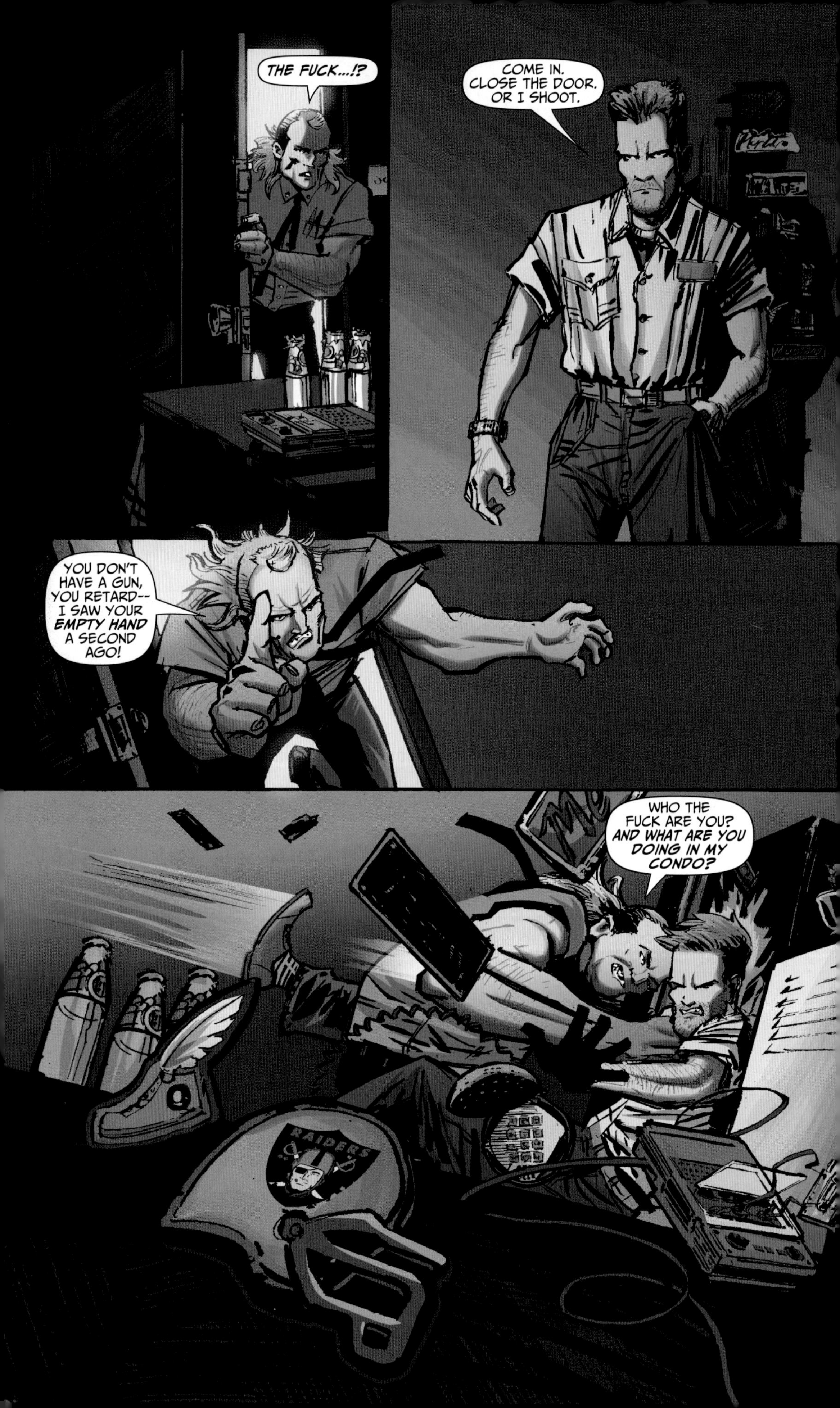
THE FUCK...!?
COME IN. CLOSE THE DOOR. OR I SHOOT.
YOU DON'T HAVE A GUN, YOU RETARD-- I SAW YOUR EMPTY HAND A SECOND AGO!
WHO THE FUCK ARE YOU? AND WHAT ARE YOU DOING IN MY CONDO?
RAIDERS

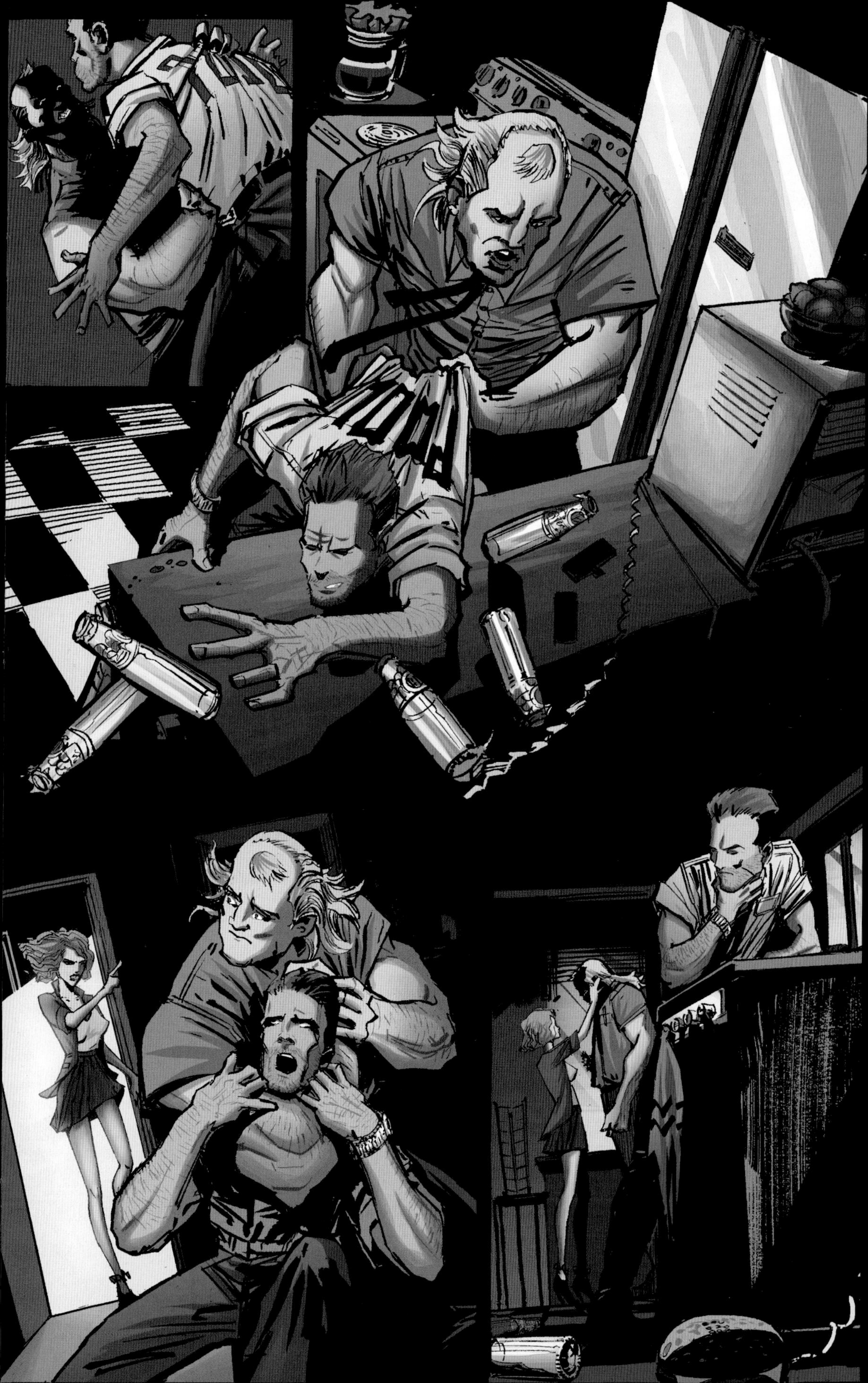

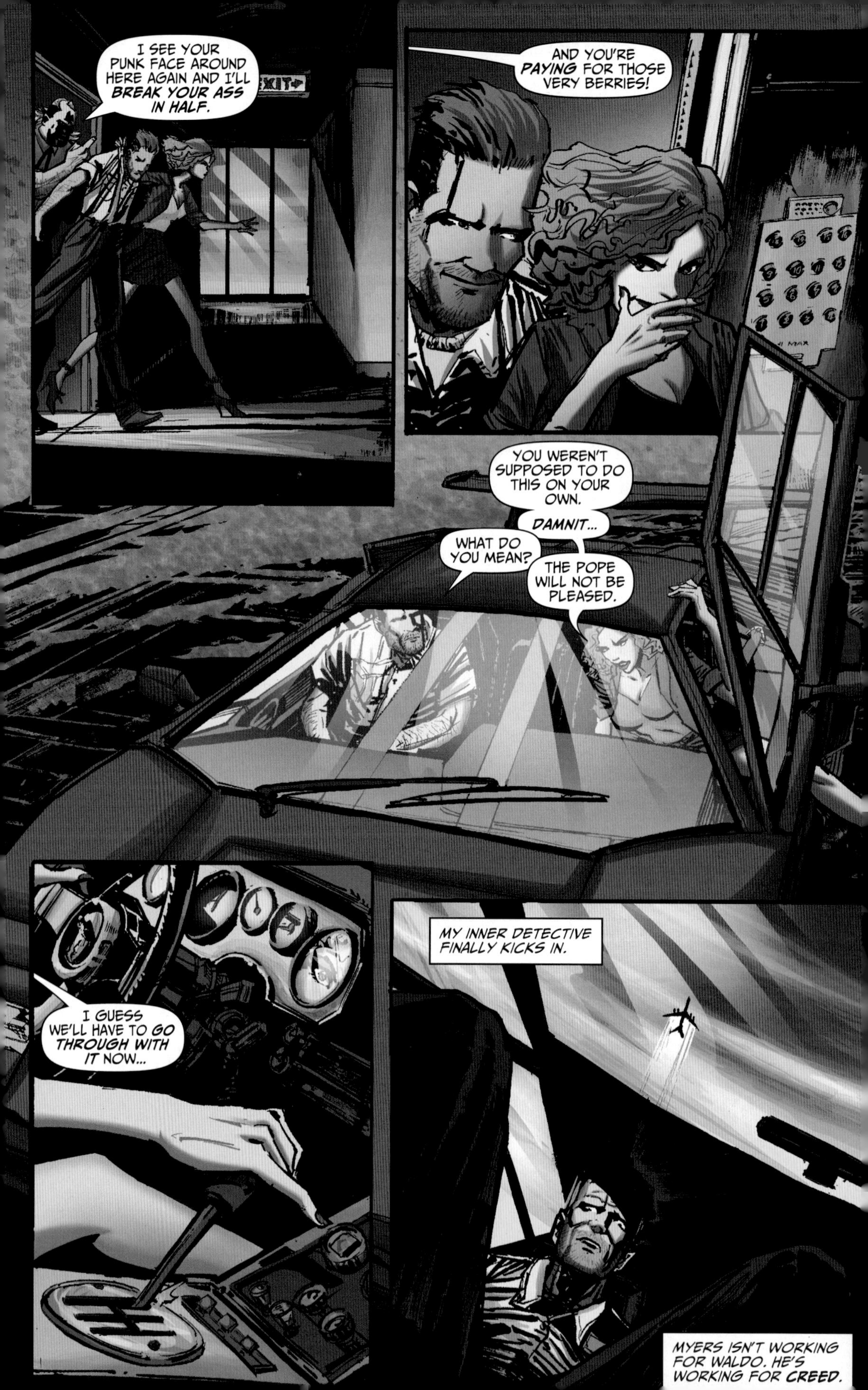
I SEE YOUR PUNK FACE AROUND HERE AGAIN AND I'LL **BREAK YOUR ASS IN HALF.**
EXIT
AND YOU'RE ***PAYING*** FOR THOSE VERY BERRIES!
YOU WEREN'T SUPPOSED TO DO THIS ON YOUR OWN.
DAMNIT...
WHAT DO YOU MEAN?
THE POPE WILL NOT BE PLEASED.
I GUESS WE'LL HAVE TO ***GO THROUGH WITH IT*** NOW...
MY INNER DETECTIVE FINALLY KICKS IN.
*MYERS ISN'T WORKING FOR WALDO. HE'S WORKING FOR **CREED**.*

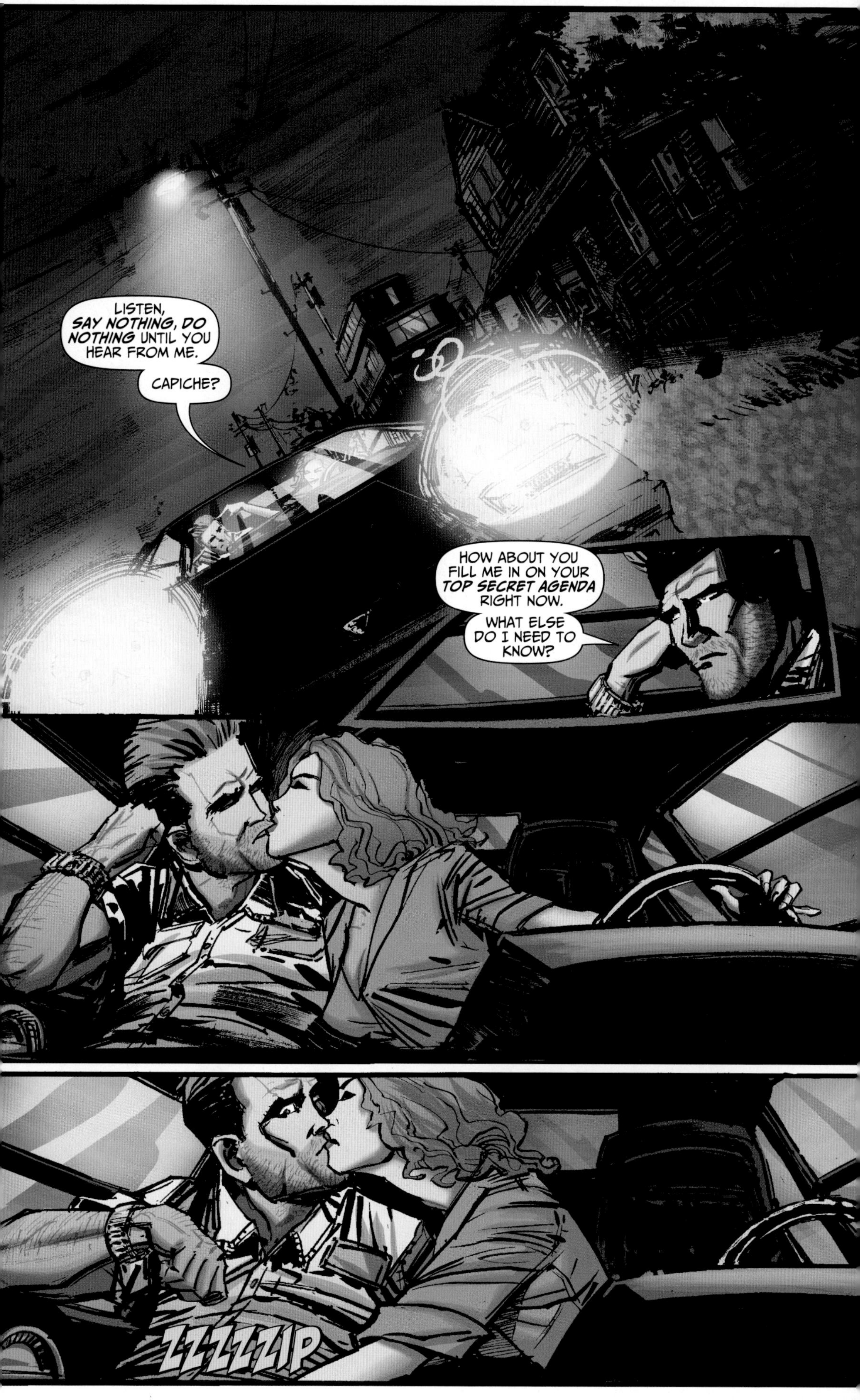
LISTEN, SAY NOTHING, DO NOTHING UNTIL YOU HEAR FROM ME.
CAPICHE?
HOW ABOUT YOU FILL ME IN ON YOUR TOP SECRET AGENDA RIGHT NOW.
WHAT ELSE DO I NEED TO KNOW?
ZZZZZIP

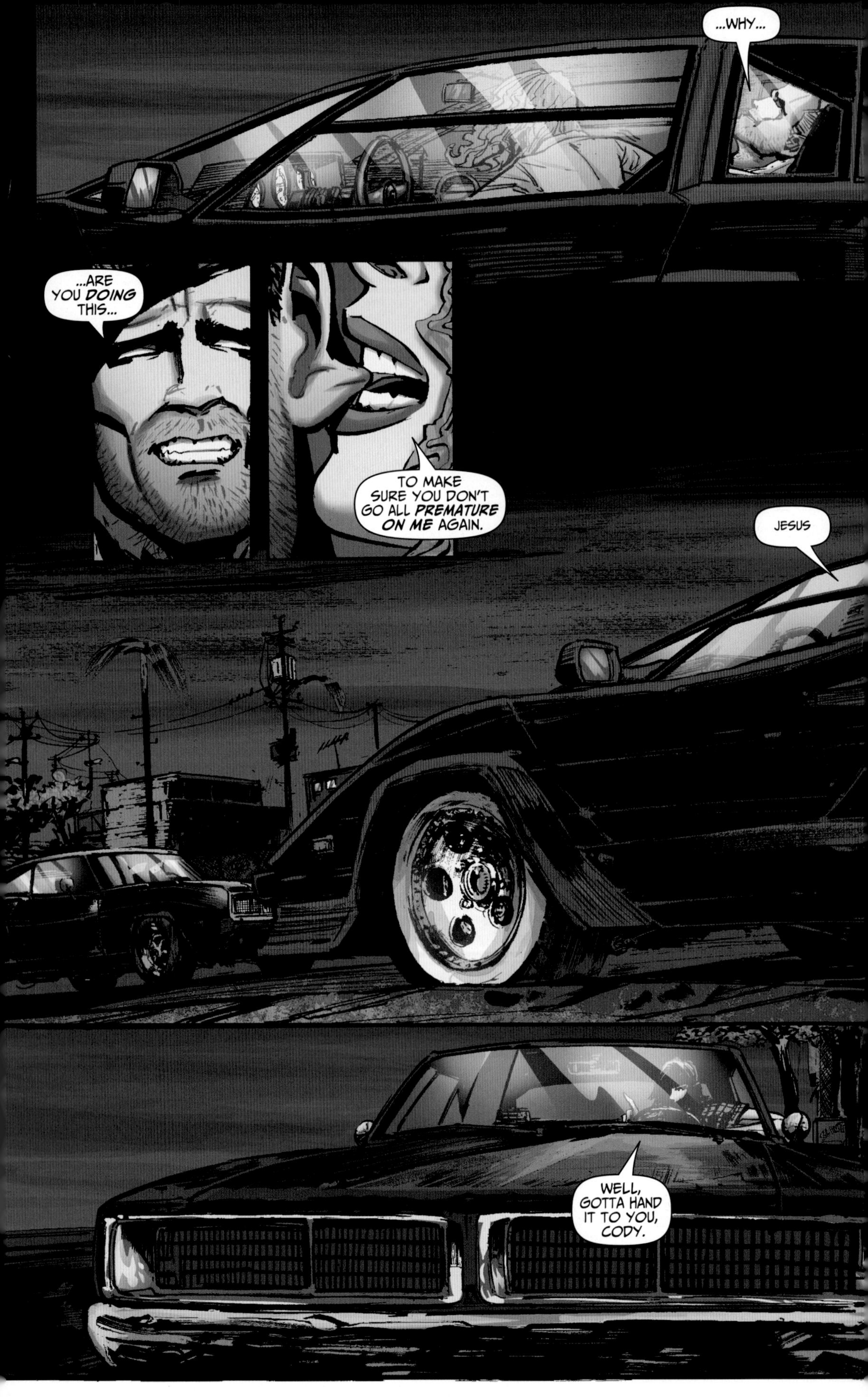
...WHY...
...ARE YOU DOING THIS...
TO MAKE SURE YOU DON'T GO ALL PREMATURE ON ME AGAIN.
JESUS
WELL, GOTTA HAND IT TO YOU, CODY.

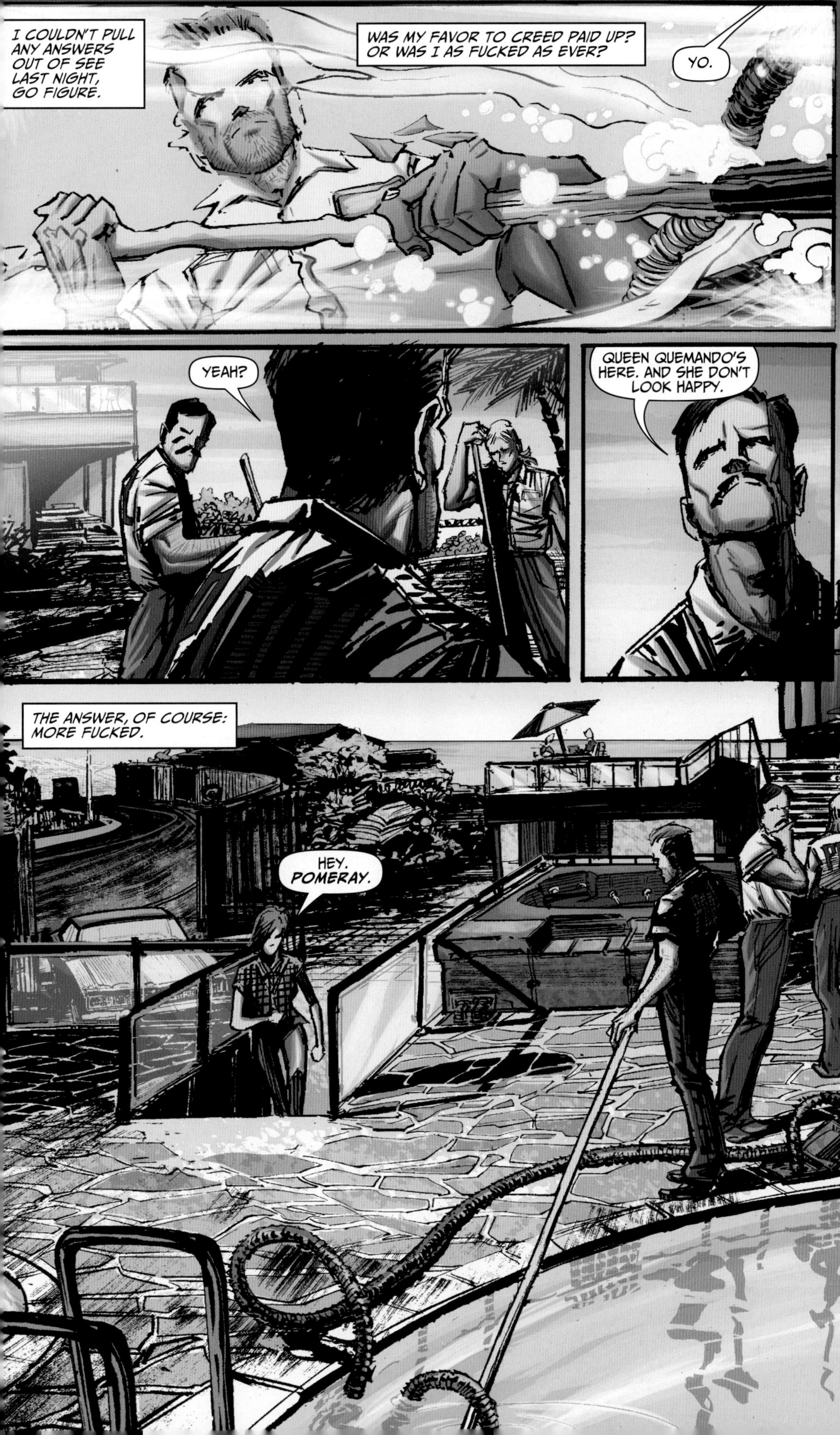
I COULDN'T PULL ANY ANSWERS OUT OF SEE LAST NIGHT, GO FIGURE.
WAS MY FAVOR TO CREED PAID UP? OR WAS I AS FUCKED AS EVER?
YO.
YEAH?
QUEEN QUEMANDO'S HERE. AND SHE DON'T LOOK HAPPY.
THE ANSWER, OF COURSE: MORE FUCKED.
HEY. **POMERAY.**

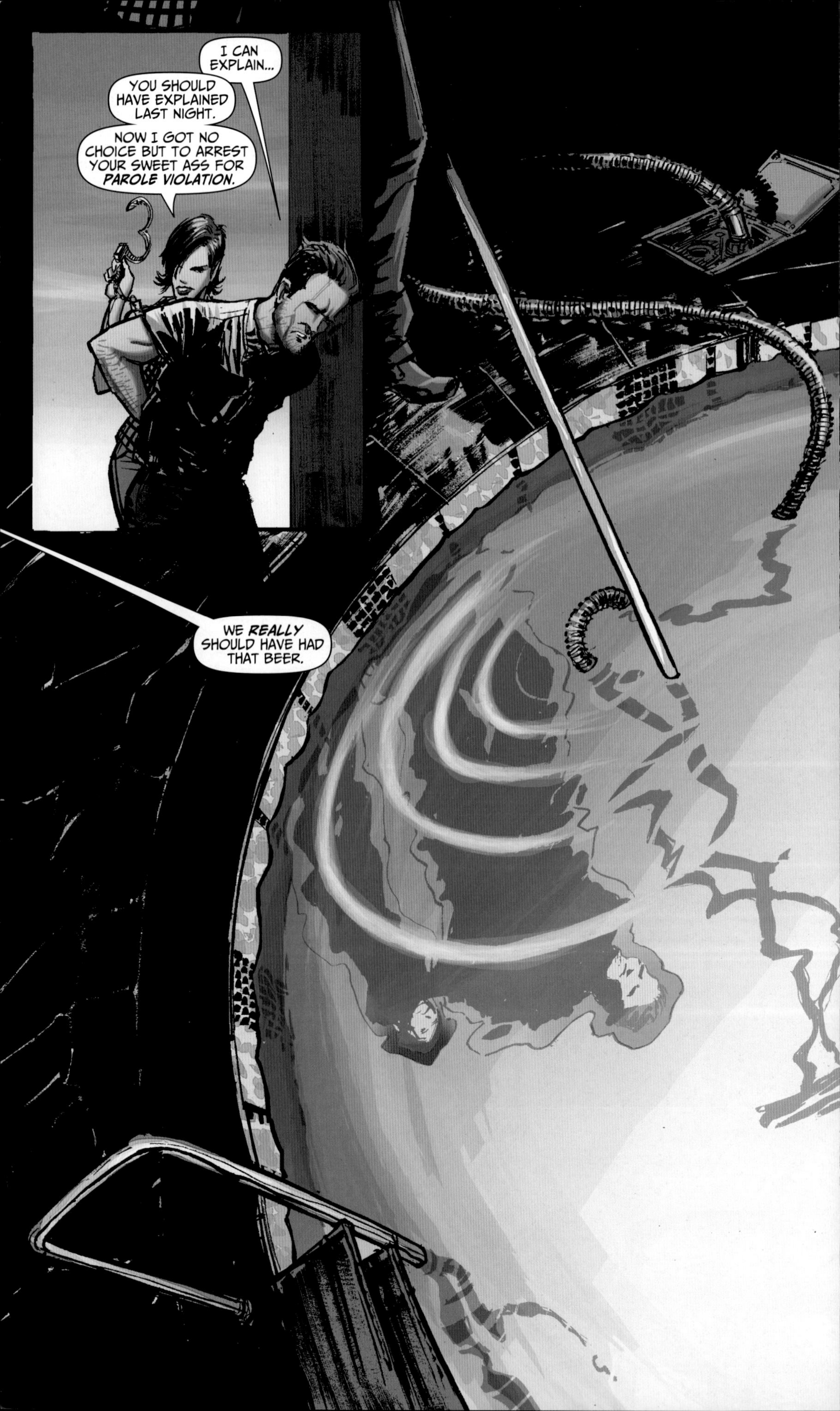
I CAN EXPLAIN...
YOU SHOULD HAVE EXPLAINED LAST NIGHT.
NOW I GOT NO CHOICE BUT TO ARREST YOUR SWEET ASS FOR PAROLE VIOLATION.
WE REALLY SHOULD HAVE HAD THAT BEER.

THREE

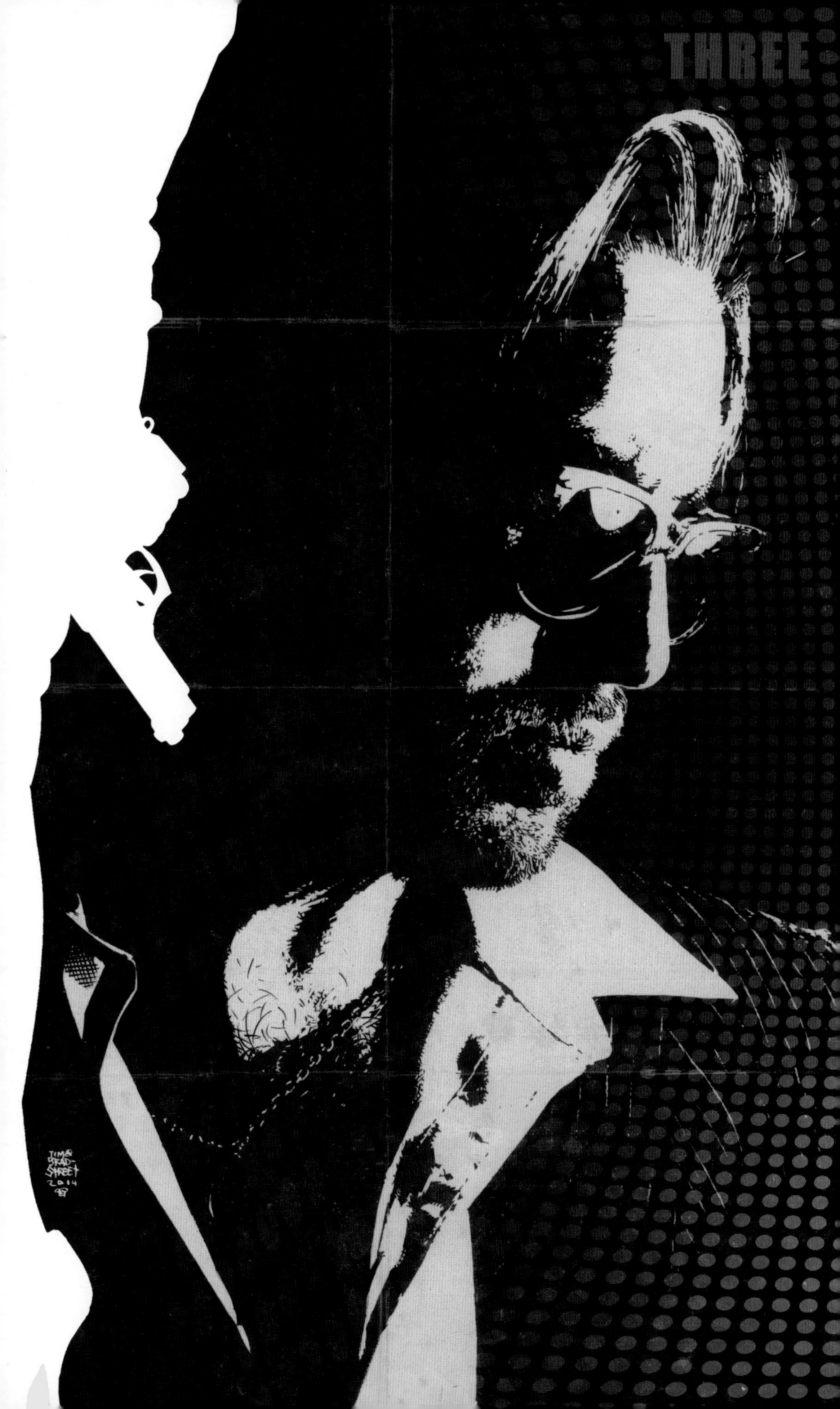

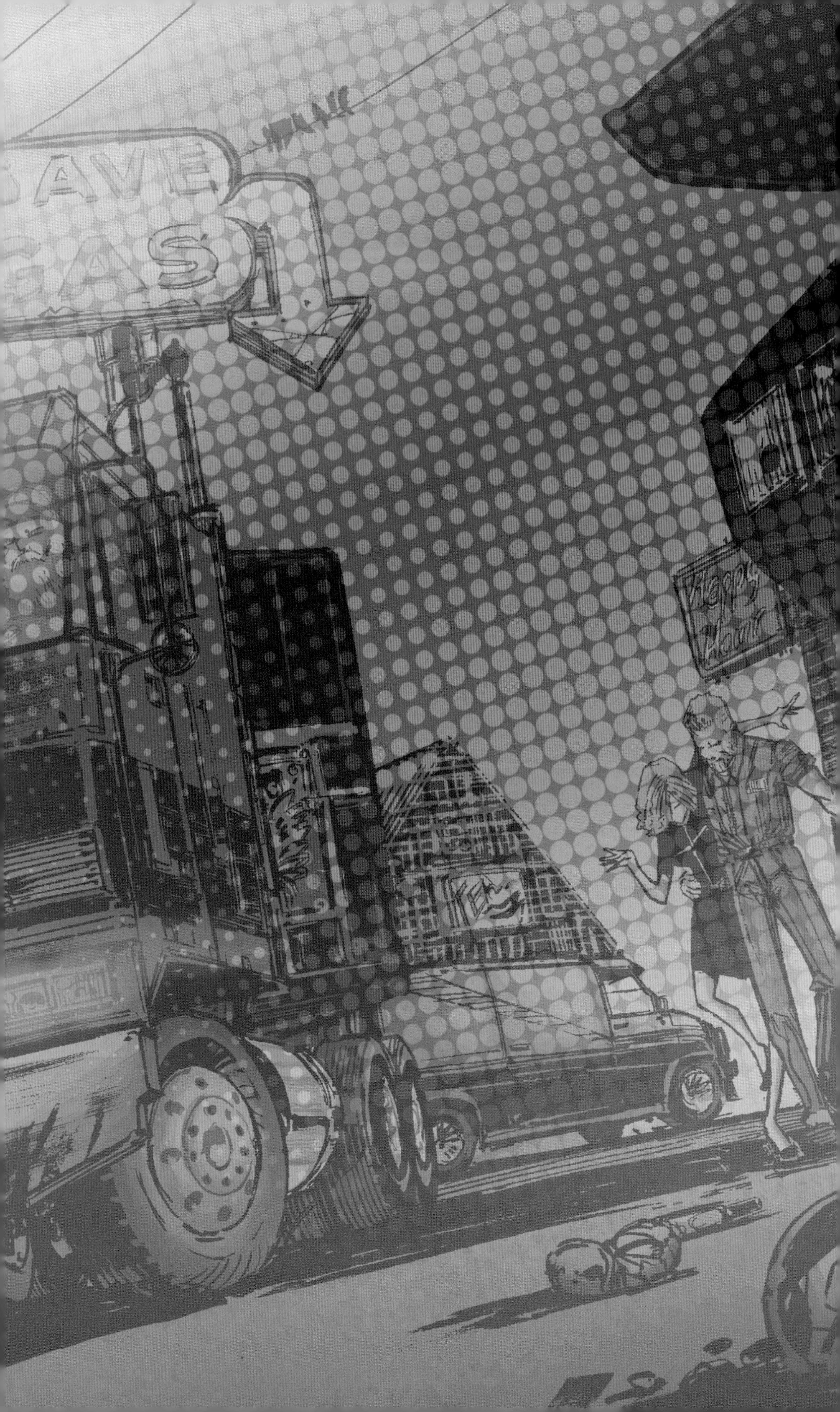
SAVE GAS
Happy Hour

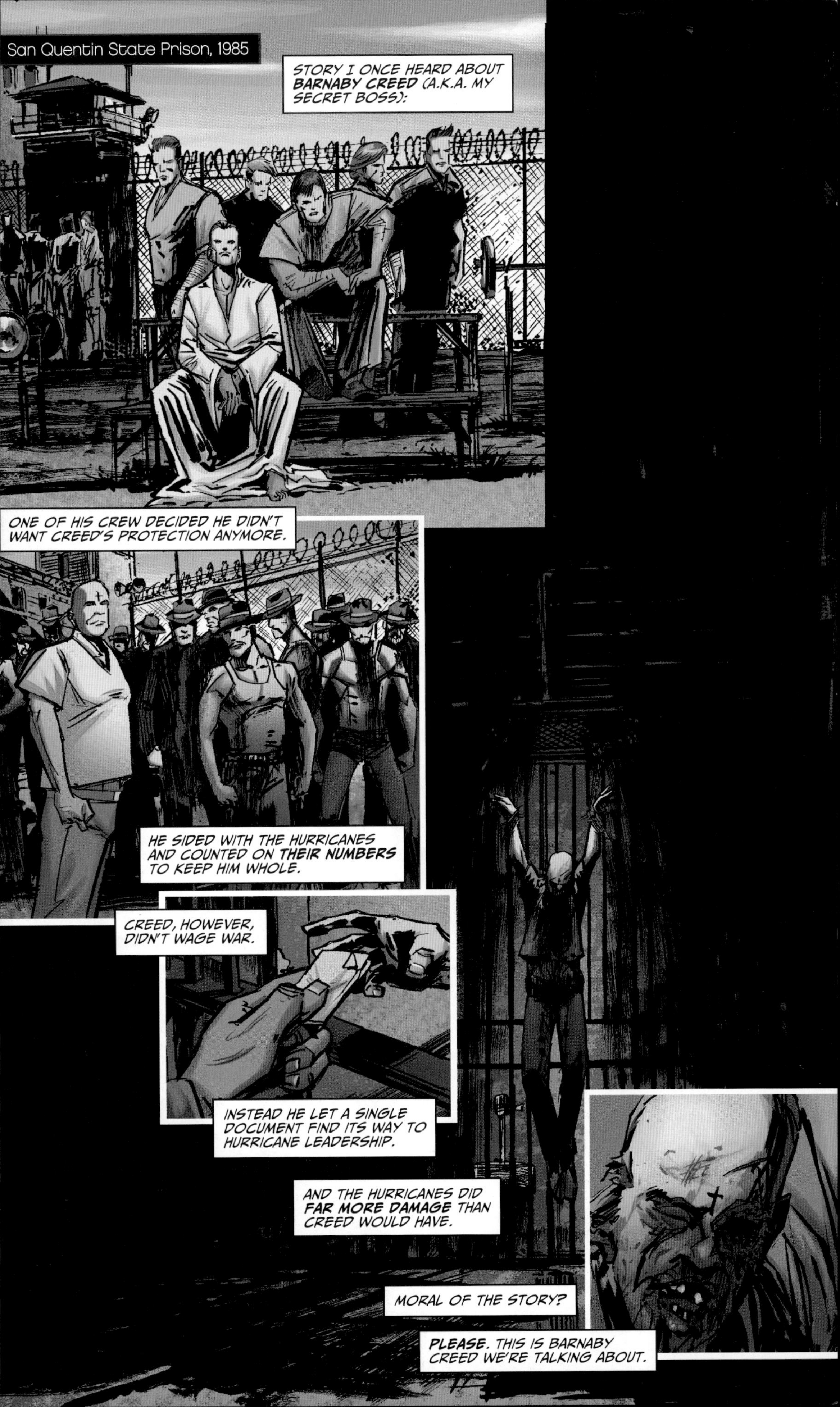
San Quentin State Prison, 1985
STORY I ONCE HEARD ABOUT BARNABY CREED (A.K.A. MY SECRET BOSS):
ONE OF HIS CREW DECIDED HE DIDN'T WANT CREED'S PROTECTION ANYMORE.
HE SIDED WITH THE HURRICANES AND COUNTED ON THEIR NUMBERS TO KEEP HIM WHOLE.
CREED, HOWEVER, DIDN'T WAGE WAR.
INSTEAD HE LET A SINGLE DOCUMENT FIND ITS WAY TO HURRICANE LEADERSHIP.
AND THE HURRICANES DID FAR MORE DAMAGE THAN CREED WOULD HAVE.
MORAL OF THE STORY?
PLEASE. THIS IS BARNABY CREED WE'RE TALKING ABOUT.

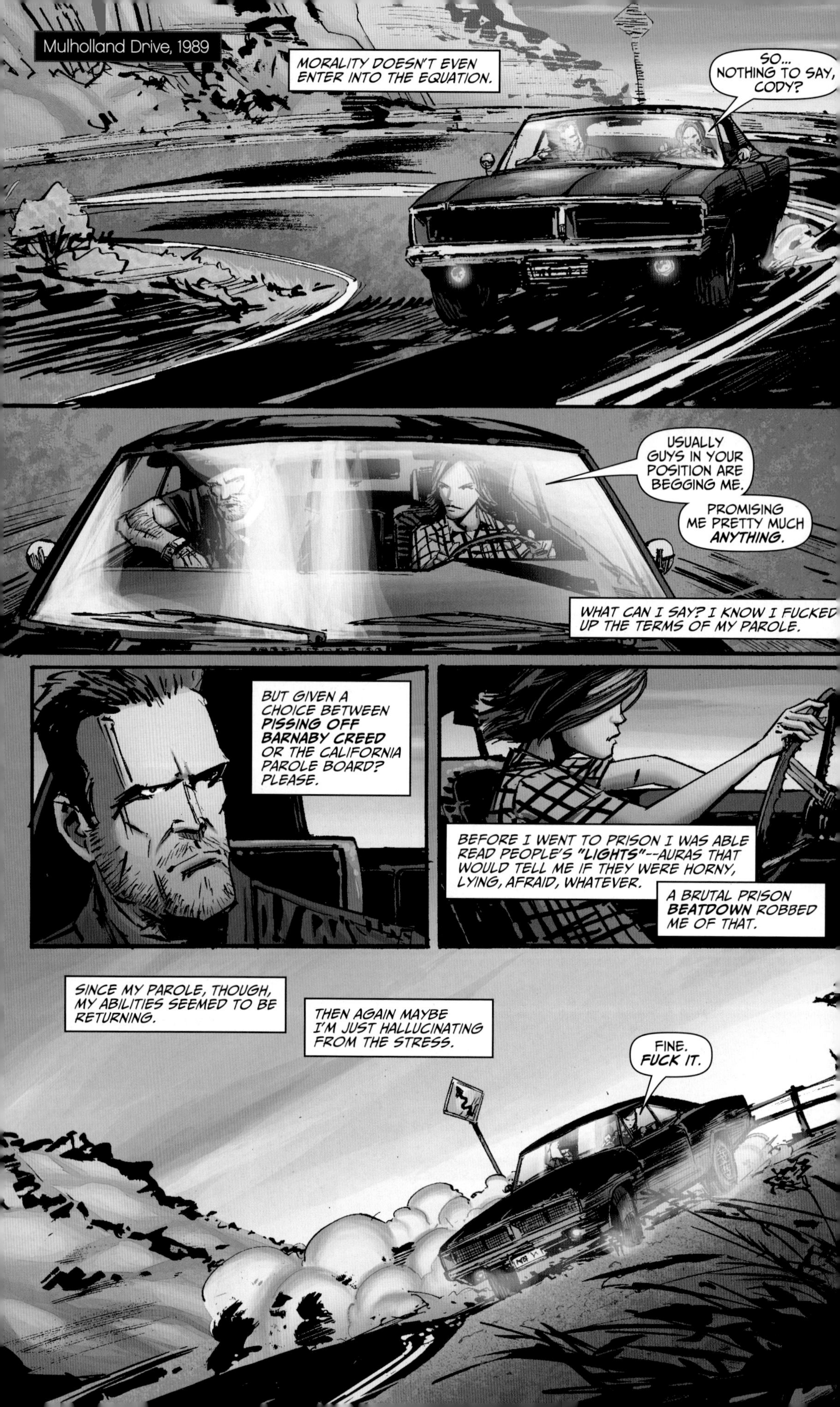

Mulholland Drive, 1989
MORALITY DOESN'T EVEN ENTER INTO THE EQUATION.
SO... NOTHING TO SAY, CODY?
USUALLY GUYS IN YOUR POSITION ARE BEGGING ME.
PROMISING ME PRETTY MUCH ANYTHING.
WHAT CAN I SAY? I KNOW I FUCKED UP THE TERMS OF MY PAROLE.
BUT GIVEN A CHOICE BETWEEN PISSING OFF BARNABY CREED OR THE CALIFORNIA PAROLE BOARD? PLEASE.
BEFORE I WENT TO PRISON I WAS ABLE READ PEOPLE'S "LIGHTS"--AURAS THAT WOULD TELL ME IF THEY WERE HORNY, LYING, AFRAID, WHATEVER.
A BRUTAL PRISON BEATDOWN ROBBED ME OF THAT.
SINCE MY PAROLE, THOUGH, MY ABILITIES SEEMED TO BE RETURNING.
THEN AGAIN MAYBE I'M JUST HALLUCINATING FROM THE STRESS.
FINE. FUCK IT.

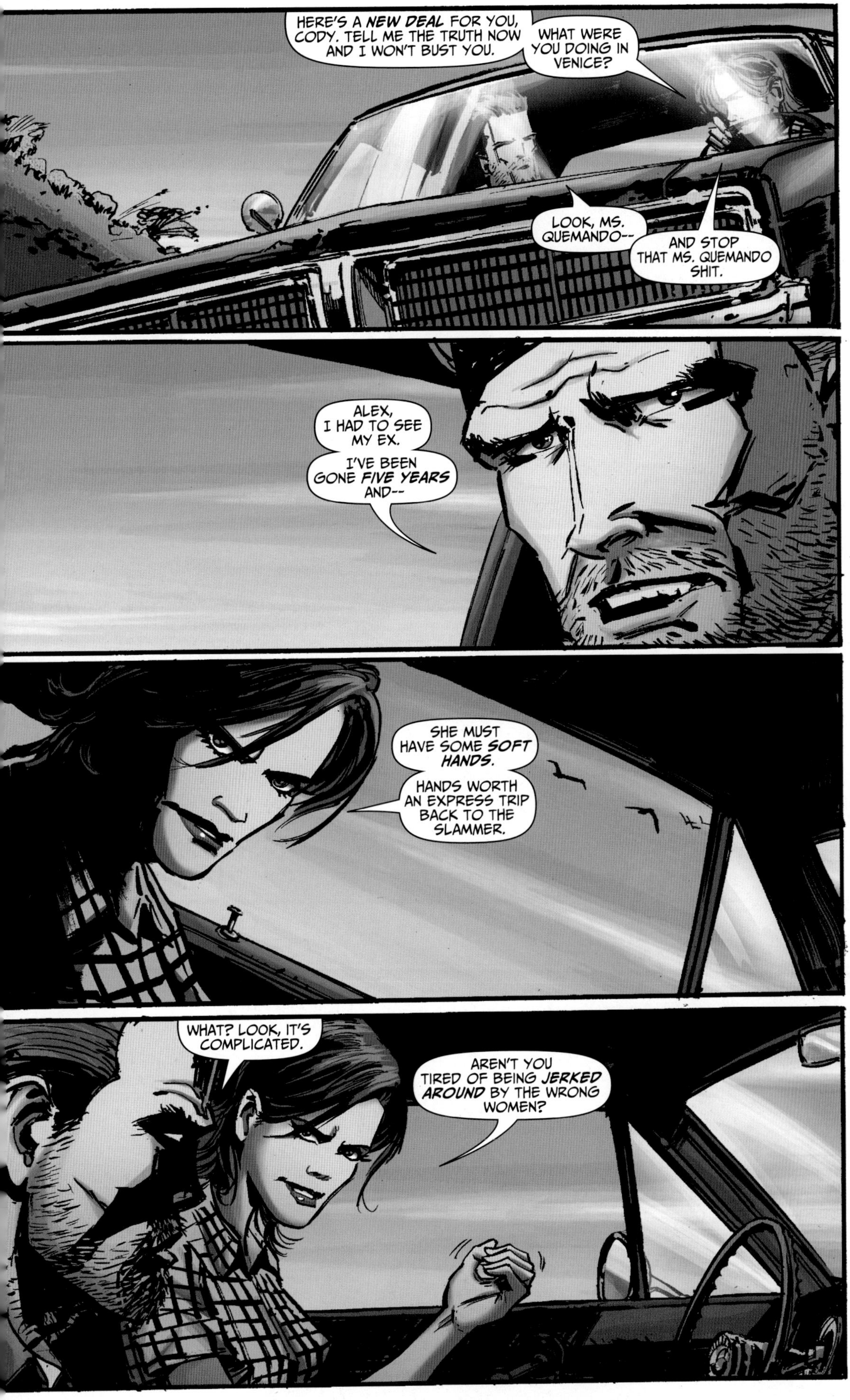
HERE'S A **NEW DEAL** FOR YOU, CODY. TELL ME THE TRUTH NOW AND I WON'T BUST YOU.
WHAT WERE YOU DOING IN VENICE?
LOOK, MS. QUEMANDO--
AND STOP THAT MS. QUEMANDO SHIT.
ALEX, I HAD TO SEE MY EX.
I'VE BEEN GONE **FIVE YEARS** AND--
SHE MUST HAVE SOME **SOFT HANDS.**
HANDS WORTH AN EXPRESS TRIP BACK TO THE SLAMMER.
WHAT? LOOK, IT'S COMPLICATED.
AREN'T YOU TIRED OF BEING **JERKED AROUND** BY THE WRONG WOMEN?

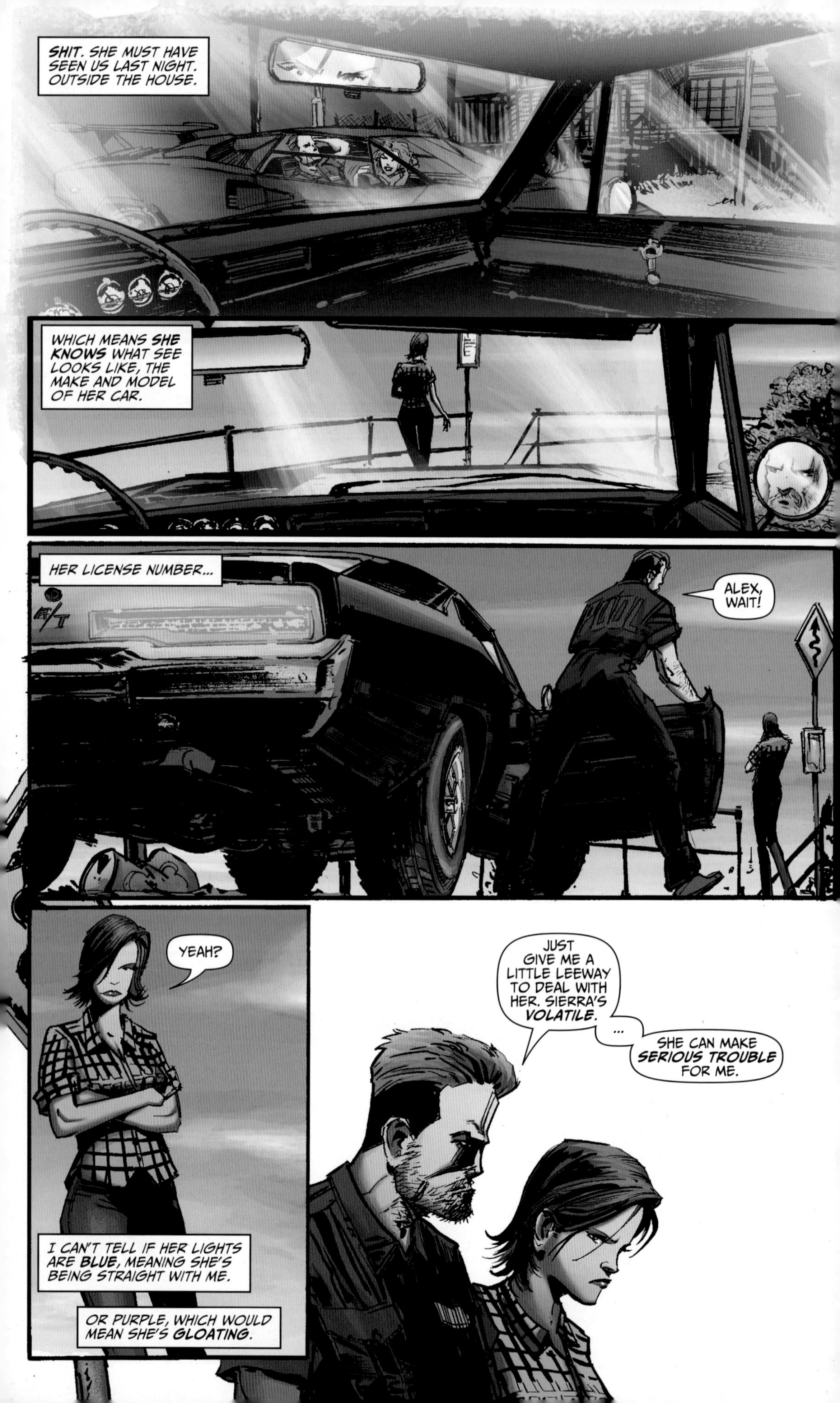

SHIT. SHE MUST HAVE SEEN US LAST NIGHT. OUTSIDE THE HOUSE.
WHICH MEANS SHE KNOWS WHAT SEE LOOKS LIKE, THE MAKE AND MODEL OF HER CAR.
HER LICENSE NUMBER...
ALEX, WAIT!
YEAH?
JUST GIVE ME A LITTLE LEEWAY TO DEAL WITH HER. SIERRA'S VOLATILE.
...
SHE CAN MAKE SERIOUS TROUBLE FOR ME.
I CAN'T TELL IF HER LIGHTS ARE BLUE, MEANING SHE'S BEING STRAIGHT WITH ME.
OR PURPLE, WHICH WOULD MEAN SHE'S GLOATING.

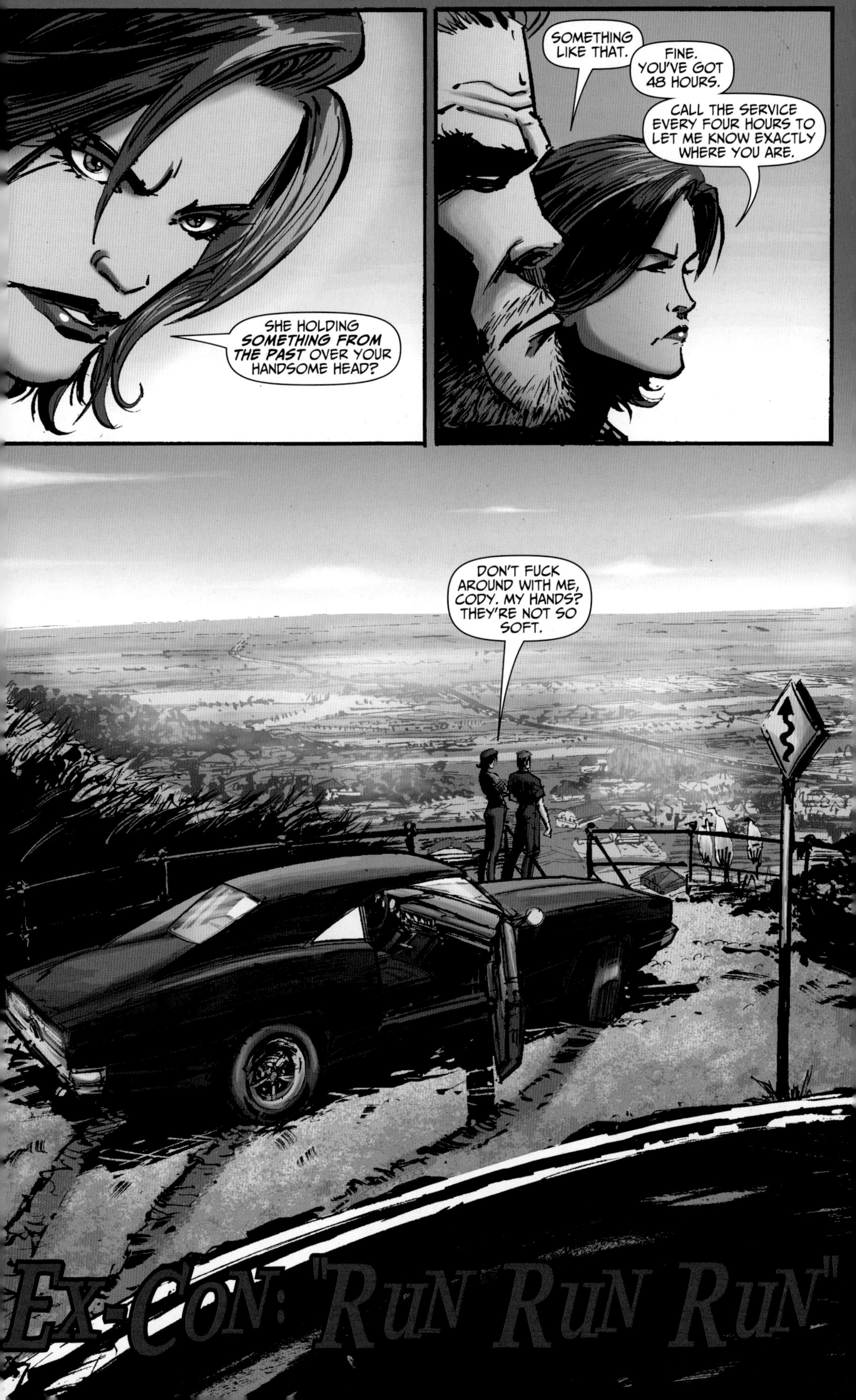
SHE HOLDING *SOMETHING FROM THE PAST* OVER YOUR HANDSOME HEAD?
SOMETHING LIKE THAT.
FINE. YOU'VE GOT 48 HOURS.
CALL THE SERVICE EVERY FOUR HOURS TO LET ME KNOW EXACTLY WHERE YOU ARE.
DON'T FUCK AROUND WITH ME, CODY. MY HANDS? THEY'RE NOT SO SOFT.
EX-CON: "RUN RUN RUN"

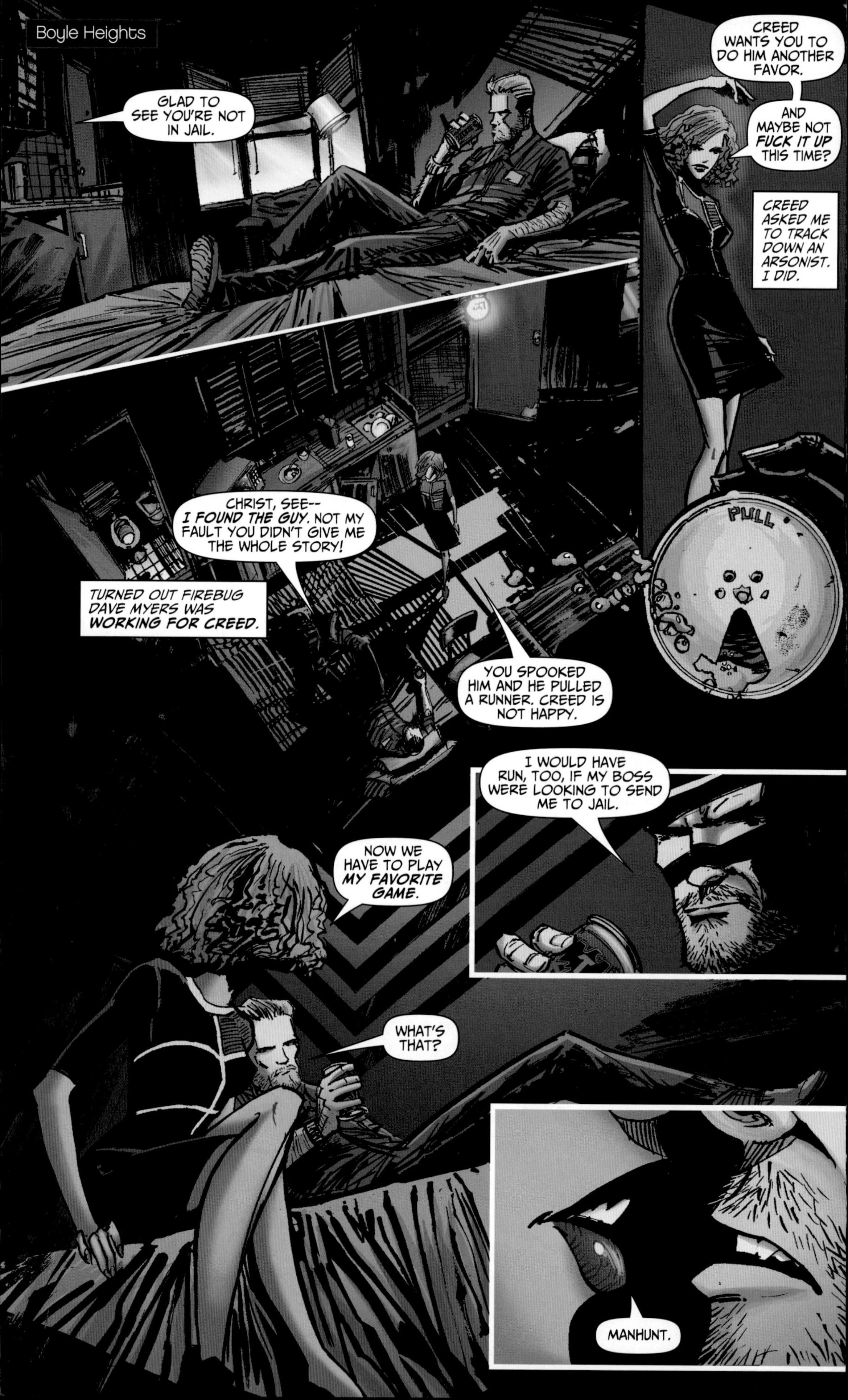
Boyle Heights
GLAD TO SEE YOU'RE NOT IN JAIL.
CREED WANTS YOU TO DO HIM ANOTHER FAVOR.
AND MAYBE NOT FUCK IT UP THIS TIME?
CREED ASKED ME TO TRACK DOWN AN ARSONIST. I DID.
CHRIST, SEE-- I FOUND THE GUY. NOT MY FAULT YOU DIDN'T GIVE ME THE WHOLE STORY!
TURNED OUT FIREBUG DAVE MYERS WAS WORKING FOR CREED.
PULL
YOU SPOOKED HIM AND HE PULLED A RUNNER. CREED IS NOT HAPPY.
I WOULD HAVE RUN, TOO, IF MY BOSS WERE LOOKING TO SEND ME TO JAIL.
NOW WE HAVE TO PLAY MY FAVORITE GAME.
WHAT'S THAT?
MANHUNT.

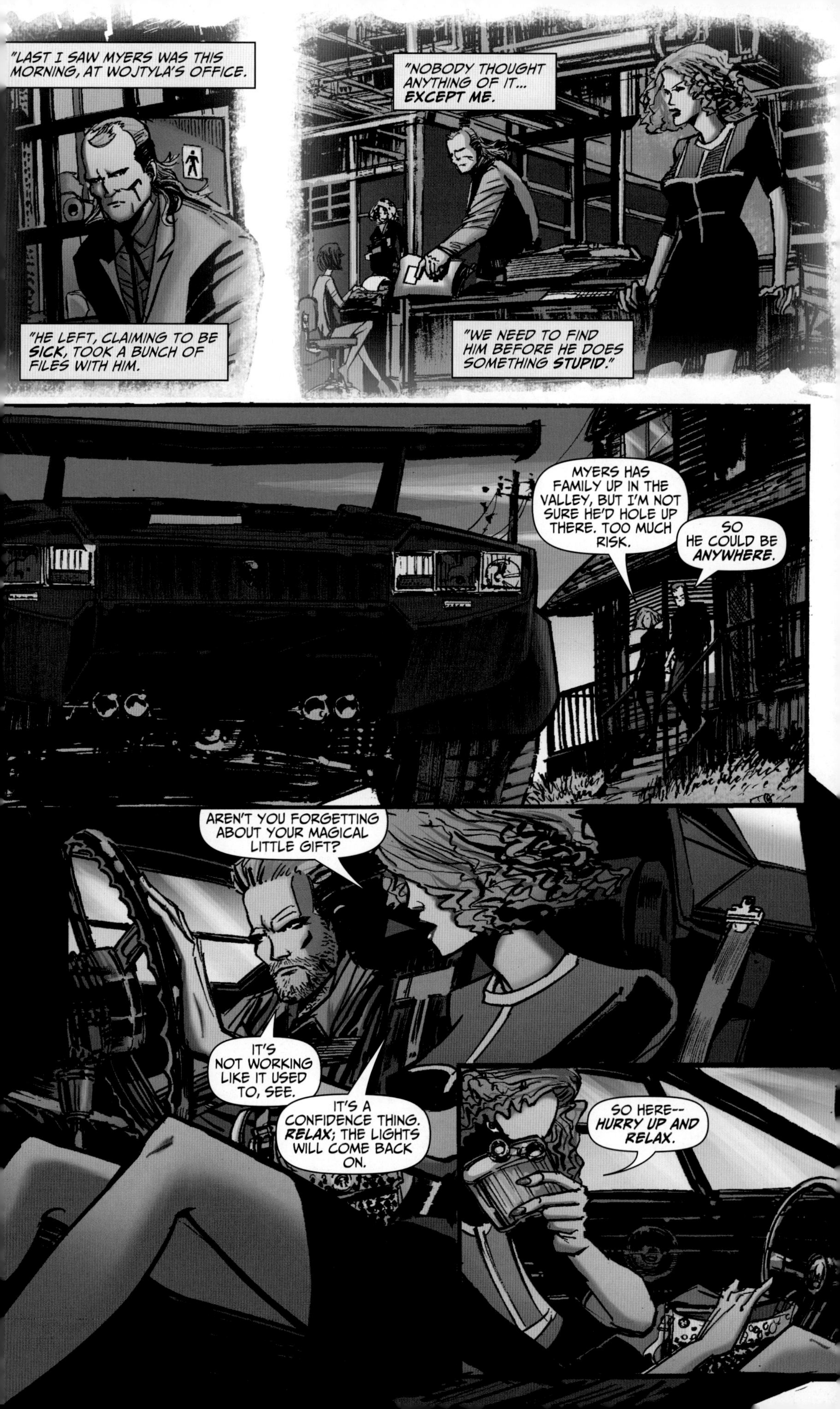
"LAST I SAW MYERS WAS THIS MORNING, AT WOJTYLA'S OFFICE.
"HE LEFT, CLAIMING TO BE SICK, TOOK A BUNCH OF FILES WITH HIM.
"NOBODY THOUGHT ANYTHING OF IT... EXCEPT ME.
"WE NEED TO FIND HIM BEFORE HE DOES SOMETHING STUPID."
MYERS HAS FAMILY UP IN THE VALLEY, BUT I'M NOT SURE HE'D HOLE UP THERE. TOO MUCH RISK.
SO HE COULD BE ANYWHERE.
AREN'T YOU FORGETTING ABOUT YOUR MAGICAL LITTLE GIFT?
IT'S NOT WORKING LIKE IT USED TO, SEE.
IT'S A CONFIDENCE THING. RELAX; THE LIGHTS WILL COME BACK ON.
SO HERE-- HURRY UP AND RELAX.

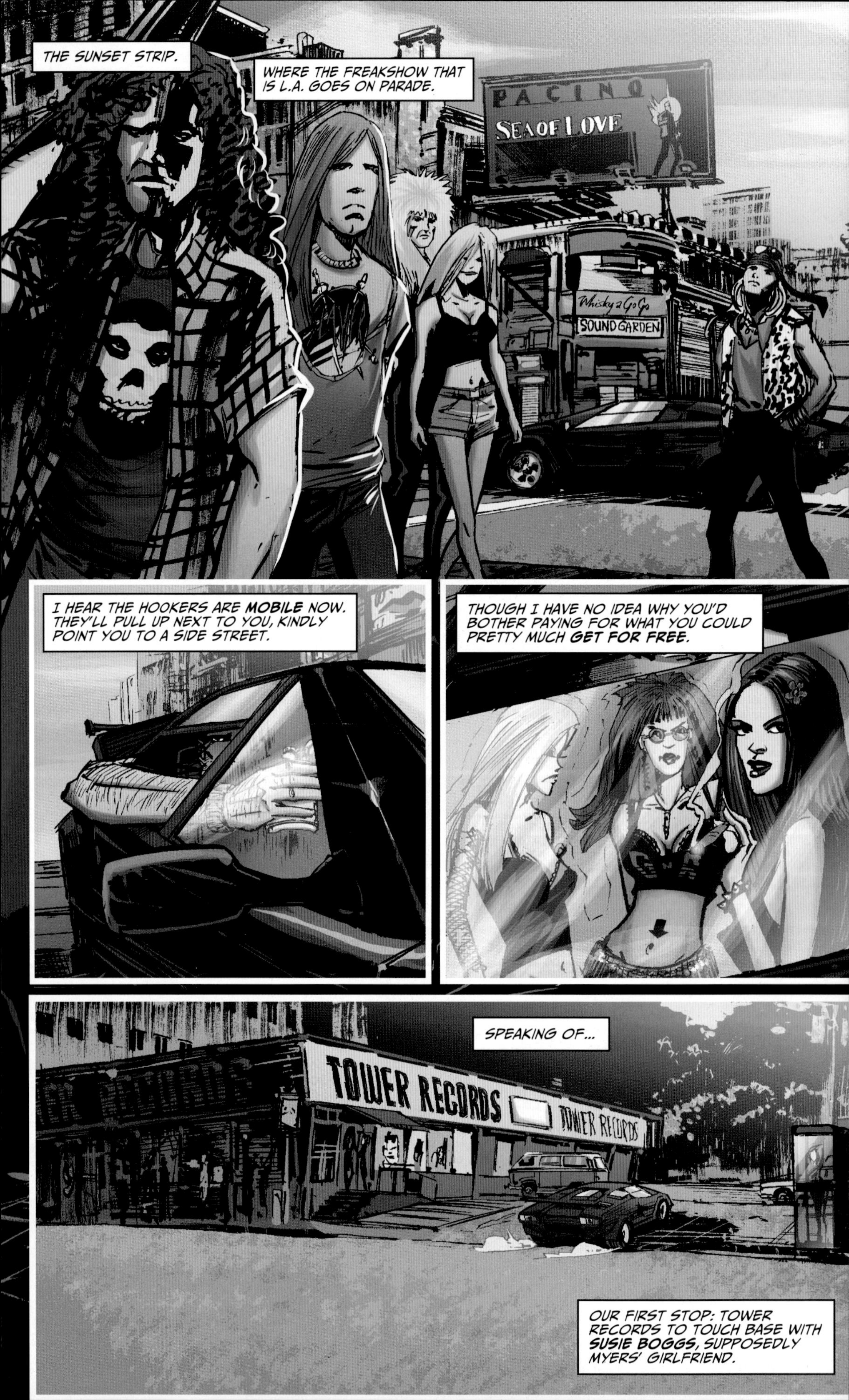
THE SUNSET STRIP.
WHERE THE FREAKSHOW THAT IS L.A. GOES ON PARADE.
PACINO
SEA OF LOVE
Whisky a Go Go
SOUND GARDEN
I HEAR THE HOOKERS ARE **MOBILE** NOW. THEY'LL PULL UP NEXT TO YOU, KINDLY POINT YOU TO A SIDE STREET.
THOUGH I HAVE NO IDEA WHY YOU'D BOTHER PAYING FOR WHAT YOU COULD PRETTY MUCH **GET FOR FREE.**
SPEAKING OF...
TOWER RECORDS
TOWER RECORDS
OUR FIRST STOP: TOWER RECORDS TO TOUCH BASE WITH **SUSIE BOGGS**, SUPPOSEDLY MYERS' GIRLFRIEND.

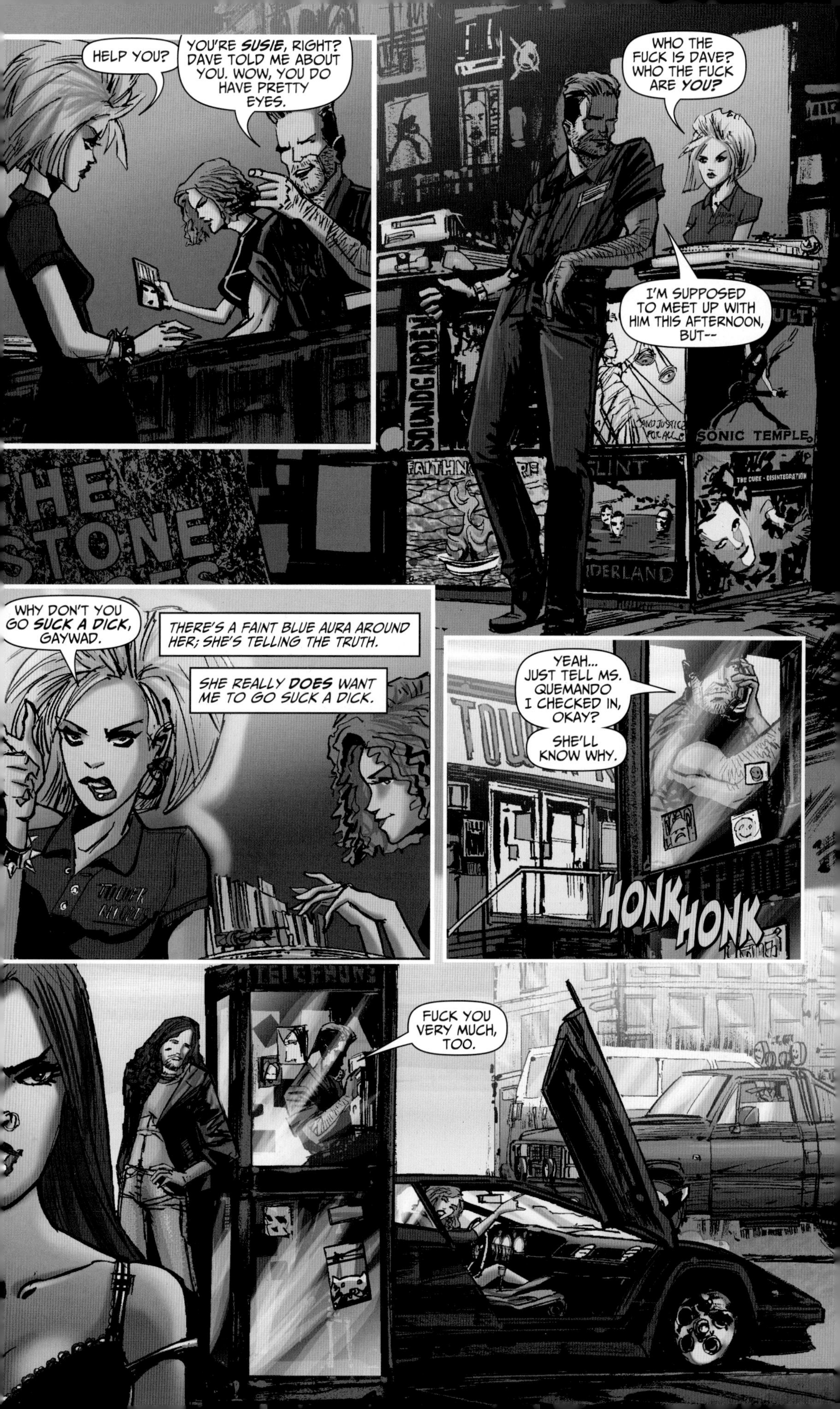
HELP YOU?
YOU'RE SUSIE, RIGHT? DAVE TOLD ME ABOUT YOU. WOW, YOU DO HAVE PRETTY EYES.
WHO THE FUCK IS DAVE? WHO THE FUCK ARE YOU?
I'M SUPPOSED TO MEET UP WITH HIM THIS AFTERNOON, BUT--
SOUNDGARDEN
SONIC TEMPLE
THE CURE · DISINTEGRATION
WHY DON'T YOU GO SUCK A DICK, GAYWAD.
THERE'S A FAINT BLUE AURA AROUND HER; SHE'S TELLING THE TRUTH.
SHE REALLY DOES WANT ME TO GO SUCK A DICK.
YEAH... JUST TELL MS. QUEMANDO I CHECKED IN, OKAY?
SHE'LL KNOW WHY.
HONK HONK
FUCK YOU VERY MUCH, TOO.

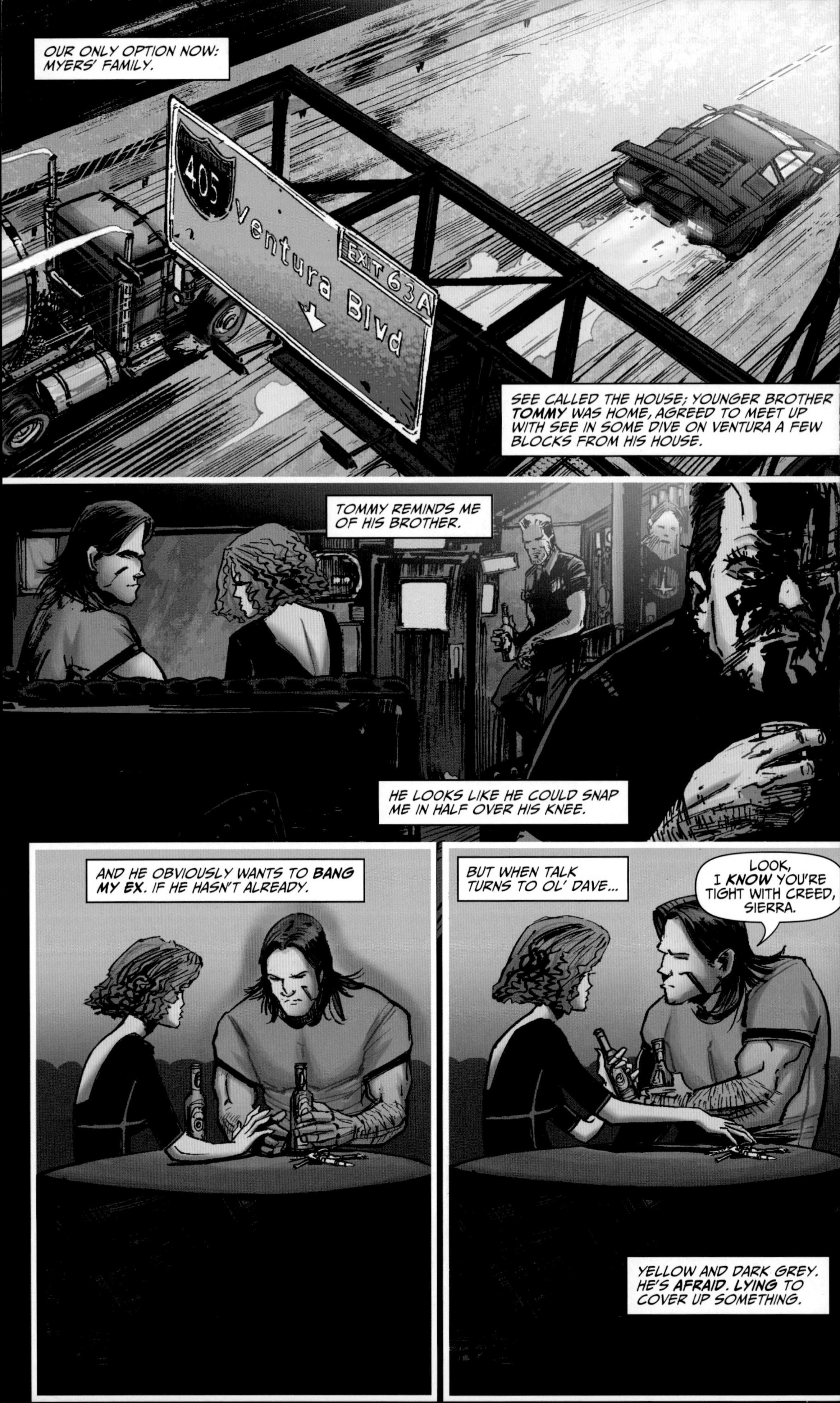

OUR ONLY OPTION NOW: MYERS' FAMILY.
405
Ventura Blvd
EXIT 63A
SEE CALLED THE HOUSE; YOUNGER BROTHER TOMMY WAS HOME, AGREED TO MEET UP WITH SEE IN SOME DIVE ON VENTURA A FEW BLOCKS FROM HIS HOUSE.
TOMMY REMINDS ME OF HIS BROTHER.
HE LOOKS LIKE HE COULD SNAP ME IN HALF OVER HIS KNEE.
AND HE OBVIOUSLY WANTS TO BANG MY EX. IF HE HASN'T ALREADY.
BUT WHEN TALK TURNS TO OL' DAVE...
LOOK, I KNOW YOU'RE TIGHT WITH CREED, SIERRA.
YELLOW AND DARK GREY. HE'S AFRAID. LYING TO COVER UP SOMETHING.

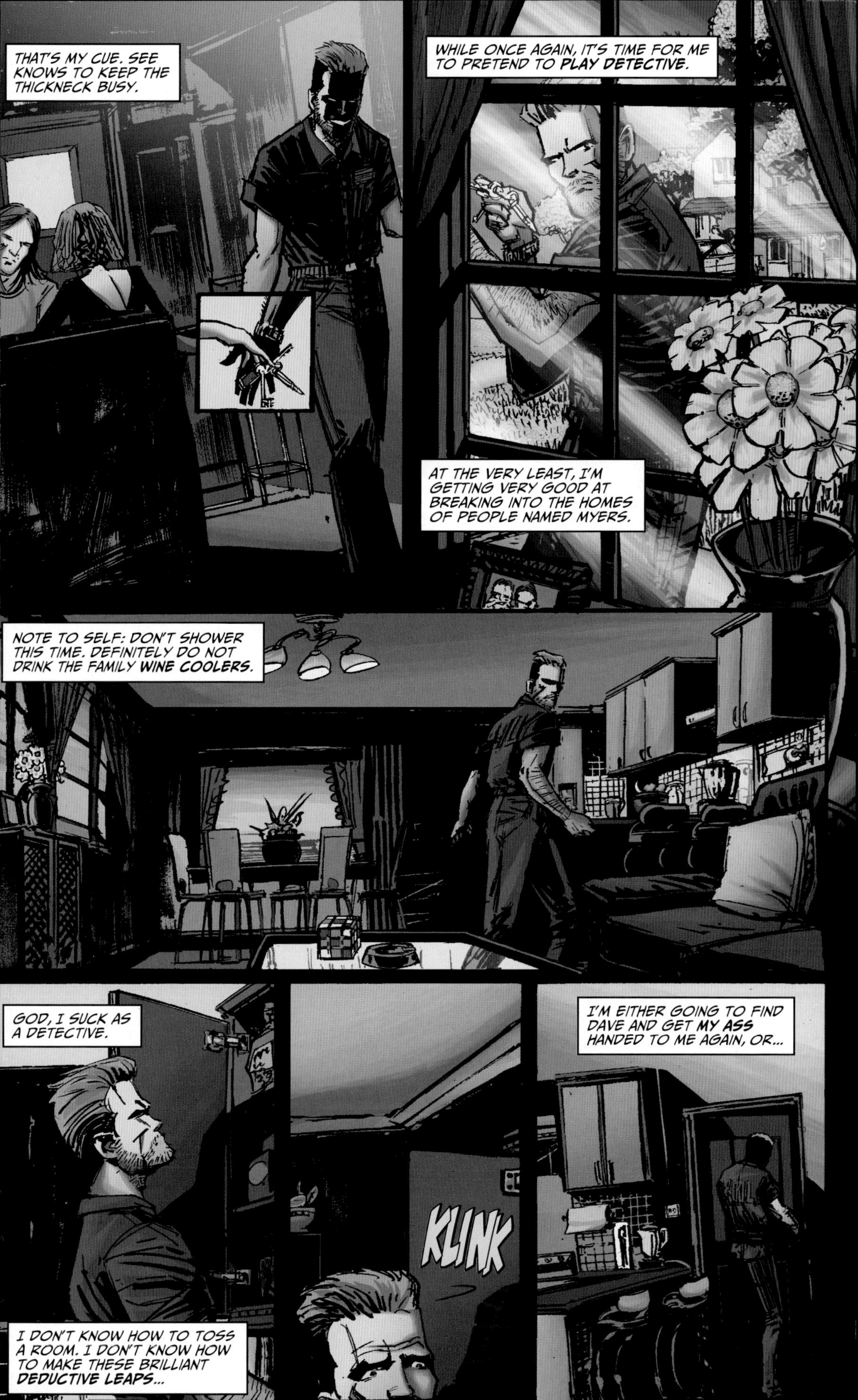
THAT'S MY CUE. SEE KNOWS TO KEEP THE THICKNECK BUSY.
WHILE ONCE AGAIN, IT'S TIME FOR ME TO PRETEND TO PLAY DETECTIVE.
AT THE VERY LEAST, I'M GETTING VERY GOOD AT BREAKING INTO THE HOMES OF PEOPLE NAMED MYERS.
NOTE TO SELF: DON'T SHOWER THIS TIME. DEFINITELY DO NOT DRINK THE FAMILY WINE COOLERS.
GOD, I SUCK AS A DETECTIVE.
I DON'T KNOW HOW TO TOSS A ROOM. I DON'T KNOW HOW TO MAKE THESE BRILLIANT DEDUCTIVE LEAPS...
KLINK
I'M EITHER GOING TO FIND DAVE AND GET MY ASS HANDED TO ME AGAIN, OR...

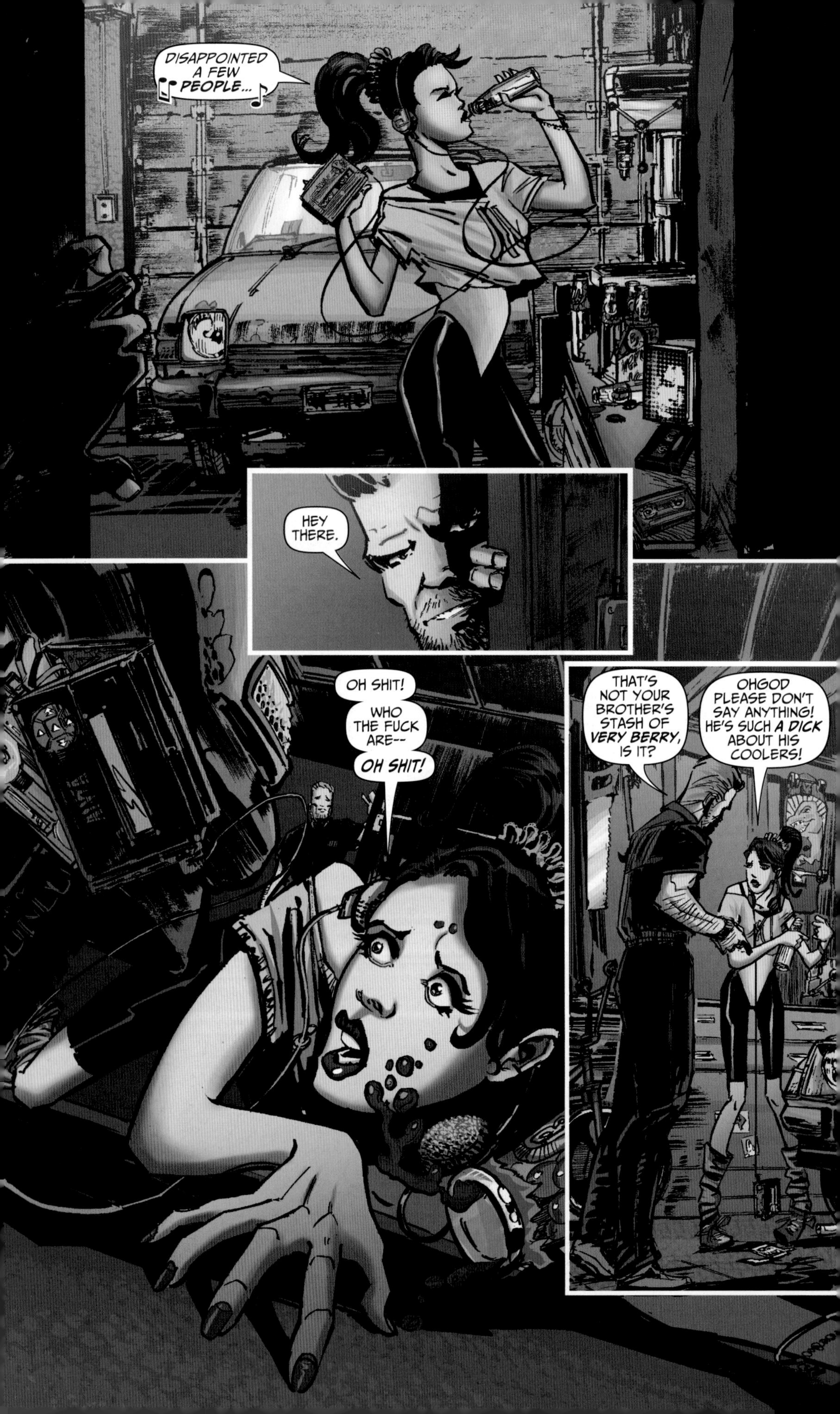
DISAPPOINTED A FEW PEOPLE...
HEY THERE.
OH SHIT!
WHO THE FUCK ARE--
OH SHIT!
THAT'S NOT YOUR BROTHER'S STASH OF VERY BERRY, IS IT?
OHGOD PLEASE DON'T SAY ANYTHING! HE'S SUCH A DICK ABOUT HIS COOLERS!

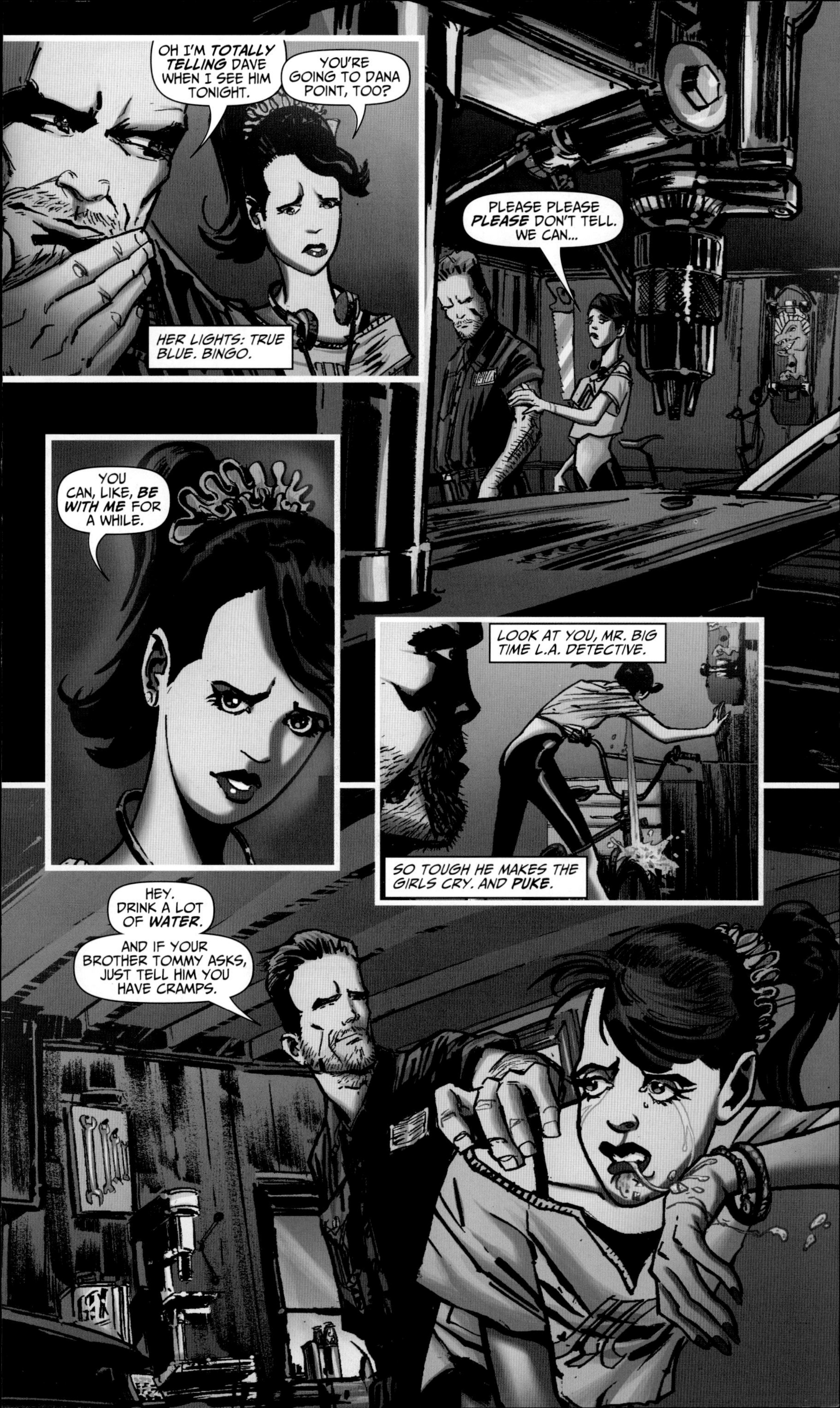
OH I'M *TOTALLY TELLING* DAVE WHEN I SEE HIM TONIGHT.
YOU'RE GOING TO DANA POINT, TOO?
HER LIGHTS: TRUE BLUE. BINGO.
PLEASE PLEASE *PLEASE* DON'T TELL. WE CAN...
YOU CAN, LIKE, *BE WITH ME* FOR A WHILE.
LOOK AT YOU, MR. BIG TIME L.A. DETECTIVE.
SO TOUGH HE MAKES THE GIRLS CRY. AND *PUKE*.
HEY. DRINK A LOT OF *WATER*.
AND IF YOUR BROTHER TOMMY ASKS, JUST TELL HIM YOU HAVE CRAMPS.

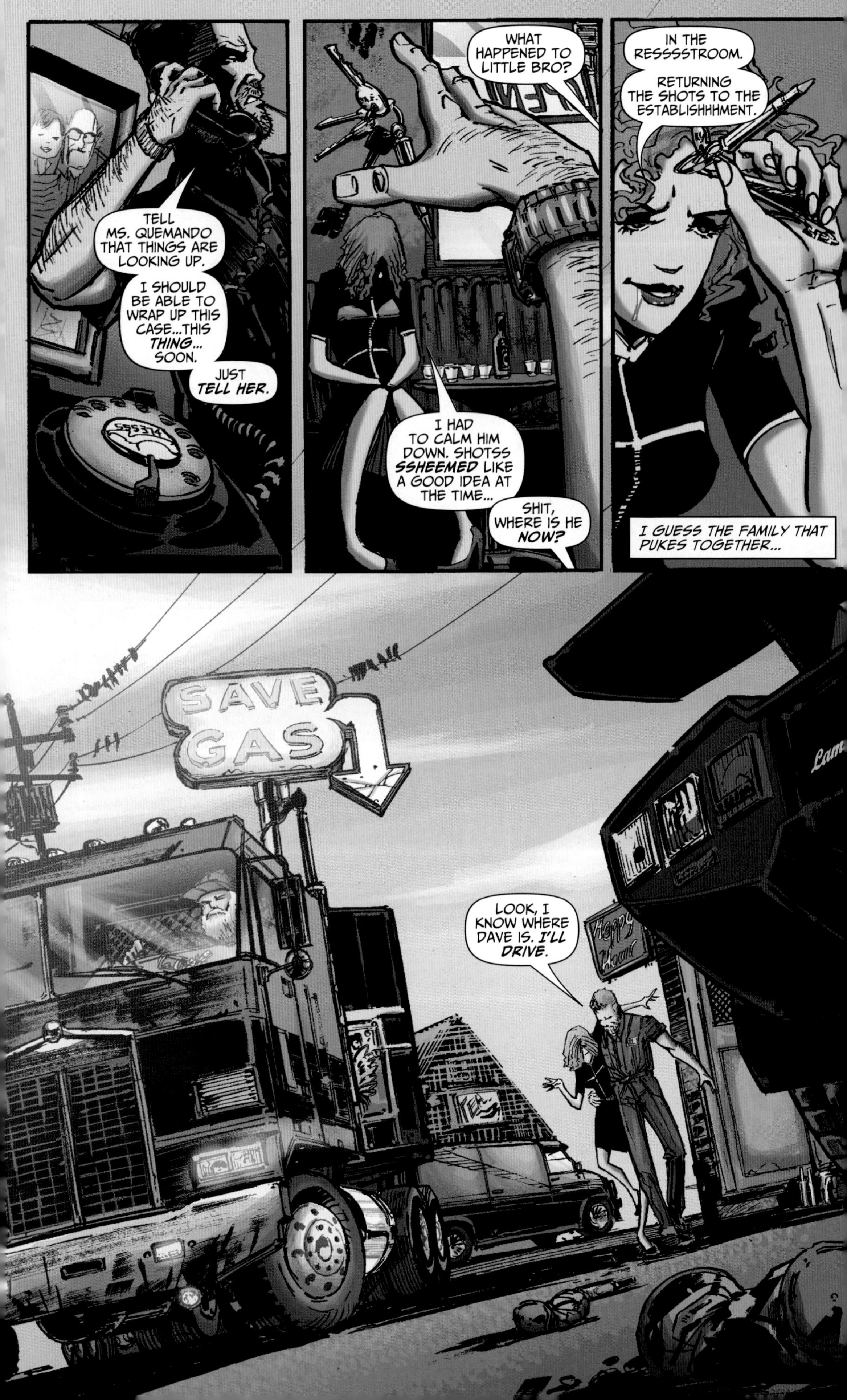
TELL MS. QUEMANDO THAT THINGS ARE LOOKING UP.
I SHOULD BE ABLE TO WRAP UP THIS CASE...THIS *THING*... SOON.
JUST *TELL HER*.
WHAT HAPPENED TO LITTLE BRO?
I HAD TO CALM HIM DOWN. SHOTSS *SSHEEMED* LIKE A GOOD IDEA AT THE TIME...
SHIT, WHERE IS HE *NOW?*
IN THE RESSSSTROOM.
RETURNING THE SHOTS TO THE ESTABLISHHHMENT.
I GUESS THE FAMILY THAT PUKES TOGETHER...
SAVE GAS
LOOK, I KNOW WHERE DAVE IS. *I'LL DRIVE*.

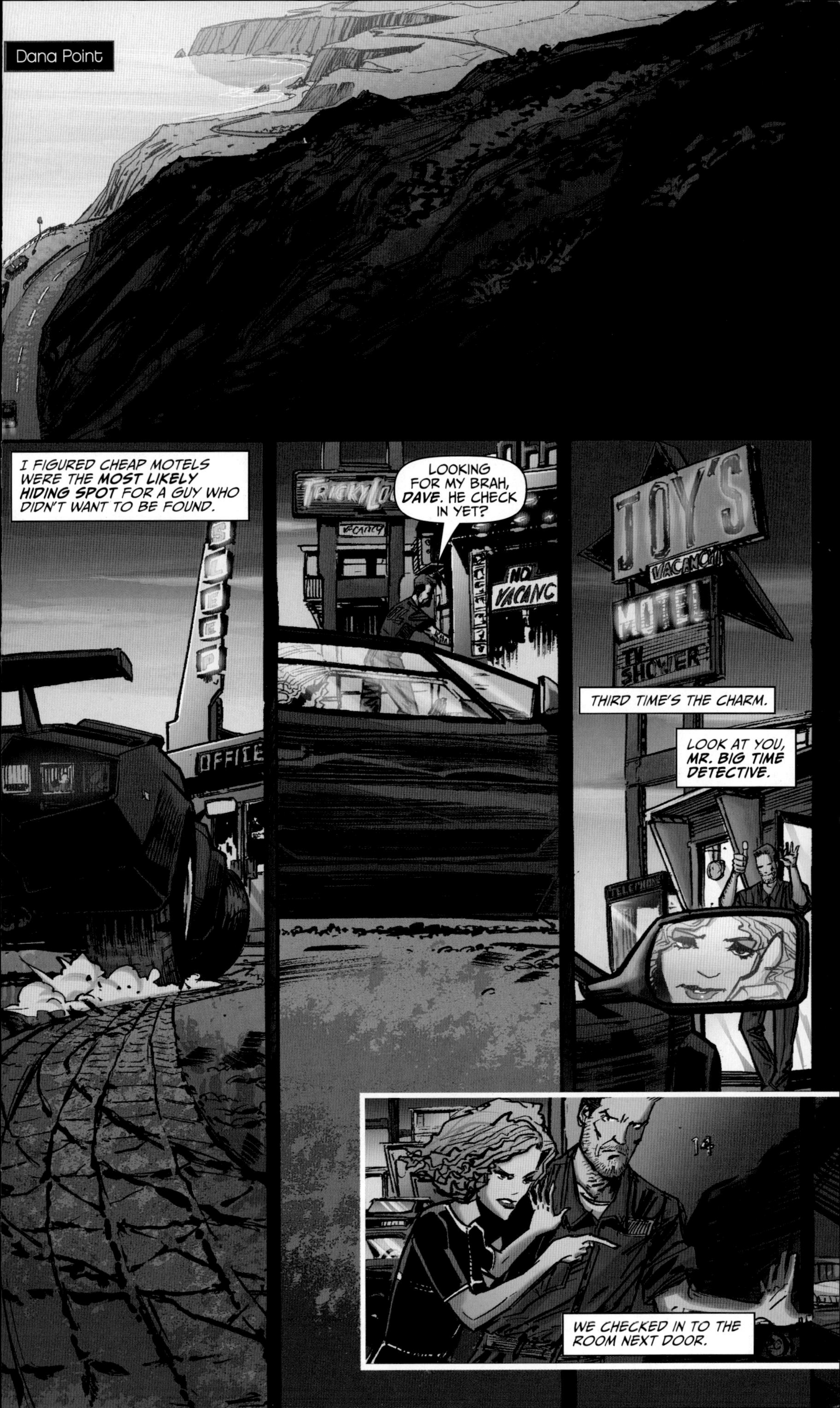
Dana Point
I FIGURED CHEAP MOTELS WERE THE MOST LIKELY HIDING SPOT FOR A GUY WHO DIDN'T WANT TO BE FOUND.
OFFICE
LOOKING FOR MY BRAH, DAVE. HE CHECK IN YET?
TOY'S
MOTEL
TV SHOWER
THIRD TIME'S THE CHARM.
LOOK AT YOU, MR. BIG TIME DETECTIVE.
14
WE CHECKED IN TO THE ROOM NEXT DOOR.

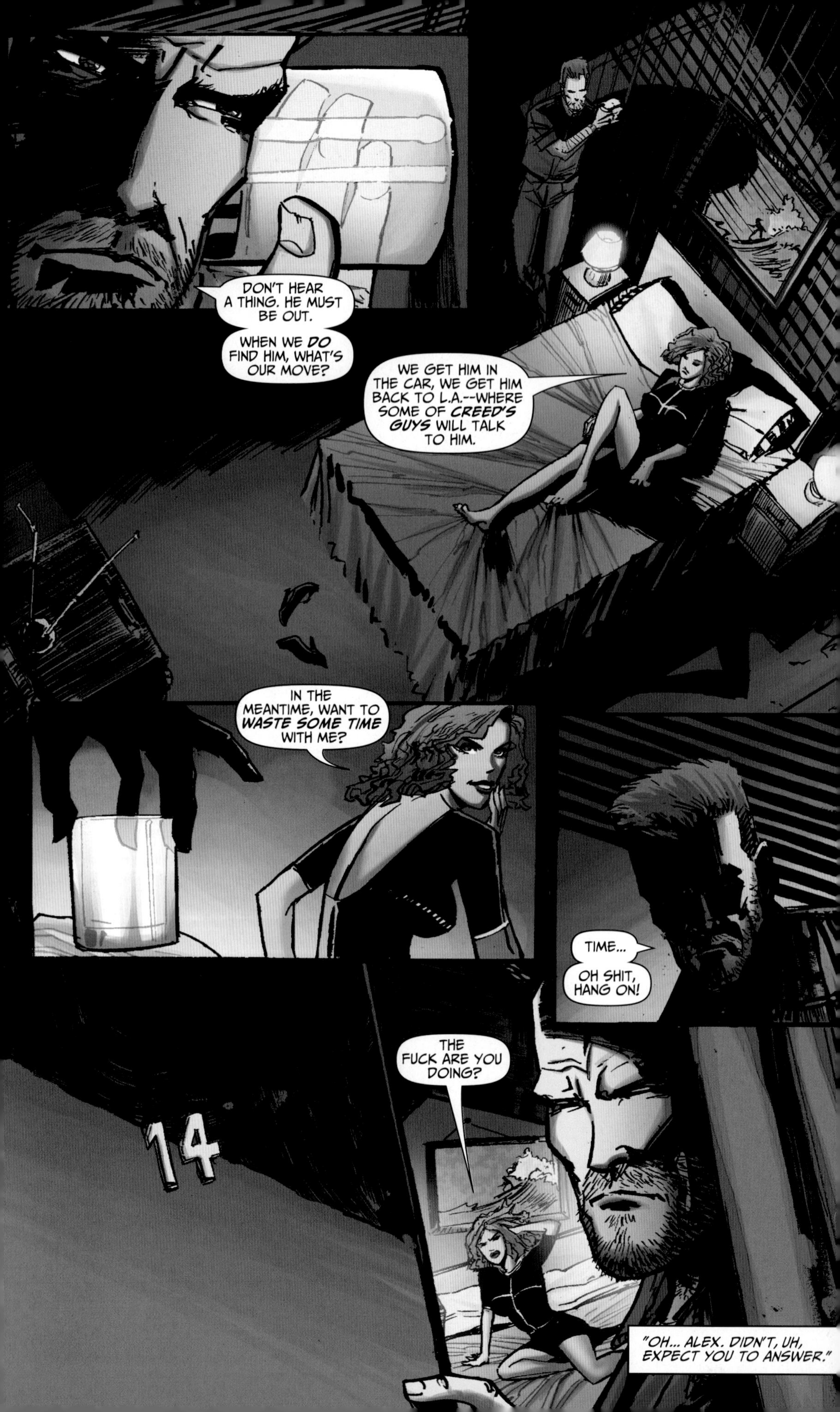
DON'T HEAR A THING. HE MUST BE OUT.
WHEN WE *DO* FIND HIM, WHAT'S OUR MOVE?
WE GET HIM IN THE CAR, WE GET HIM BACK TO L.A.--WHERE SOME OF ***CREED'S GUYS*** WILL TALK TO HIM.
IN THE MEANTIME, WANT TO ***WASTE SOME TIME*** WITH ME?
TIME...
OH SHIT, HANG ON!
THE FUCK ARE YOU DOING?
14
"OH... ALEX. DIDN'T, UH, EXPECT YOU TO ANSWER."

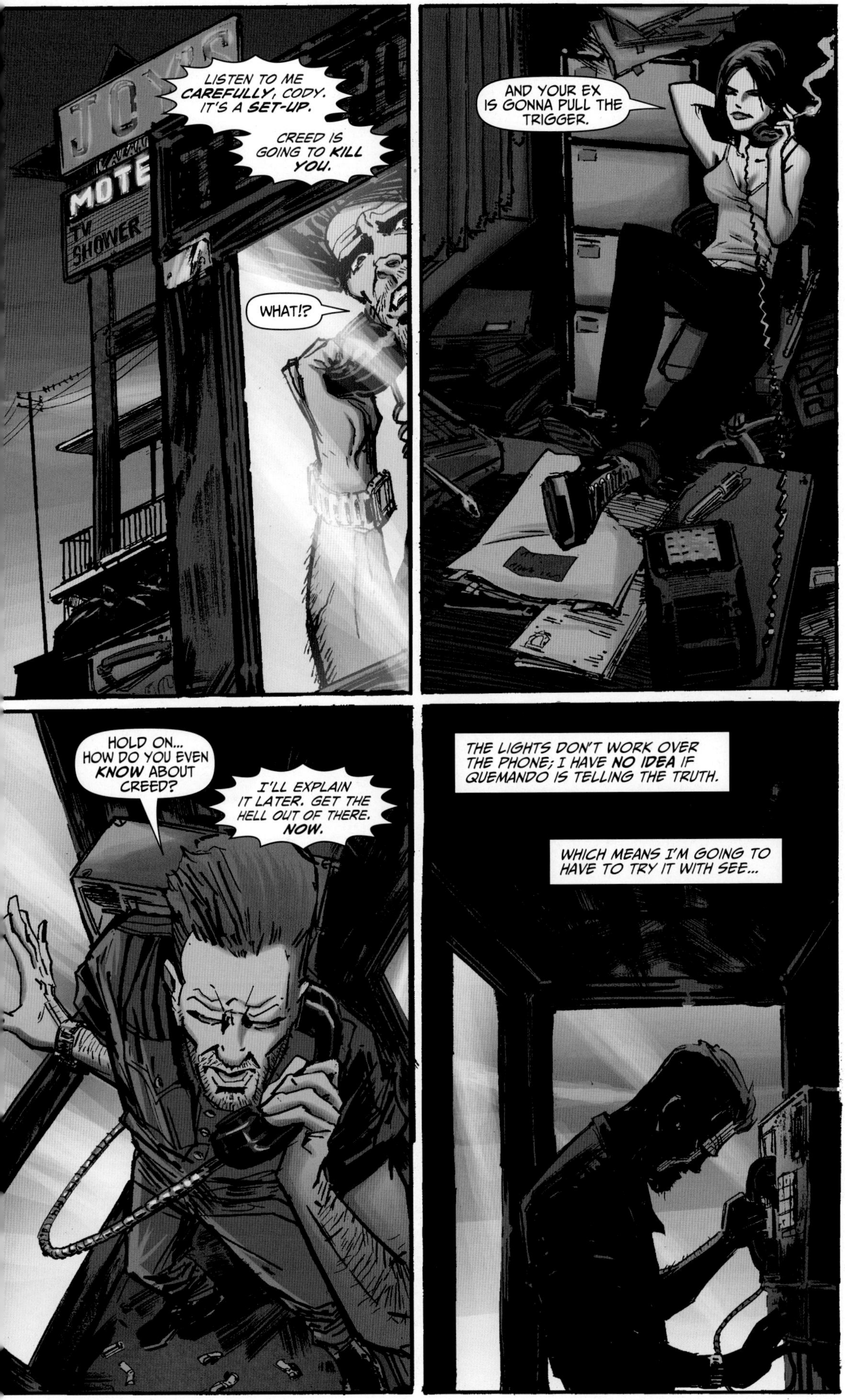

LISTEN TO ME CAREFULLY, CODY. IT'S A SET-UP.
CREED IS GOING TO KILL YOU.
MOTE
TV
SHOWER
WHAT!?
AND YOUR EX IS GONNA PULL THE TRIGGER.
HOLD ON... HOW DO YOU EVEN KNOW ABOUT CREED?
I'LL EXPLAIN IT LATER. GET THE HELL OUT OF THERE. NOW.
THE LIGHTS DON'T WORK OVER THE PHONE; I HAVE NO IDEA IF QUEMANDO IS TELLING THE TRUTH.
WHICH MEANS I'M GOING TO HAVE TO TRY IT WITH SEE...

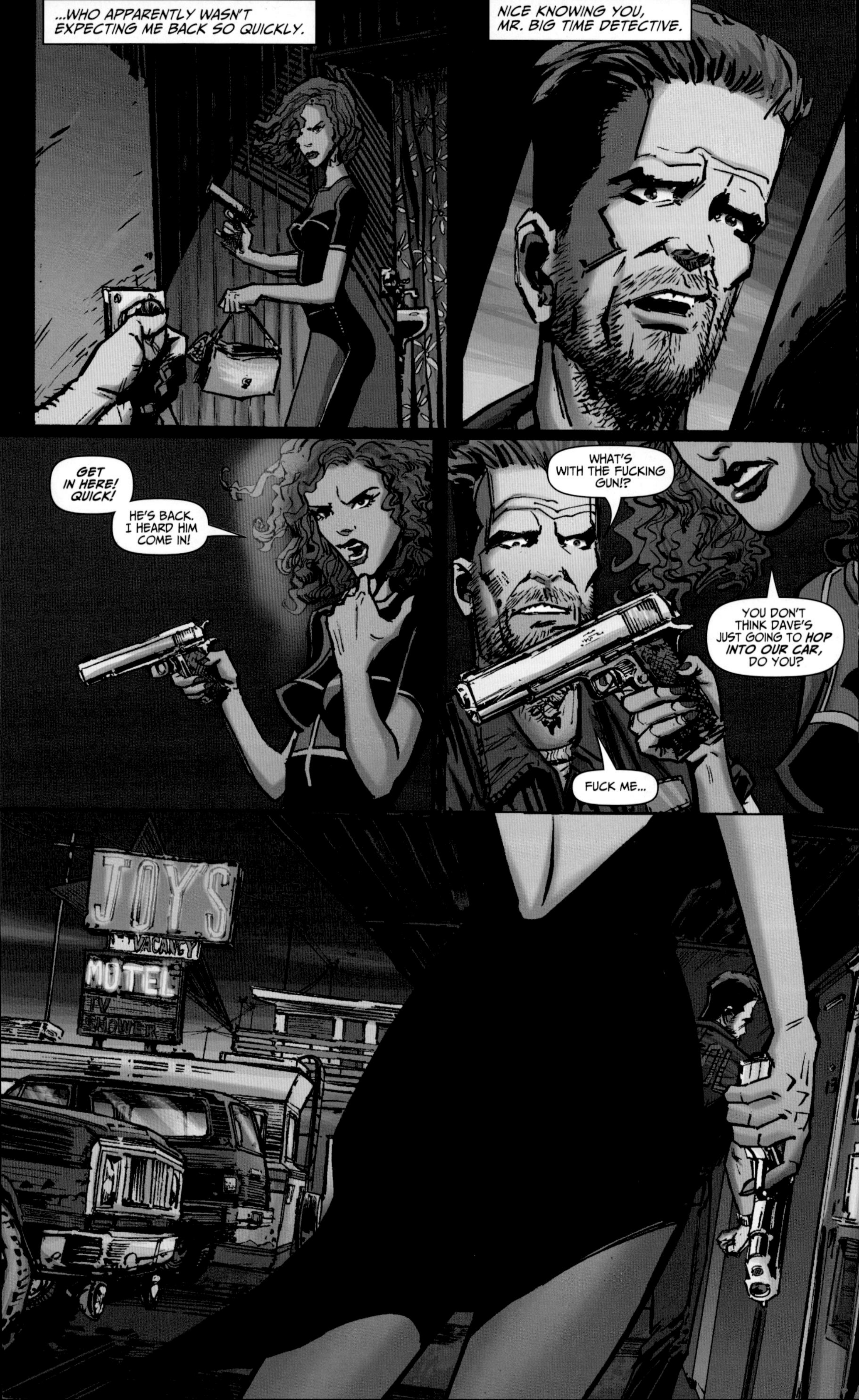
...WHO APPARENTLY WASN'T EXPECTING ME BACK SO QUICKLY.
NICE KNOWING YOU, MR. BIG TIME DETECTIVE.
GET IN HERE! QUICK!
HE'S BACK. I HEARD HIM COME IN!
WHAT'S WITH THE FUCKING GUN!?
YOU DON'T THINK DAVE'S JUST GOING TO HOP INTO OUR CAR, DO YOU?
FUCK ME...
JOY'S
VACANCY
MOTEL
TV
SHOWER

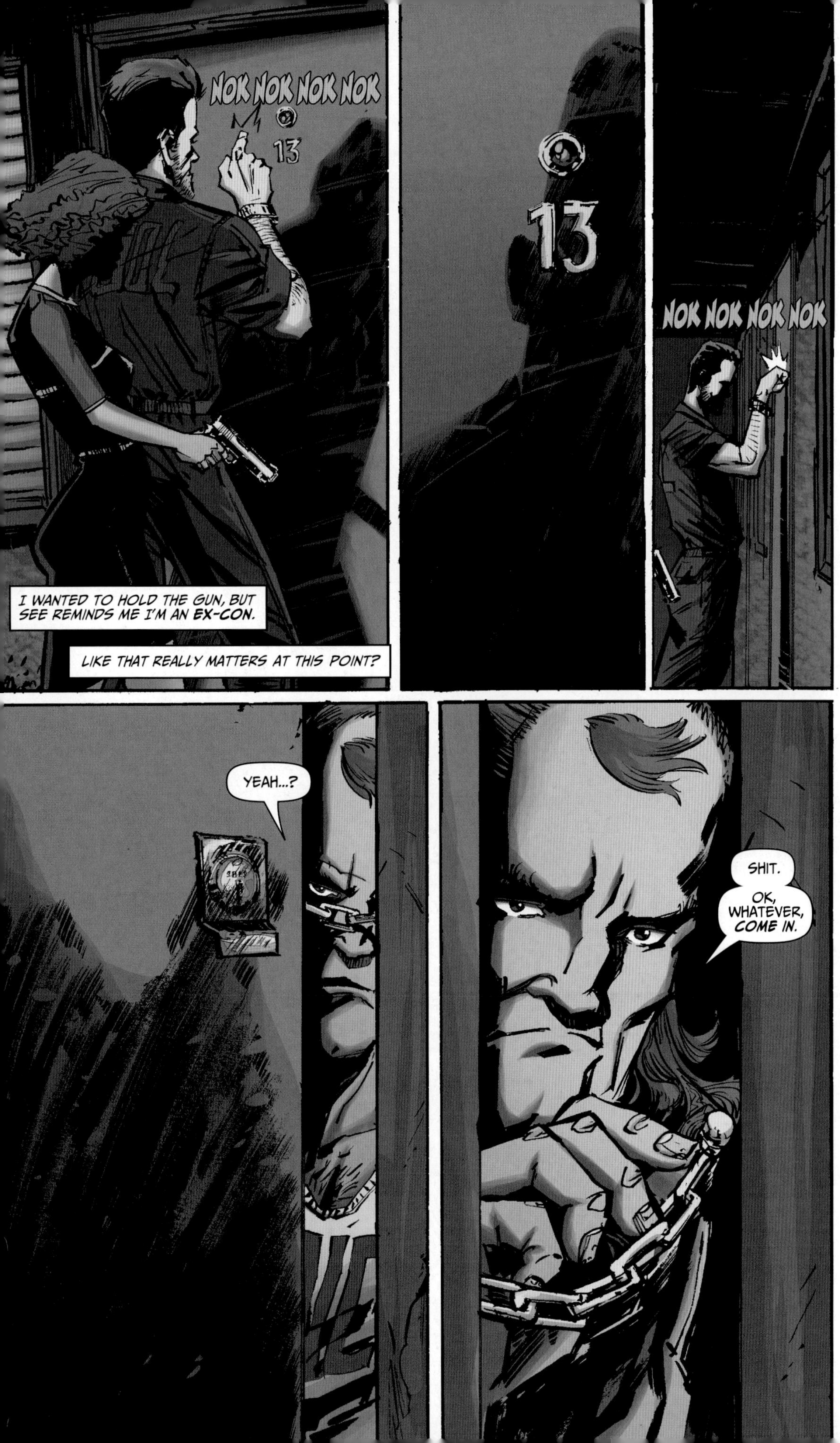
NOK NOK NOK NOK
13
I WANTED TO HOLD THE GUN, BUT SEE REMINDS ME I'M AN EX-CON.
LIKE THAT REALLY MATTERS AT THIS POINT?
13
NOK NOK NOK NOK
YEAH...?
SHIT.
OK, WHATEVER, COME IN.

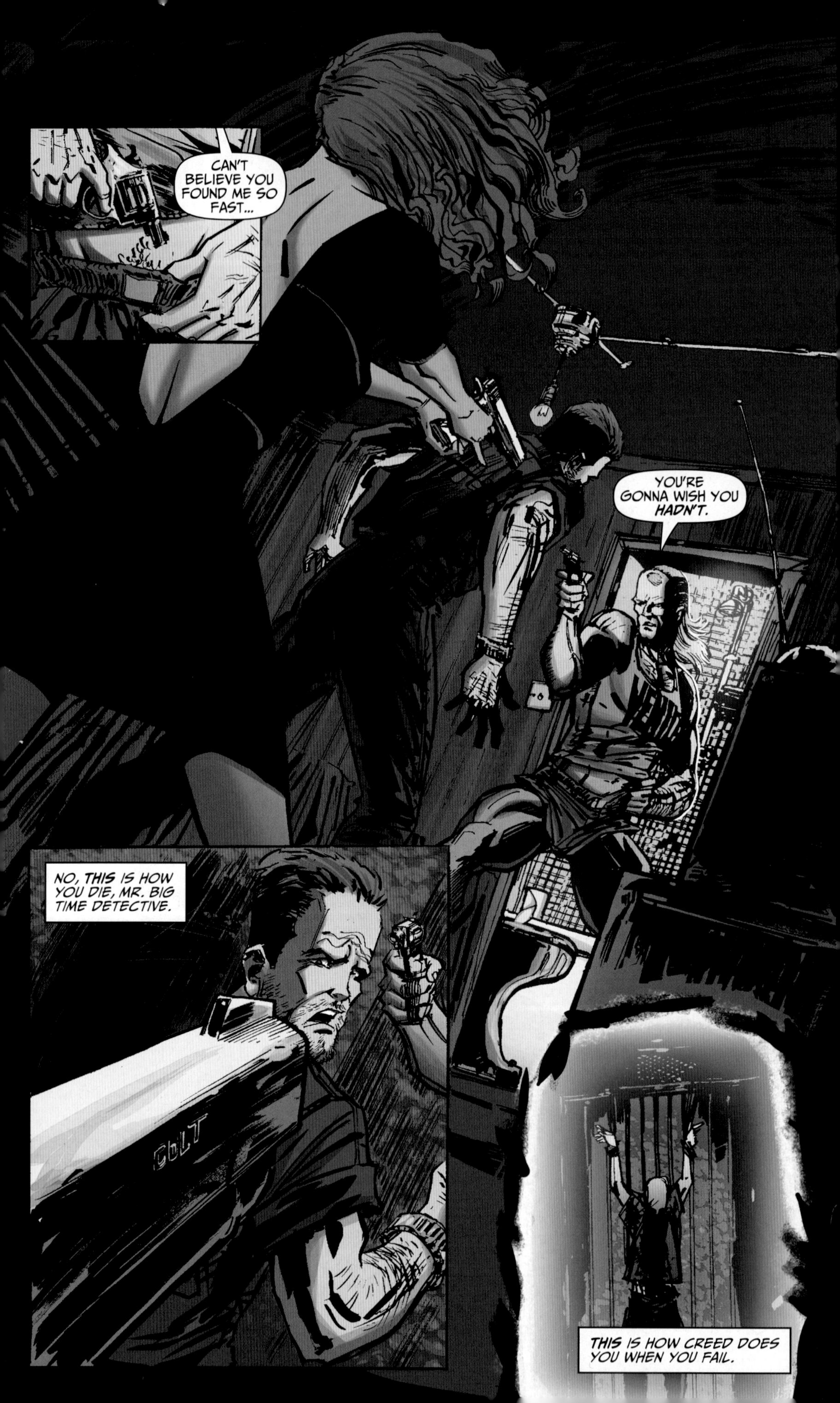
CAN'T BELIEVE YOU FOUND ME SO FAST...
YOU'RE GONNA WISH YOU HADN'T.
NO, THIS IS HOW YOU DIE, MR. BIG TIME DETECTIVE.
COLT
THIS IS HOW CREED DOES YOU WHEN YOU FAIL.

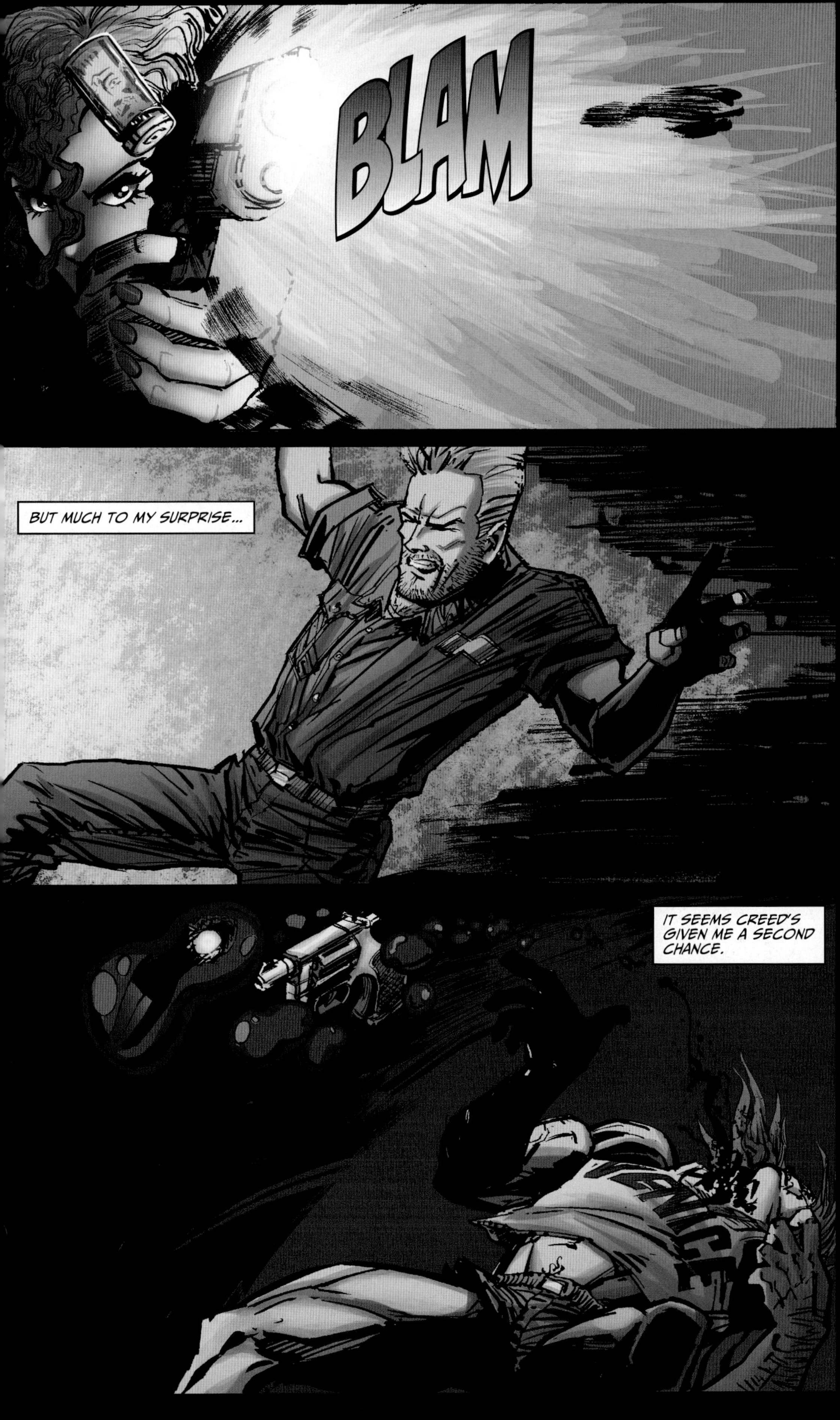

BLAM
BUT MUCH TO MY SURPRISE...
IT SEEMS CREED'S GIVEN ME A SECOND CHANCE.

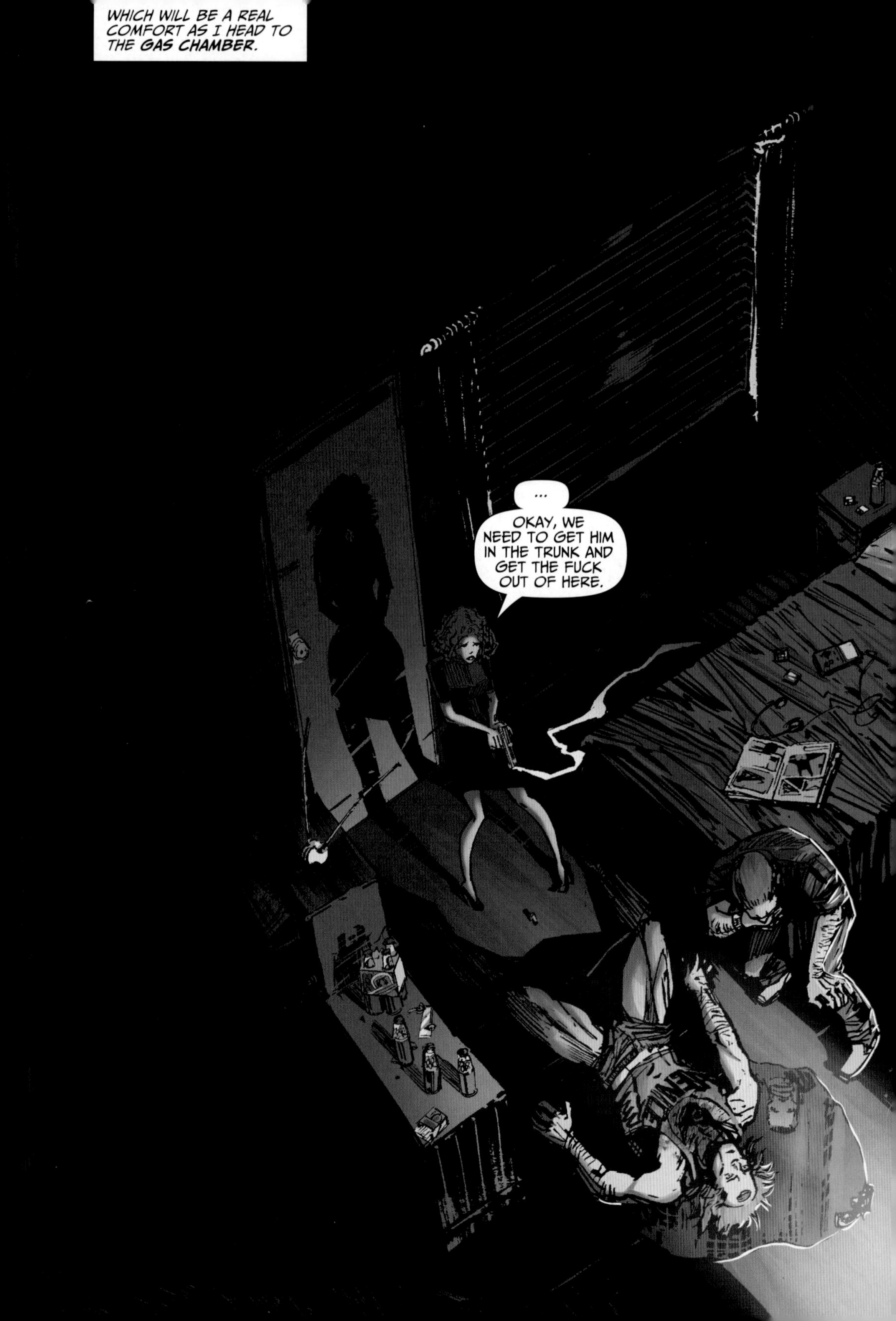
WHICH WILL BE A REAL COMFORT AS I HEAD TO THE **GAS CHAMBER**.
...
OKAY, WE NEED TO GET HIM IN THE TRUNK AND GET THE FUCK OUT OF HERE.

FOUR

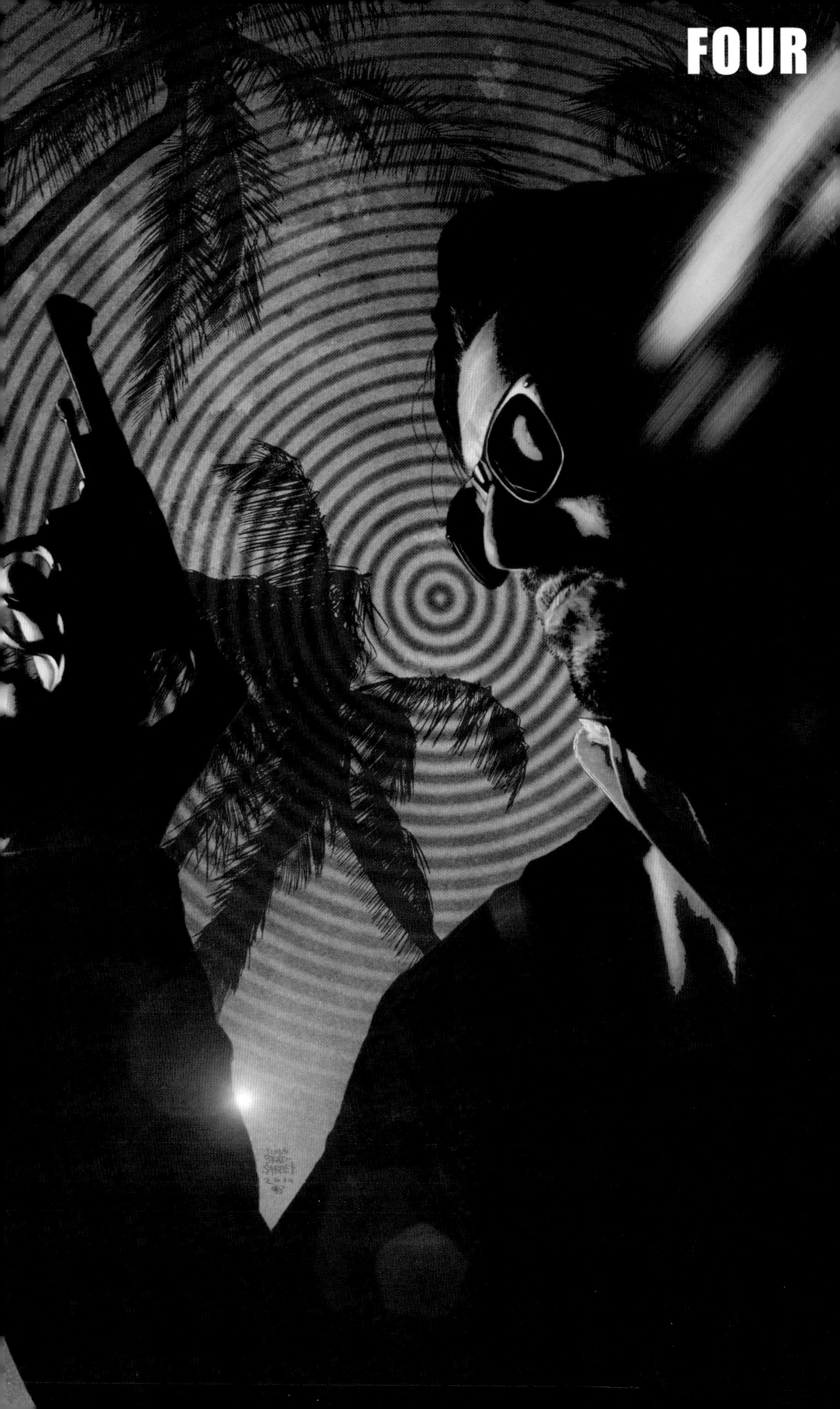

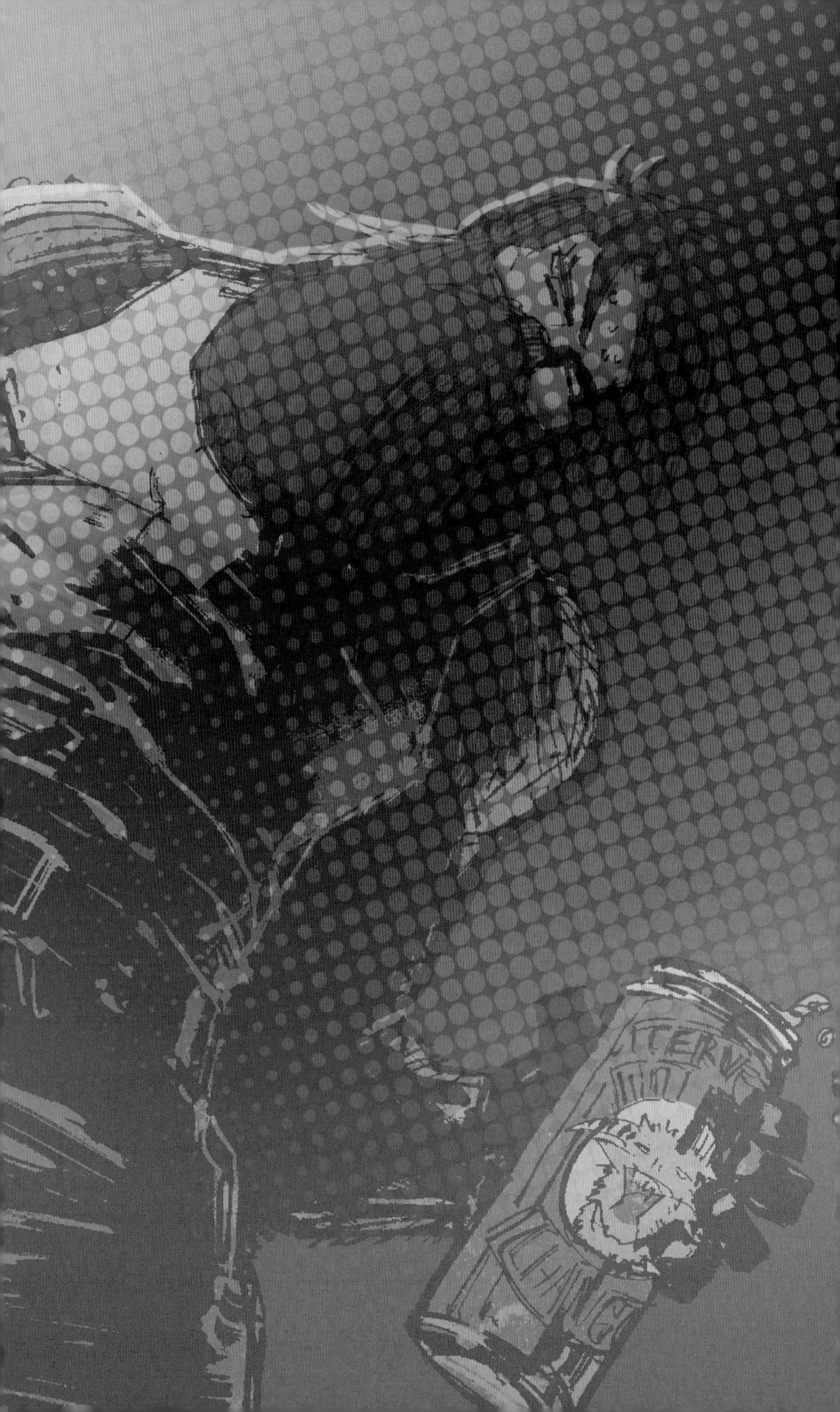

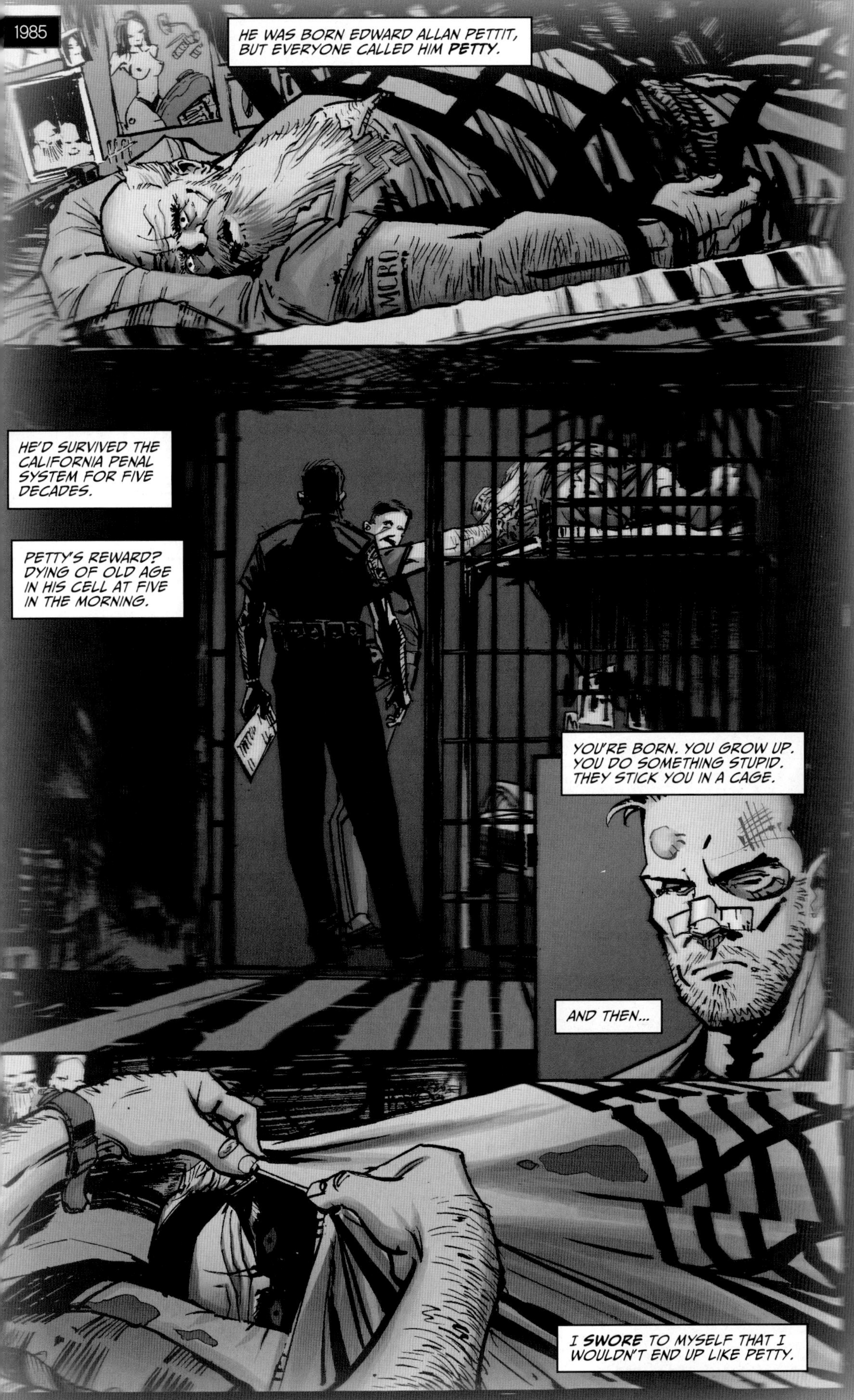
1985
HE WAS BORN EDWARD ALLAN PETTIT, BUT EVERYONE CALLED HIM PETTY.
HE'D SURVIVED THE CALIFORNIA PENAL SYSTEM FOR FIVE DECADES.
PETTY'S REWARD? DYING OF OLD AGE IN HIS CELL AT FIVE IN THE MORNING.
YOU'RE BORN. YOU GROW UP. YOU DO SOMETHING STUPID. THEY STICK YOU IN A CAGE.
AND THEN...
I SWORE TO MYSELF THAT I WOULDN'T END UP LIKE PETTY.

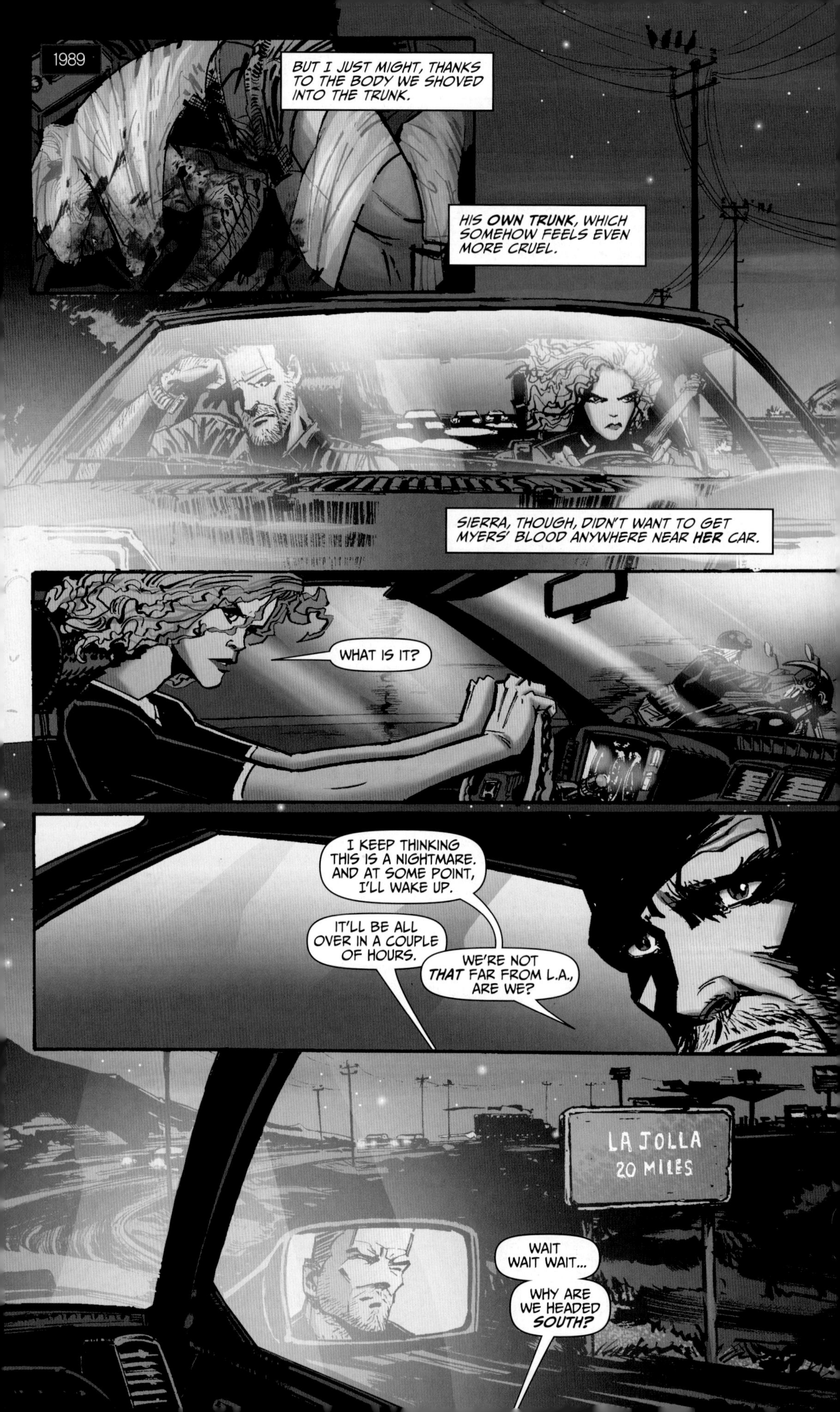
1989
BUT I JUST MIGHT, THANKS TO THE BODY WE SHOVED INTO THE TRUNK.
HIS OWN TRUNK, WHICH SOMEHOW FEELS EVEN MORE CRUEL.
SIERRA, THOUGH, DIDN'T WANT TO GET MYERS' BLOOD ANYWHERE NEAR HER CAR.
WHAT IS IT?
I KEEP THINKING THIS IS A NIGHTMARE. AND AT SOME POINT, I'LL WAKE UP.
IT'LL BE ALL OVER IN A COUPLE OF HOURS.
WE'RE NOT THAT FAR FROM L.A., ARE WE?
LA JOLLA 20 MILES
WAIT WAIT WAIT...
WHY ARE WE HEADED SOUTH?

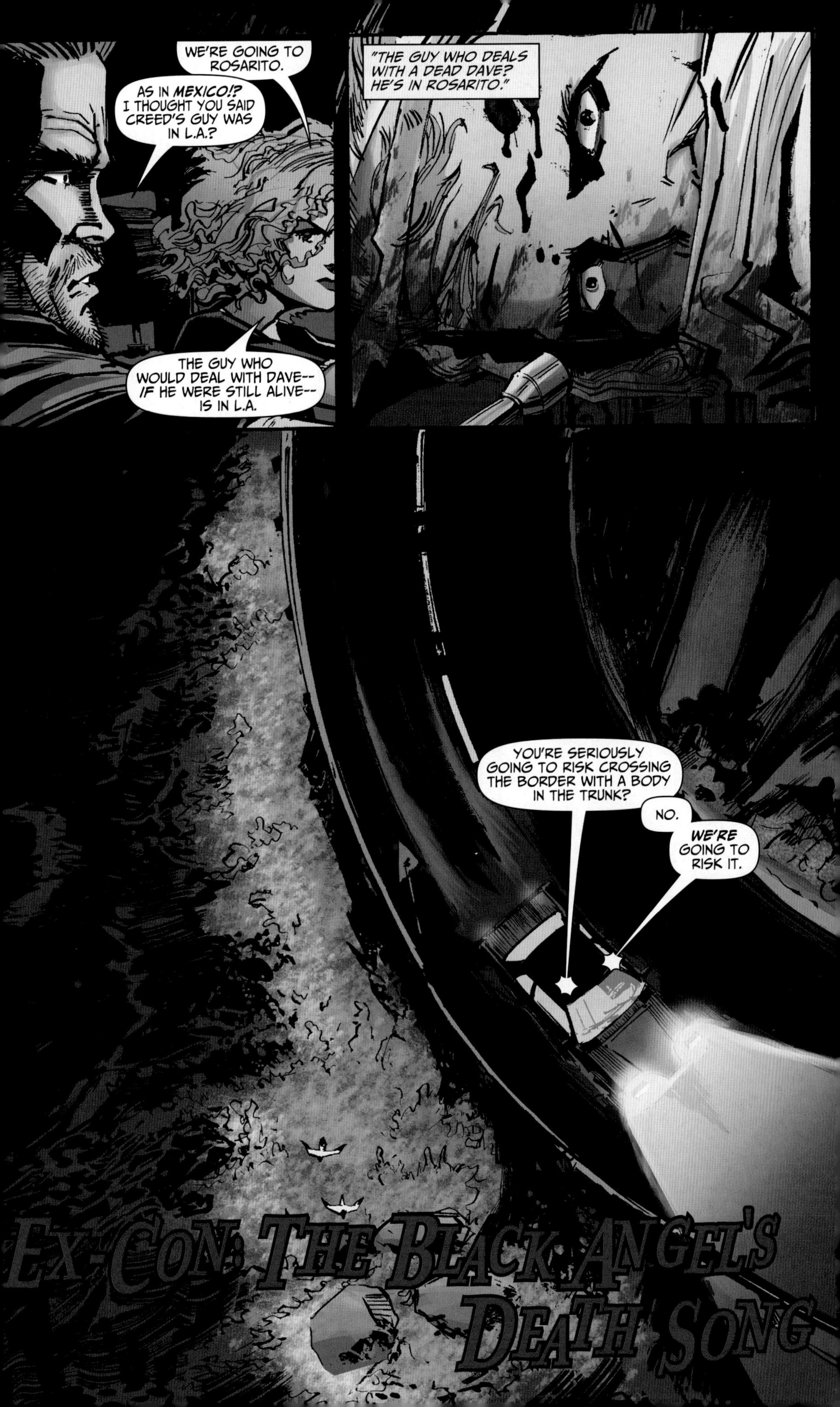
WE'RE GOING TO ROSARITO.
AS IN MEXICO!? I THOUGHT YOU SAID CREED'S GUY WAS IN L.A.?
THE GUY WHO WOULD DEAL WITH DAVE-- IF HE WERE STILL ALIVE-- IS IN L.A.
"THE GUY WHO DEALS WITH A DEAD DAVE? HE'S IN ROSARITO."
YOU'RE SERIOUSLY GOING TO RISK CROSSING THE BORDER WITH A BODY IN THE TRUNK?
NO.
WE'RE GOING TO RISK IT.
EX-CON: THE BLACK ANGEL'S DEATH SONG

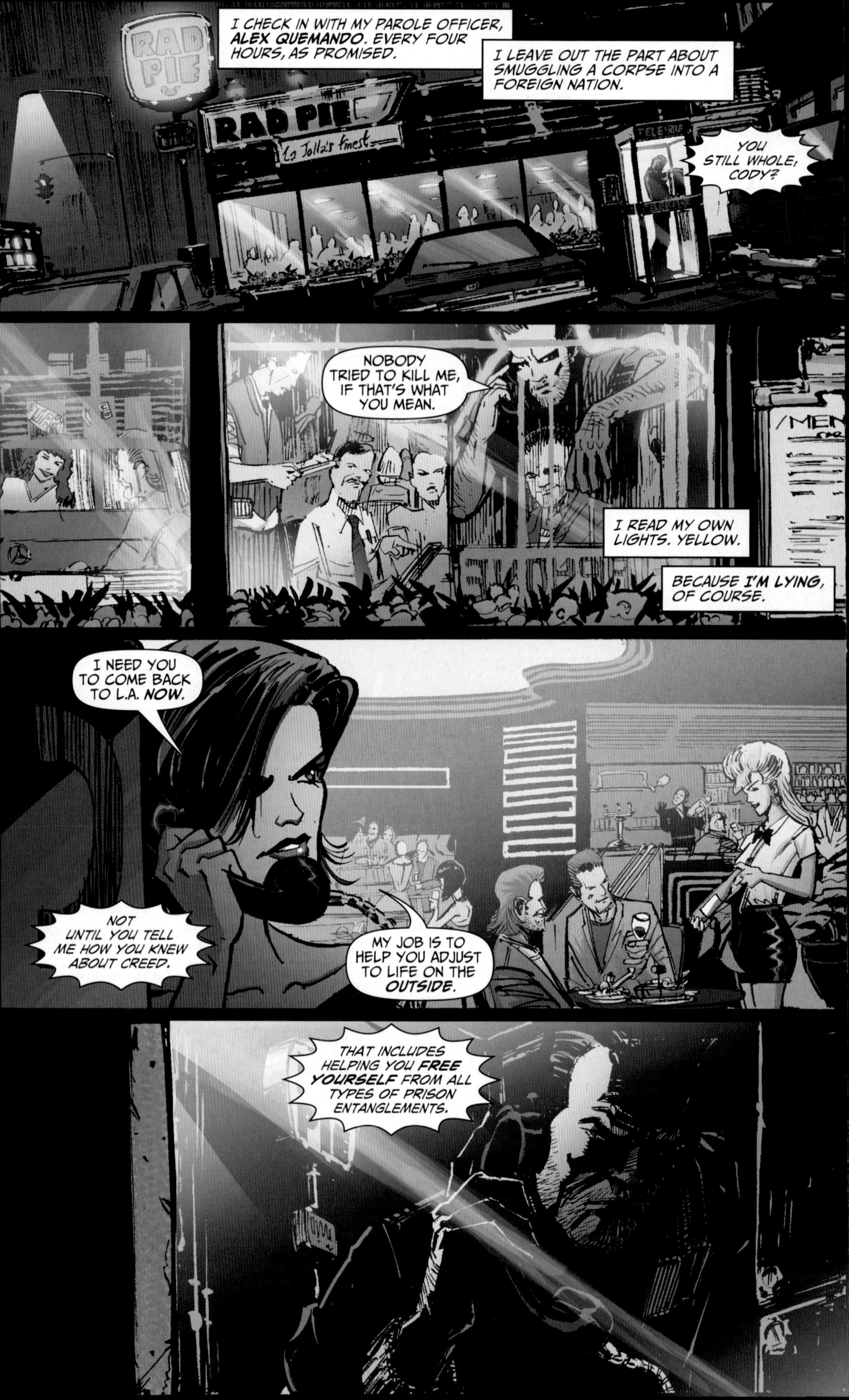
RAD PIE
I CHECK IN WITH MY PAROLE OFFICER, ALEX QUEMANDO. EVERY FOUR HOURS, AS PROMISED.
I LEAVE OUT THE PART ABOUT SMUGGLING A CORPSE INTO A FOREIGN NATION.
RAD PIE
La Jolla's Finest
YOU STILL WHOLE, CODY?
NOBODY TRIED TO KILL ME, IF THAT'S WHAT YOU MEAN.
I READ MY OWN LIGHTS. YELLOW.
BECAUSE I'M LYING, OF COURSE.
I NEED YOU TO COME BACK TO L.A. NOW.
NOT UNTIL YOU TELL ME HOW YOU KNEW ABOUT CREED.
MY JOB IS TO HELP YOU ADJUST TO LIFE ON THE OUTSIDE.
THAT INCLUDES HELPING YOU FREE YOURSELF FROM ALL TYPES OF PRISON ENTANGLEMENTS.

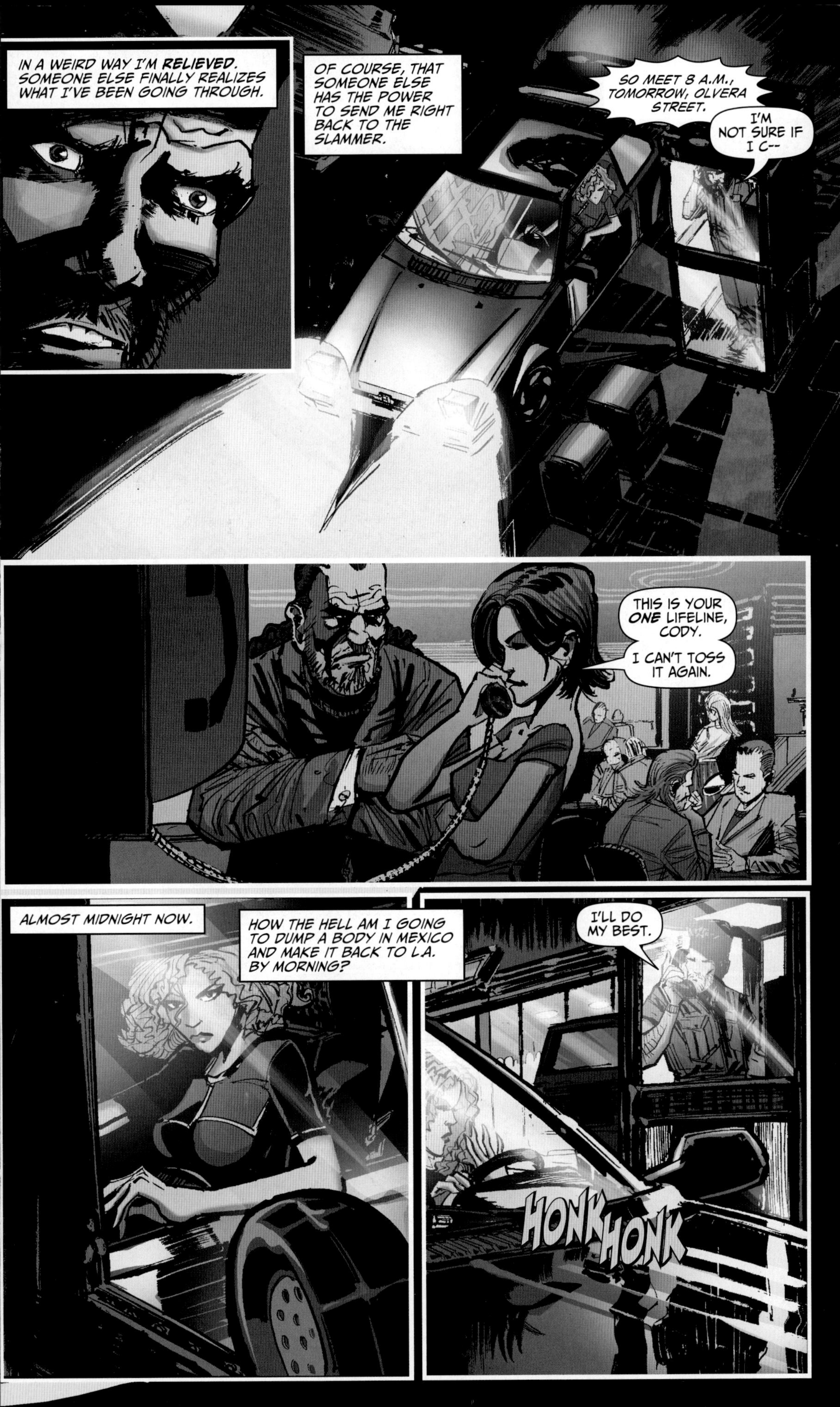
IN A WEIRD WAY I'M **RELIEVED**. SOMEONE ELSE FINALLY REALIZES WHAT I'VE BEEN GOING THROUGH.
OF COURSE, THAT SOMEONE ELSE HAS THE POWER TO SEND ME RIGHT BACK TO THE SLAMMER.
SO MEET 8 A.M., TOMORROW, OLVERA STREET.
I'M NOT SURE IF I C--
THIS IS YOUR ***ONE*** LIFELINE, CODY.
I CAN'T TOSS IT AGAIN.
ALMOST MIDNIGHT NOW.
HOW THE HELL AM I GOING TO DUMP A BODY IN MEXICO AND MAKE IT BACK TO L.A. BY MORNING?
I'LL DO MY BEST.
HONK HONK

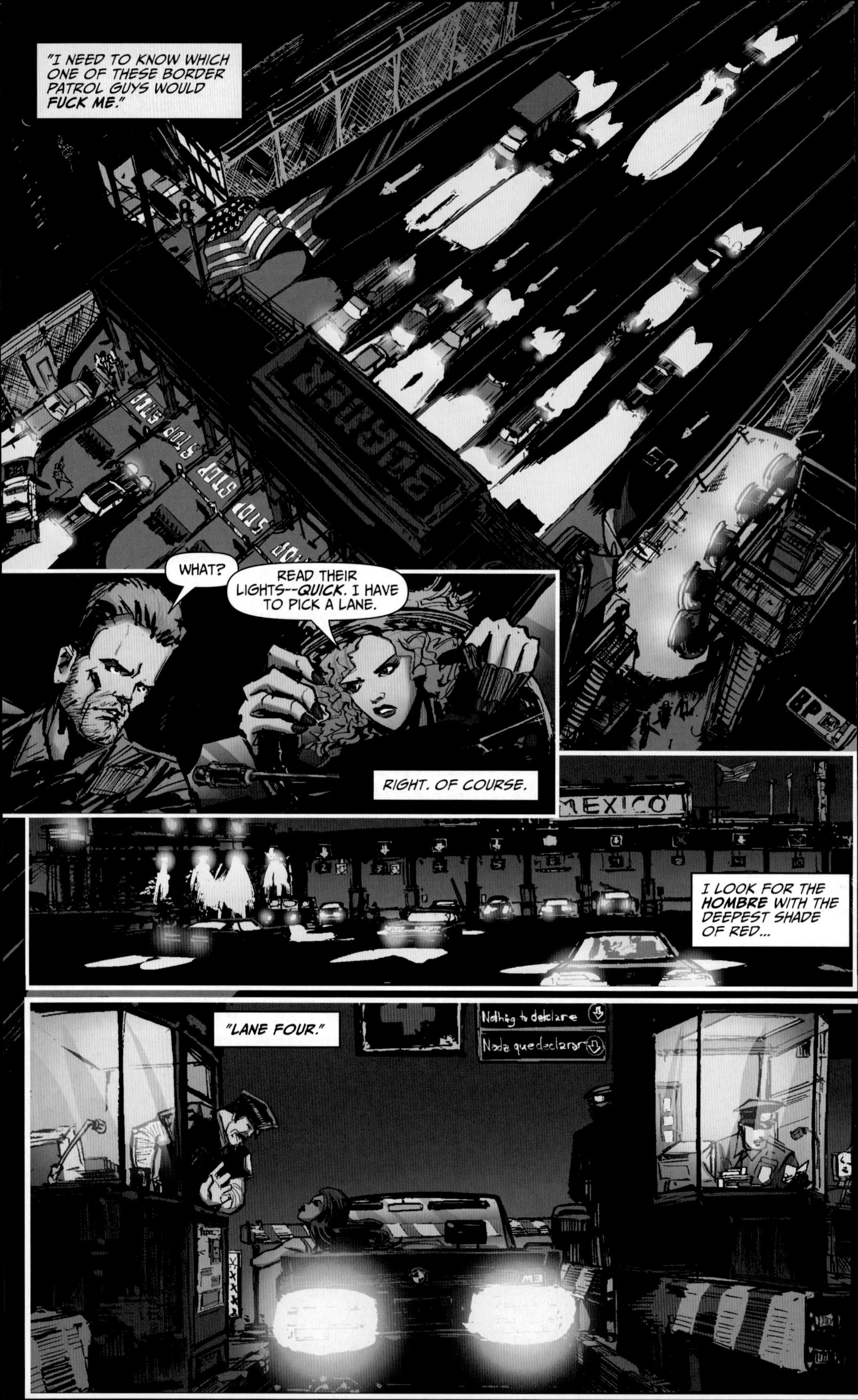
"I NEED TO KNOW WHICH ONE OF THESE BORDER PATROL GUYS WOULD FUCK ME."
STOP
WHAT?
READ THEIR LIGHTS--QUICK. I HAVE TO PICK A LANE.
RIGHT. OF COURSE.
MEXICO
I LOOK FOR THE HOMBRE WITH THE DEEPEST SHADE OF RED...
"LANE FOUR."
Nothing to declare
Nada que declarar

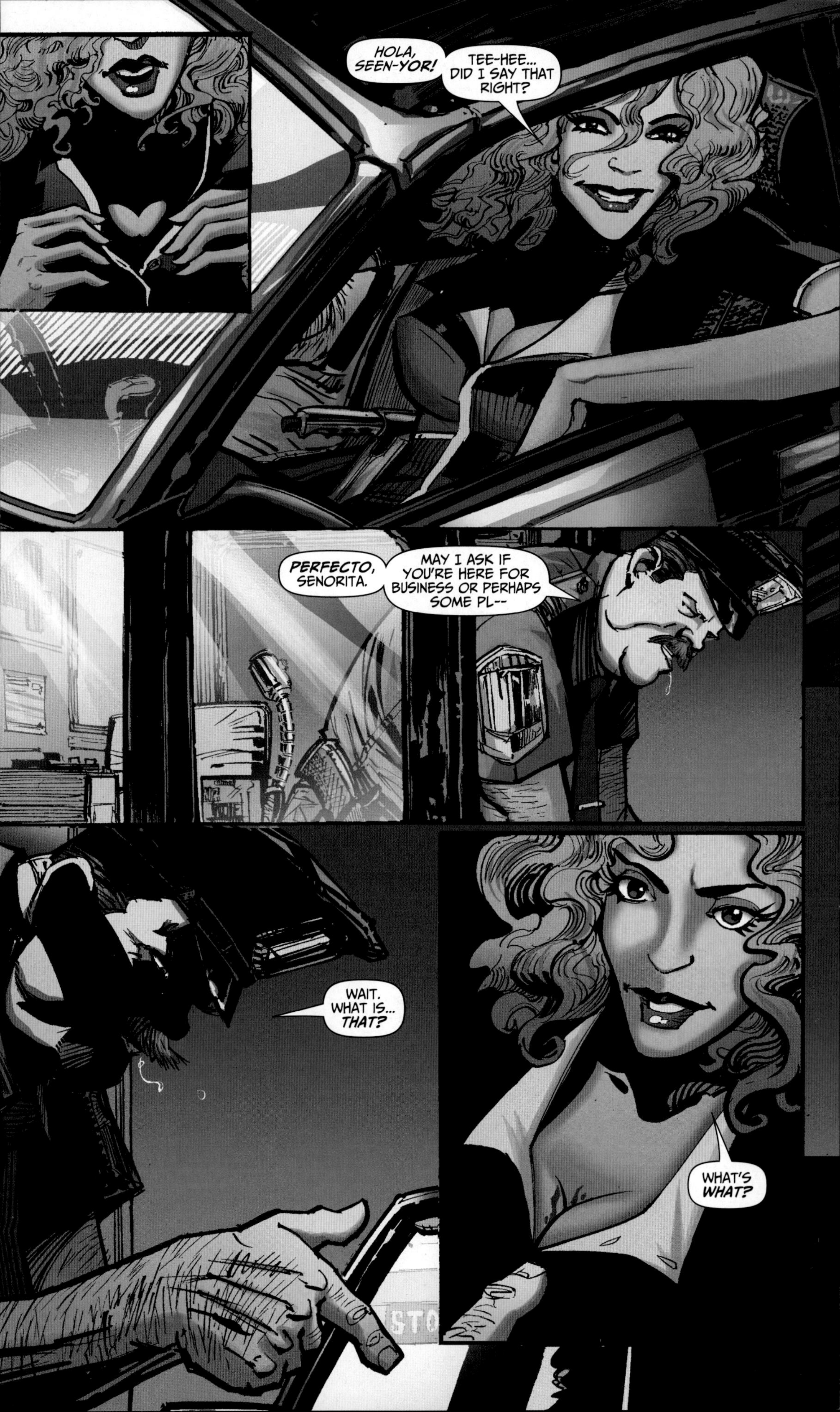

HOLA, SEEN-YOR!
TEE-HEE... DID I SAY THAT RIGHT?
PERFECTO, SENORITA.
MAY I ASK IF YOU'RE HERE FOR BUSINESS OR PERHAPS SOME PL--
WAIT. WHAT IS... THAT?
WHAT'S WHAT?

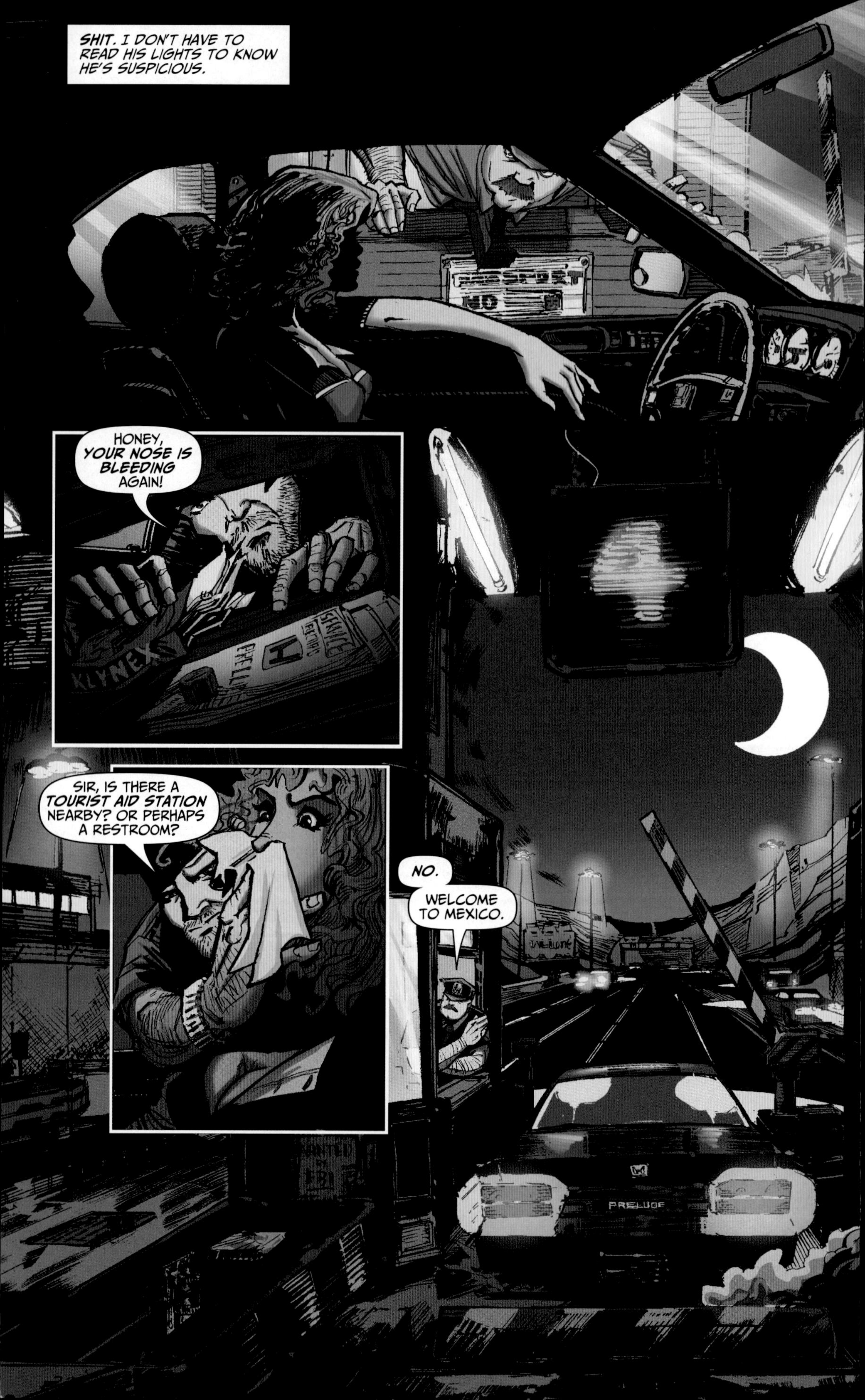
SHIT. I DON'T HAVE TO READ HIS LIGHTS TO KNOW HE'S SUSPICIOUS.
PASSPORT
NO
HONEY, YOUR NOSE IS BLEEDING AGAIN!
KLYNEX
SIR, IS THERE A TOURIST AID STATION NEARBY? OR PERHAPS A RESTROOM?
NO.
WELCOME TO MEXICO.
PRELUDE

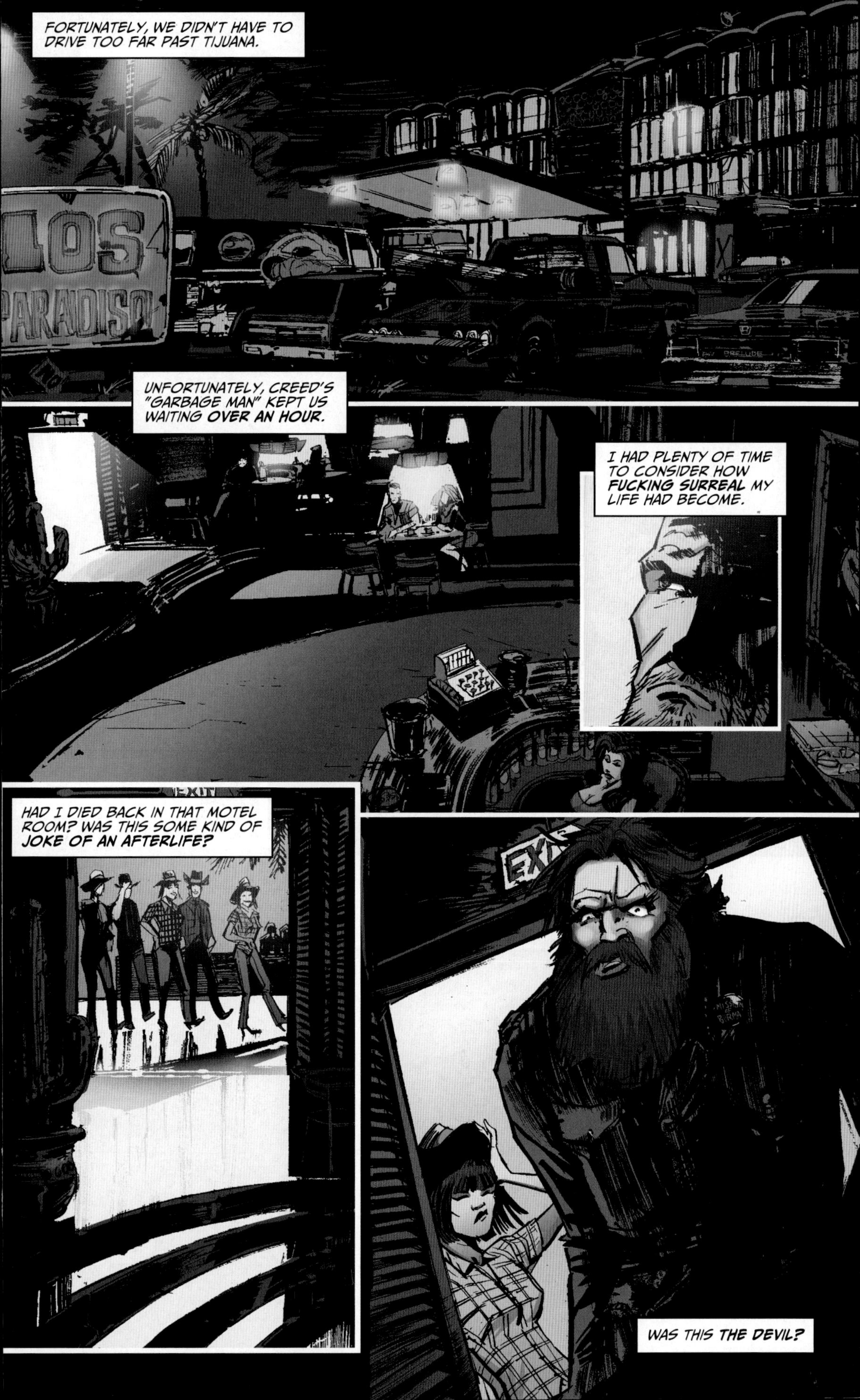
FORTUNATELY, WE DIDN'T HAVE TO DRIVE TOO FAR PAST TIJUANA.
LOS PARADISO
UNFORTUNATELY, CREED'S "GARBAGE MAN" KEPT US WAITING OVER AN HOUR.
I HAD PLENTY OF TIME TO CONSIDER HOW FUCKING SURREAL MY LIFE HAD BECOME.
HAD I DIED BACK IN THAT MOTEL ROOM? WAS THIS SOME KIND OF JOKE OF AN AFTERLIFE?
EXIT
WAS THIS THE DEVIL?

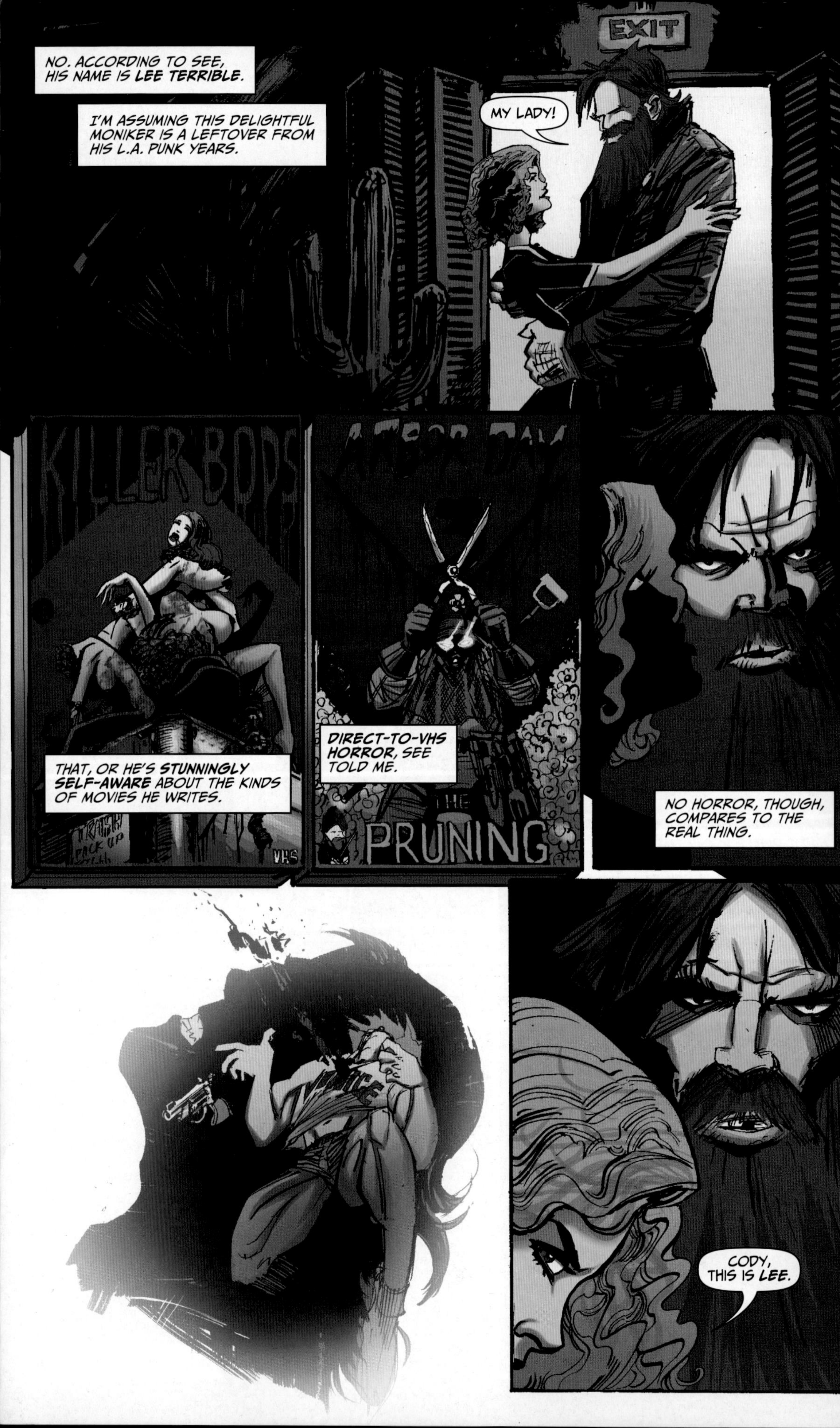
EXIT
NO. ACCORDING TO SEE, HIS NAME IS **LEE TERRIBLE.**
I'M ASSUMING THIS DELIGHTFUL MONIKER IS A LEFTOVER FROM HIS L.A. PUNK YEARS.
MY LADY!
KILLER BODS
THAT, OR HE'S **STUNNINGLY SELF-AWARE** ABOUT THE KINDS OF MOVIES HE WRITES.
VHS
DIRECT-TO-VHS HORROR, SEE TOLD ME.
THE PRUNING
NO HORROR, THOUGH, COMPARES TO THE REAL THING.
CODY, THIS IS **LEE.**

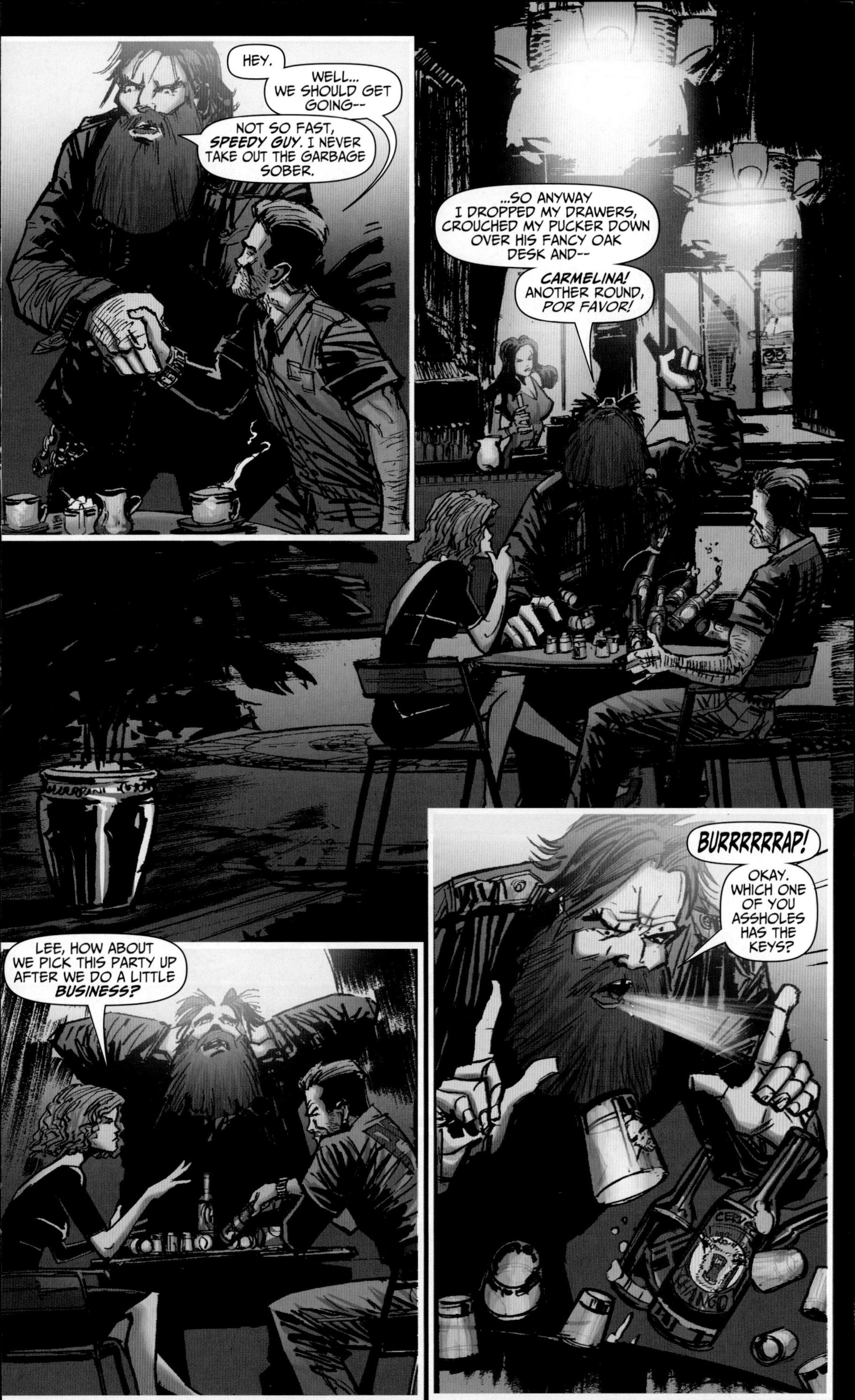
HEY.
WELL... WE SHOULD GET GOING--
NOT SO FAST, *SPEEDY GUY*. I NEVER TAKE OUT THE GARBAGE SOBER.
...SO ANYWAY I DROPPED MY DRAWERS, CROUCHED MY PUCKER DOWN OVER HIS FANCY OAK DESK AND--
CARMELINA! ANOTHER ROUND, *POR FAVOR!*
LEE, HOW ABOUT WE PICK THIS PARTY UP AFTER WE DO A LITTLE *BUSINESS?*
BURRRRRRAP!
OKAY. WHICH ONE OF YOU ASSHOLES HAS THE KEYS?

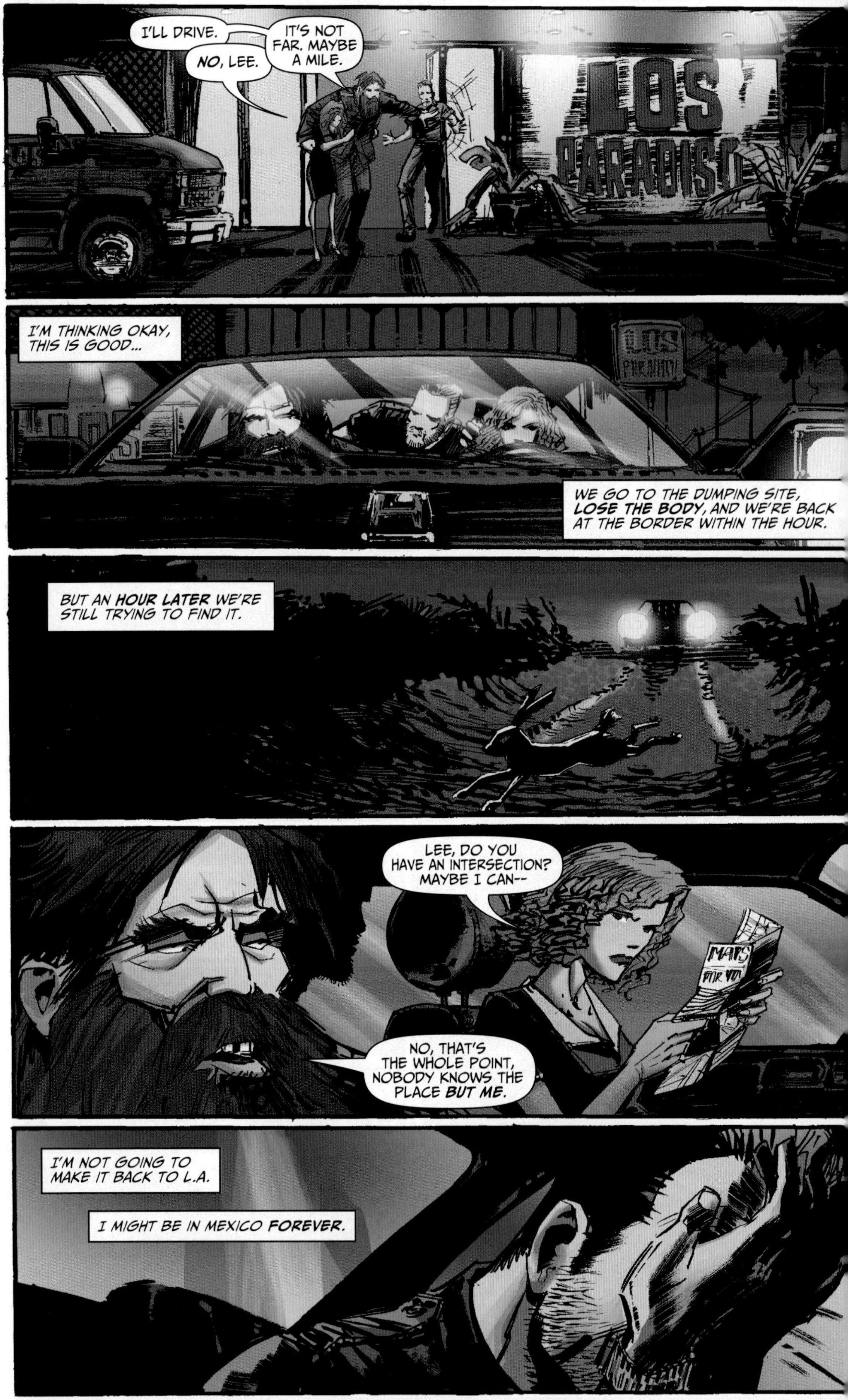

I'LL DRIVE.
NO, LEE.
IT'S NOT FAR. MAYBE A MILE.
LOS PARADISO
I'M THINKING OKAY, THIS IS GOOD...
WE GO TO THE DUMPING SITE, LOSE THE BODY, AND WE'RE BACK AT THE BORDER WITHIN THE HOUR.
BUT AN HOUR LATER WE'RE STILL TRYING TO FIND IT.
LEE, DO YOU HAVE AN INTERSECTION? MAYBE I CAN--
NO, THAT'S THE WHOLE POINT, NOBODY KNOWS THE PLACE BUT ME.
I'M NOT GOING TO MAKE IT BACK TO L.A.
I MIGHT BE IN MEXICO FOREVER.

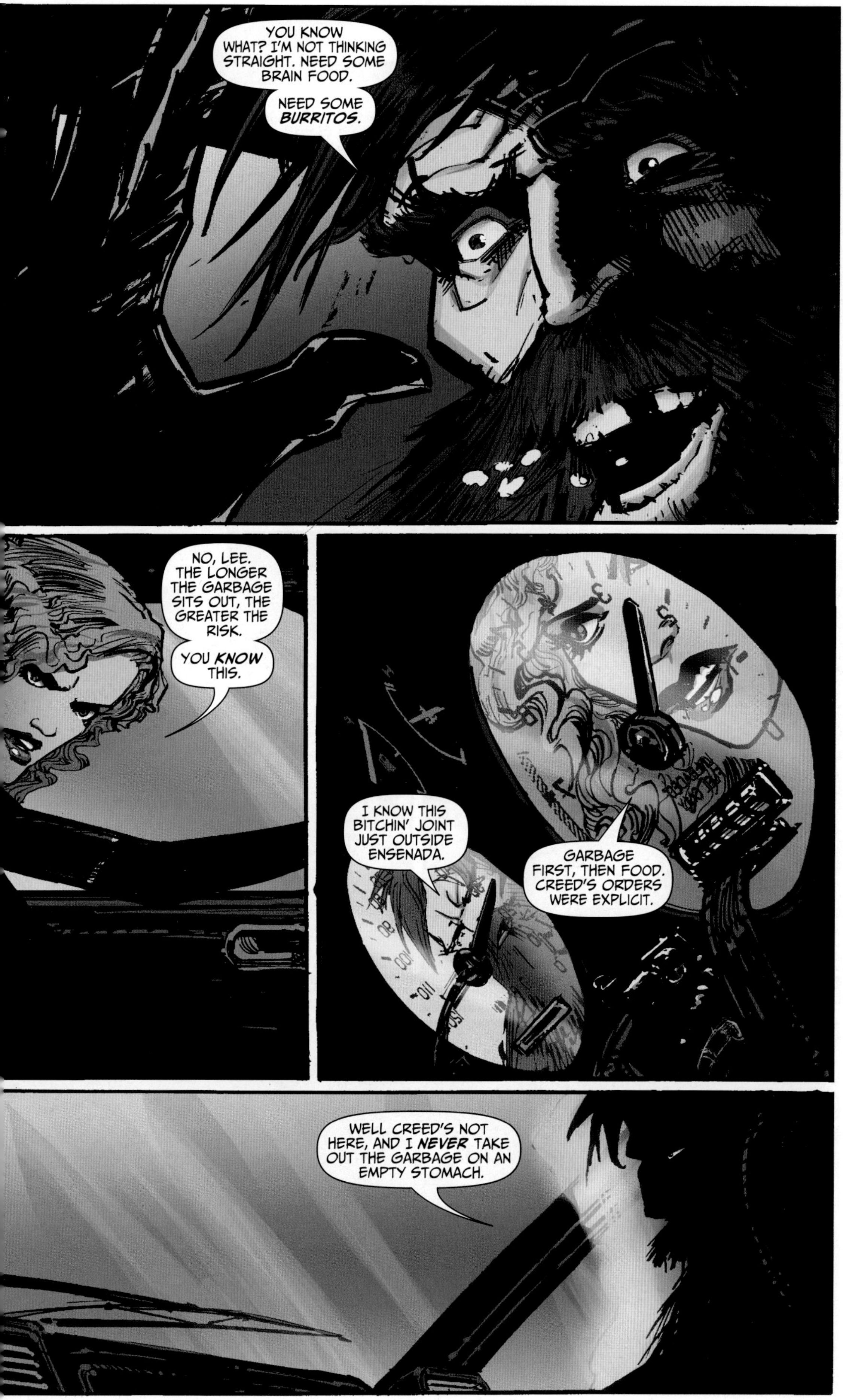
YOU KNOW WHAT? I'M NOT THINKING STRAIGHT. NEED SOME BRAIN FOOD.
NEED SOME *BURRITOS*.
NO, LEE. THE LONGER THE GARBAGE SITS OUT, THE GREATER THE RISK.
YOU *KNOW* THIS.
I KNOW THIS BITCHIN' JOINT JUST OUTSIDE ENSENADA.
GARBAGE FIRST, THEN FOOD. CREED'S ORDERS WERE EXPLICIT.
WELL CREED'S NOT HERE, AND I *NEVER* TAKE OUT THE GARBAGE ON AN EMPTY STOMACH.

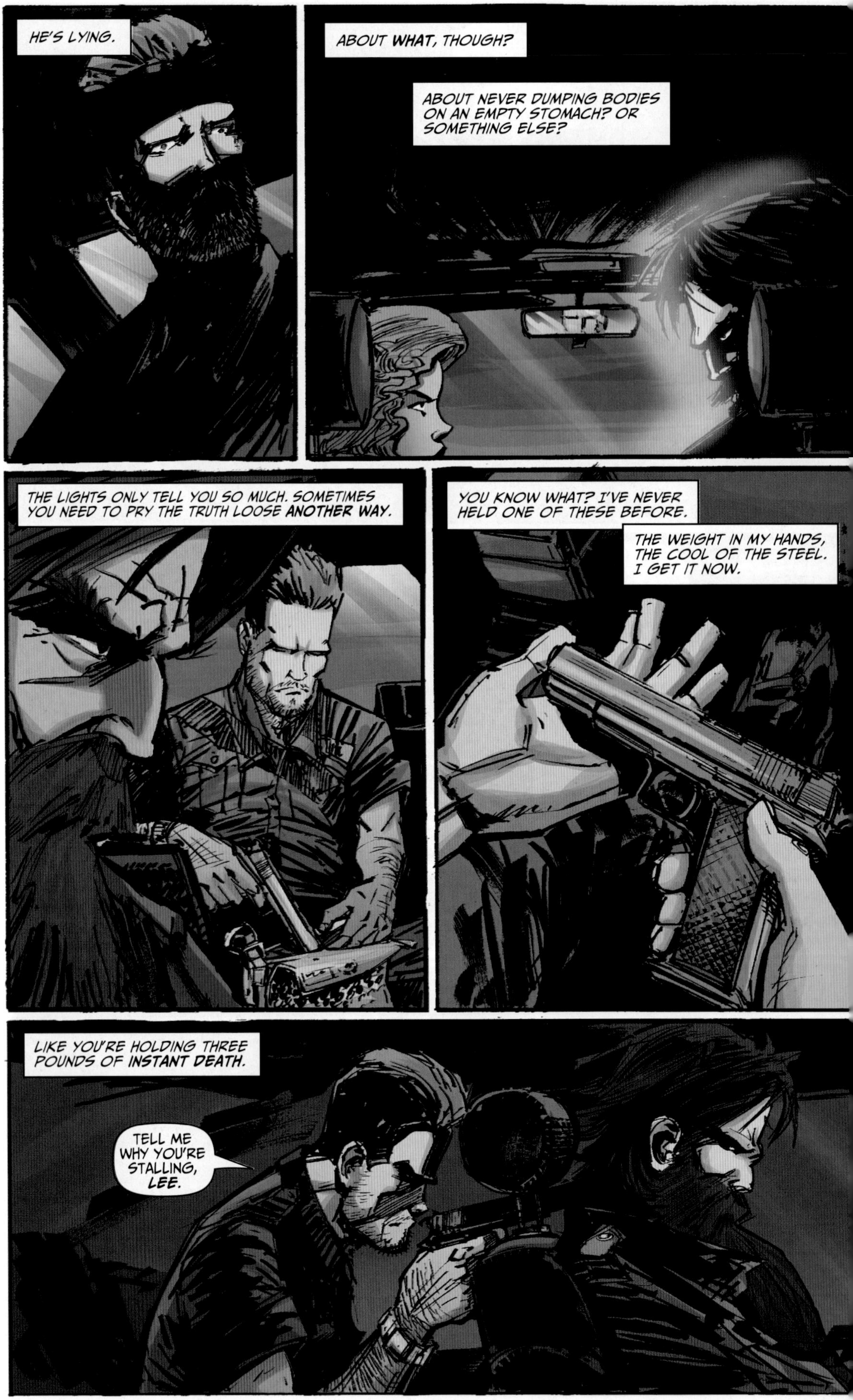
HE'S LYING.
ABOUT WHAT, THOUGH?
ABOUT NEVER DUMPING BODIES ON AN EMPTY STOMACH? OR SOMETHING ELSE?
THE LIGHTS ONLY TELL YOU SO MUCH. SOMETIMES YOU NEED TO PRY THE TRUTH LOOSE ANOTHER WAY.
YOU KNOW WHAT? I'VE NEVER HELD ONE OF THESE BEFORE.
THE WEIGHT IN MY HANDS, THE COOL OF THE STEEL. I GET IT NOW.
LIKE YOU'RE HOLDING THREE POUNDS OF INSTANT DEATH.
TELL ME WHY YOU'RE STALLING, LEE.

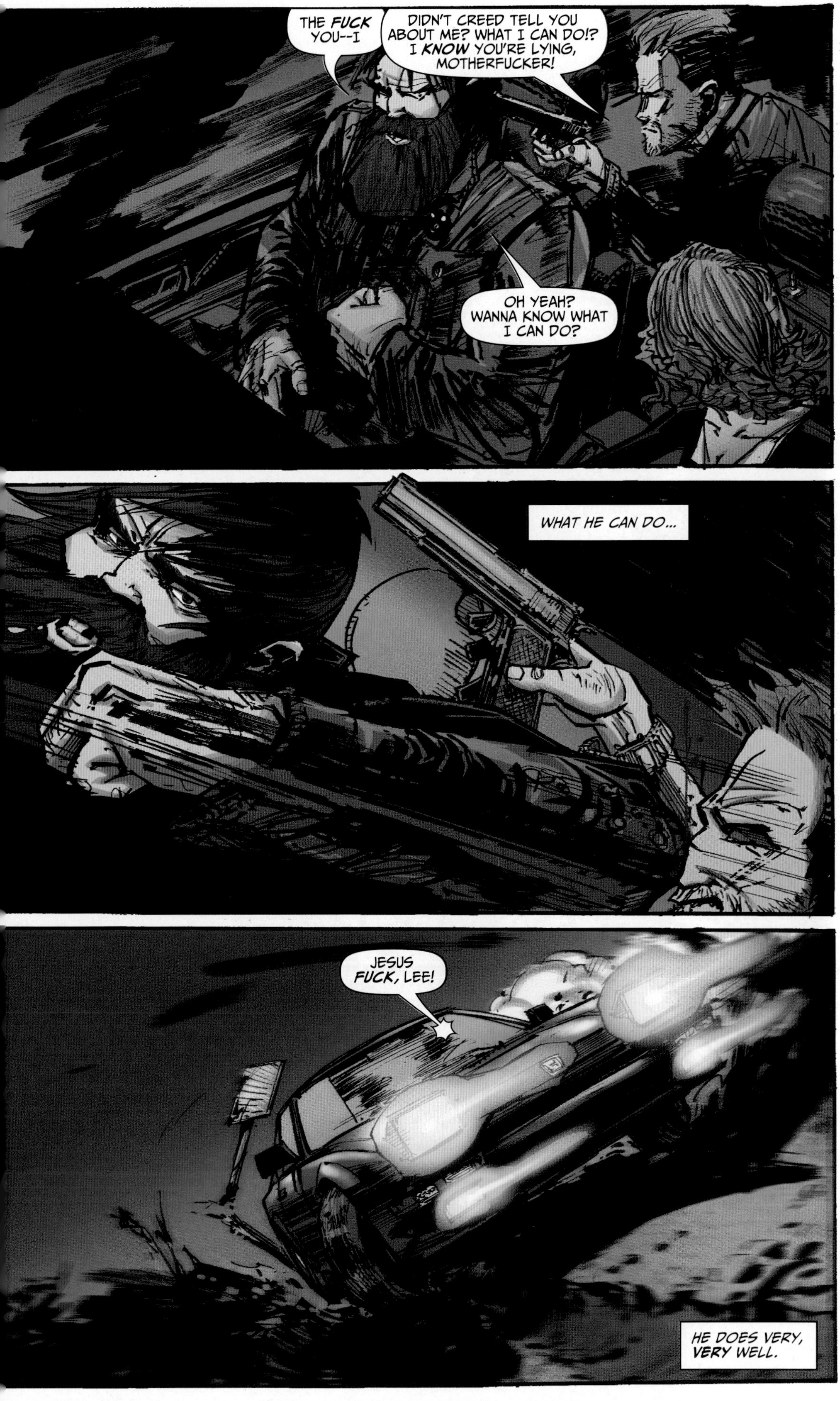
THE *FUCK* YOU--I
DIDN'T CREED TELL YOU ABOUT ME? WHAT I CAN DO!? I *KNOW* YOU'RE LYING, MOTHERFUCKER!
OH YEAH? WANNA KNOW WHAT I CAN DO?
WHAT HE CAN DO...
JESUS *FUCK*, LEE!
HE DOES VERY, *VERY* WELL.

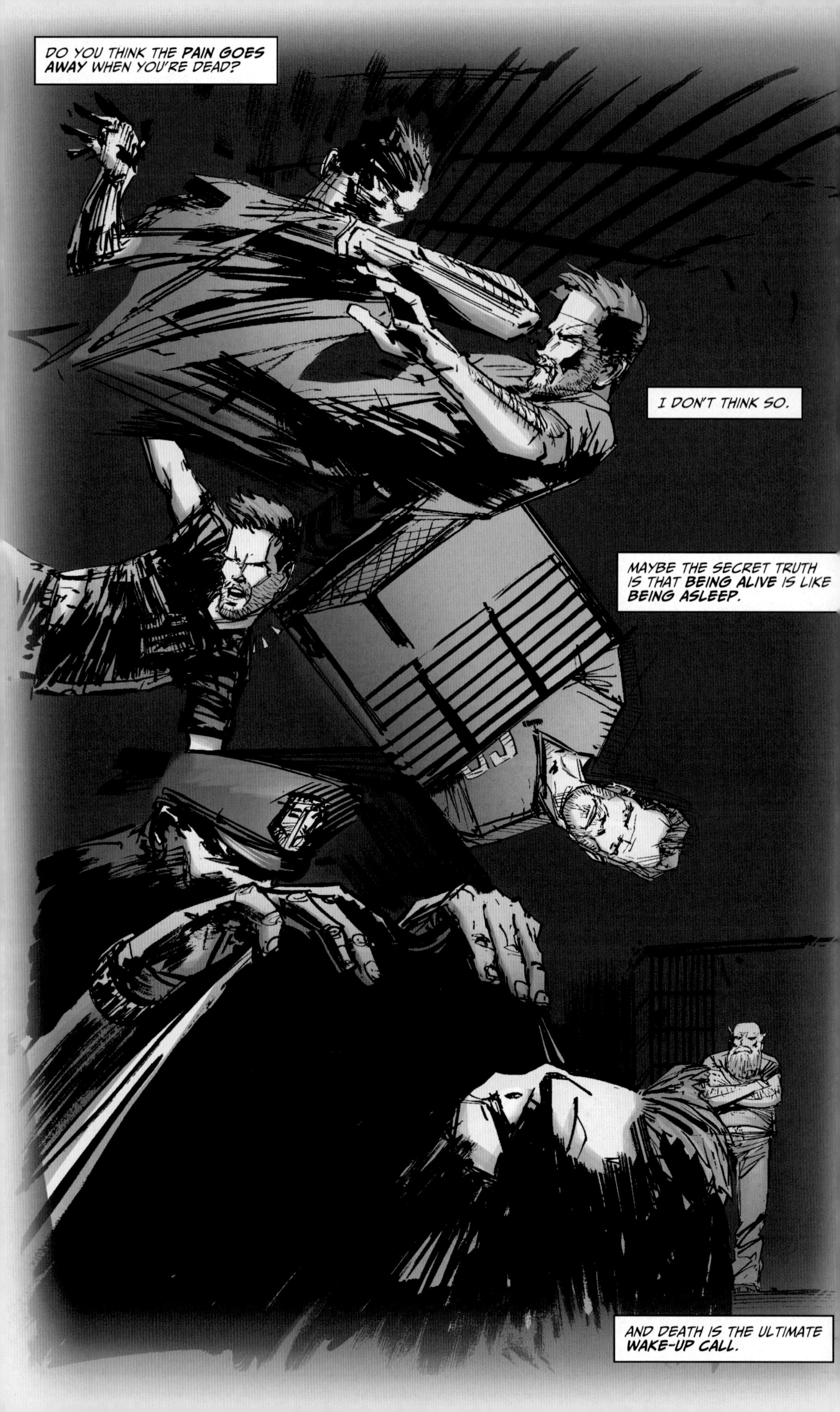
DO YOU THINK THE PAIN GOES AWAY WHEN YOU'RE DEAD?
I DON'T THINK SO.
MAYBE THE SECRET TRUTH IS THAT BEING ALIVE IS LIKE BEING ASLEEP.
AND DEATH IS THE ULTIMATE WAKE-UP CALL.

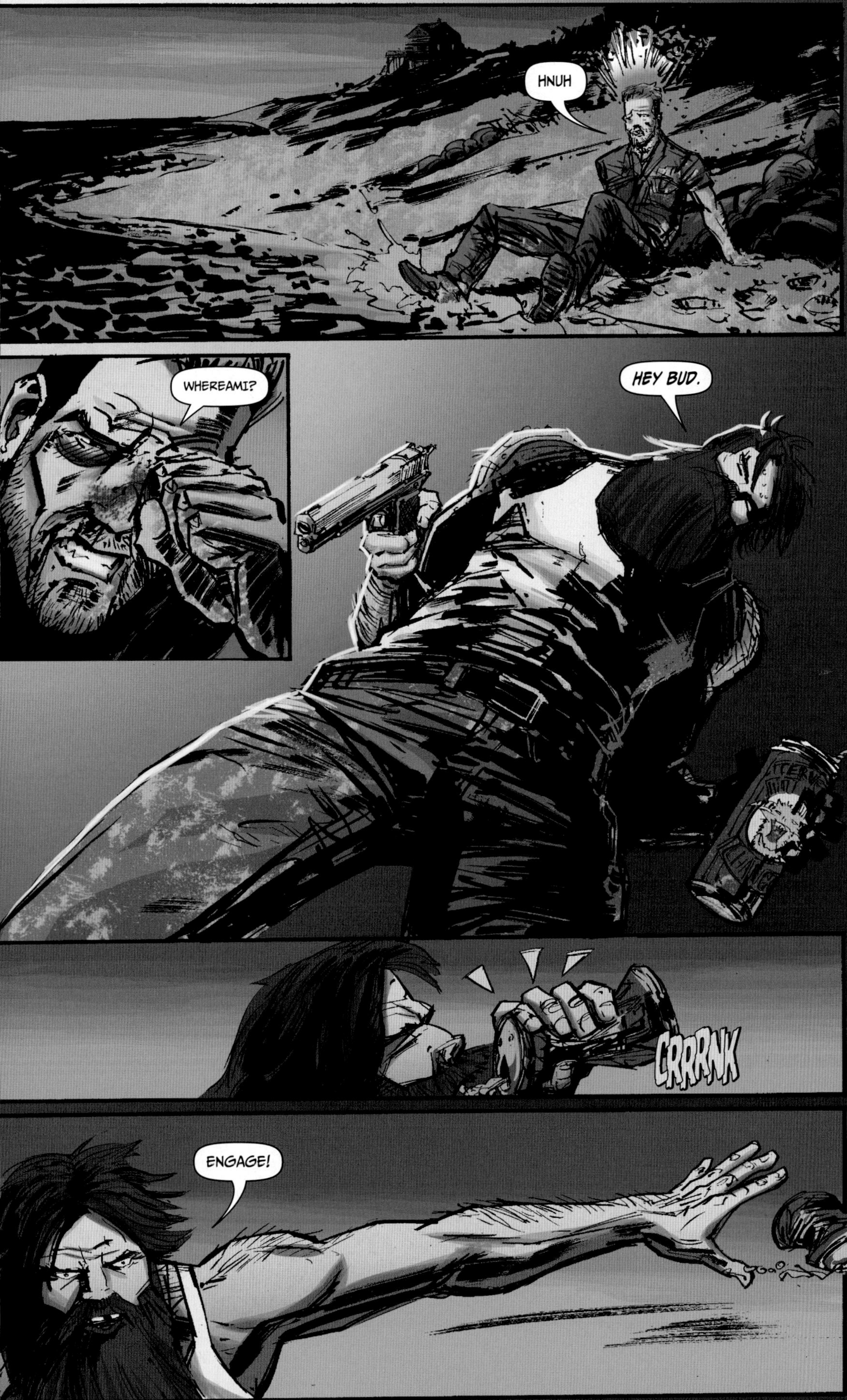
HNUH
WHEREAMI?
HEY BUD.
CRRRNK
ENGAGE!

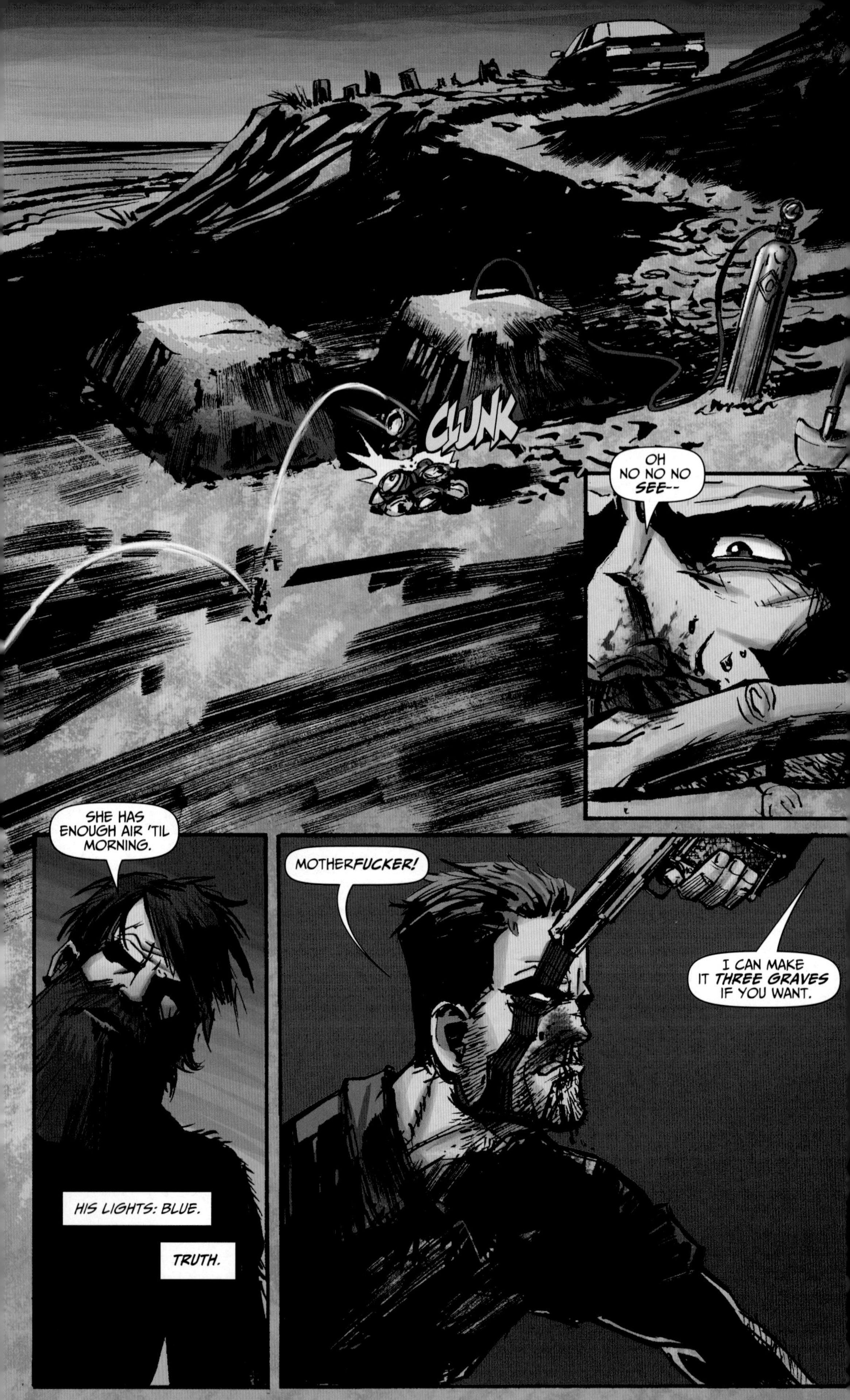
CLUNK
OH NO NO NO SEE--
SHE HAS ENOUGH AIR 'TIL MORNING.
HIS LIGHTS: BLUE.
TRUTH.
MOTHERFUCKER!
I CAN MAKE IT THREE GRAVES IF YOU WANT.

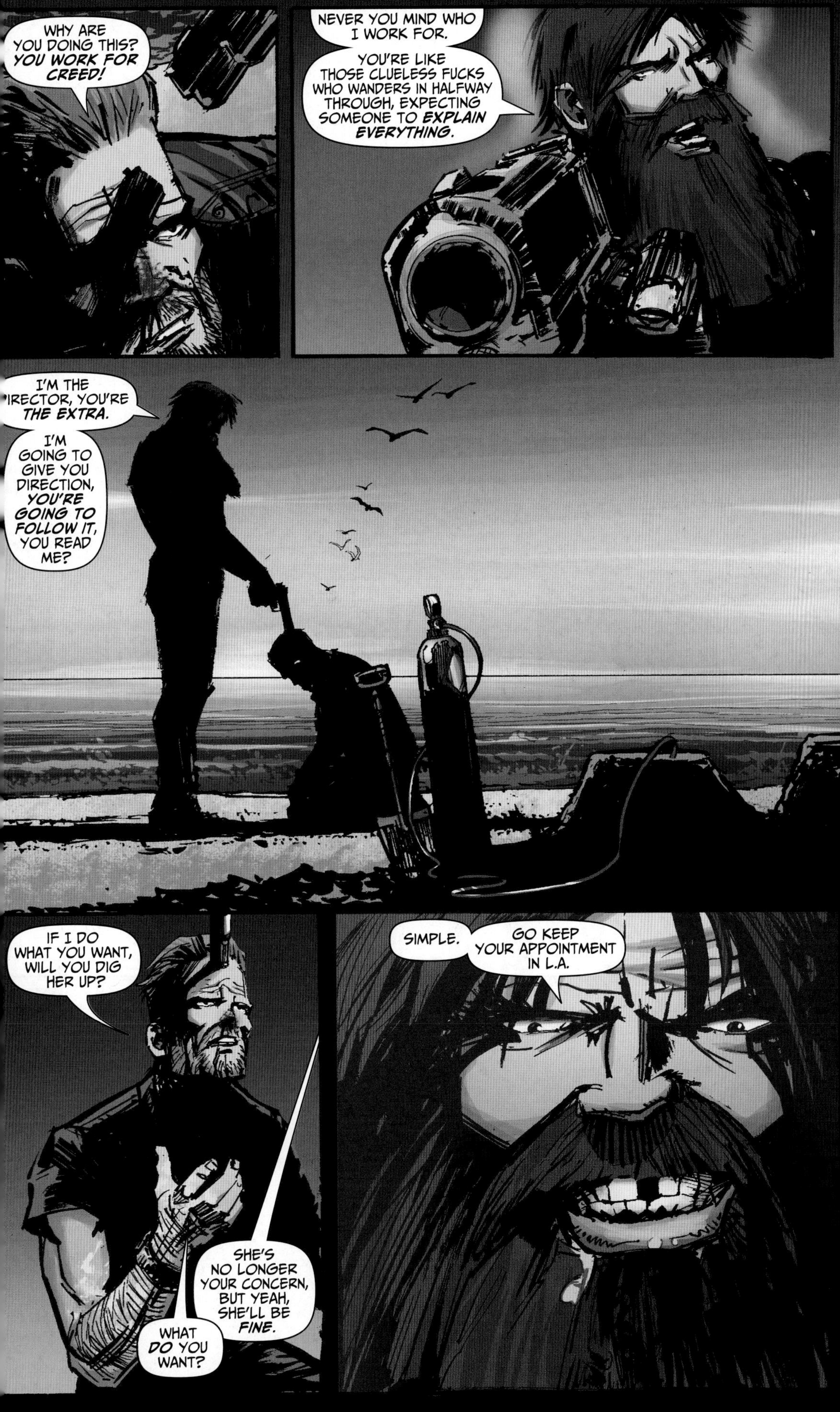
WHY ARE YOU DOING THIS? *YOU WORK FOR CREED!*
NEVER YOU MIND WHO I WORK FOR.
YOU'RE LIKE THOSE CLUELESS FUCKS WHO WANDERS IN HALFWAY THROUGH, EXPECTING SOMEONE TO *EXPLAIN EVERYTHING*.
I'M THE IRECTOR, YOU'RE *THE EXTRA*.
I'M GOING TO GIVE YOU DIRECTION, *YOU'RE GOING TO FOLLOW IT*, YOU READ ME?
IF I DO WHAT YOU WANT, WILL YOU DIG HER UP?
SHE'S NO LONGER YOUR CONCERN, BUT YEAH, SHE'LL BE *FINE*.
WHAT *DO* YOU WANT?
SIMPLE.
GO KEEP YOUR APPOINTMENT IN L.A.

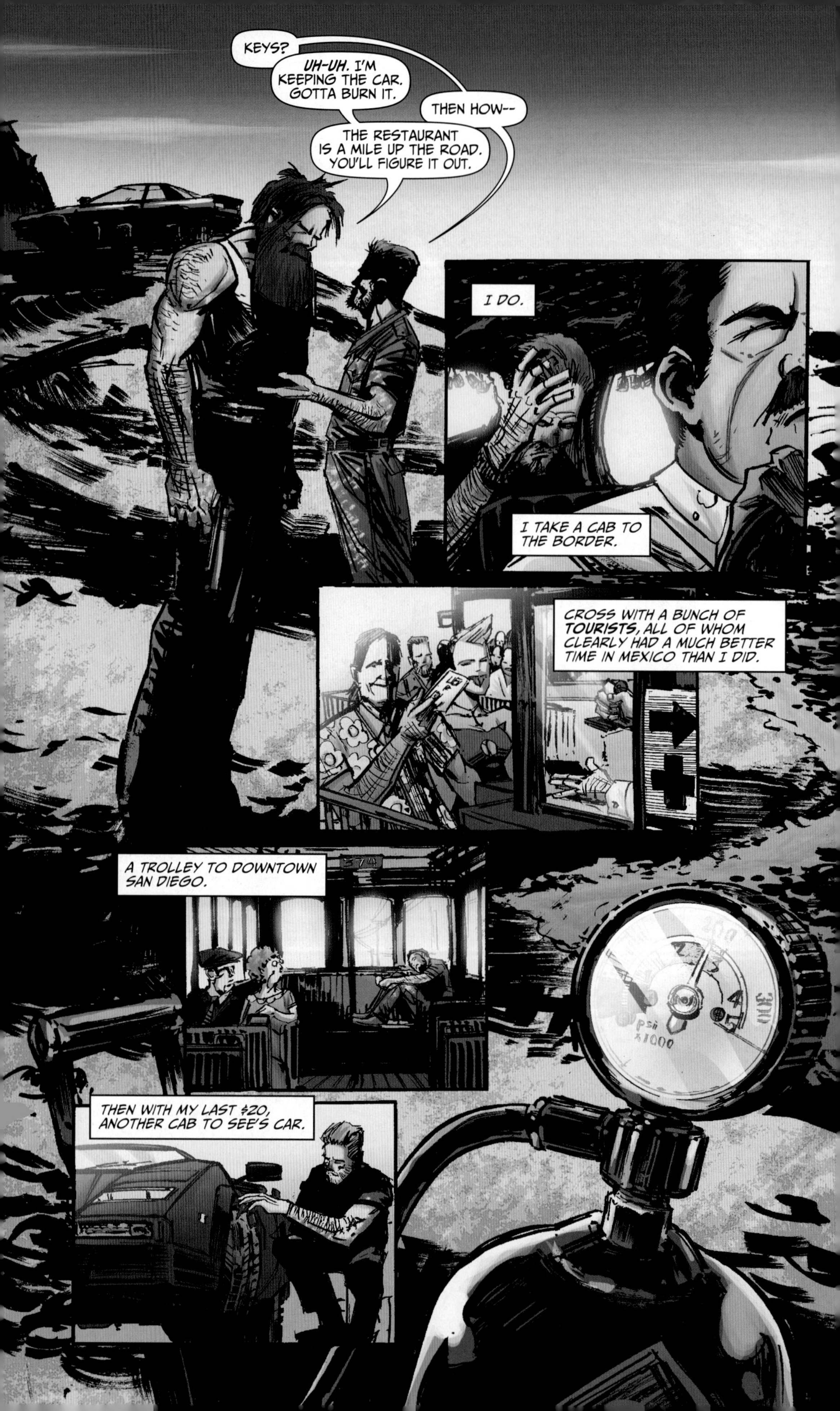
KEYS?
UH-UH. I'M KEEPING THE CAR. GOTTA BURN IT.
THEN HOW--
THE RESTAURANT IS A MILE UP THE ROAD. YOU'LL FIGURE IT OUT.
I DO.
I TAKE A CAB TO THE BORDER.
CROSS WITH A BUNCH OF TOURISTS, ALL OF WHOM CLEARLY HAD A MUCH BETTER TIME IN MEXICO THAN I DID.
A TROLLEY TO DOWNTOWN SAN DIEGO.
THEN WITH MY LAST $20, ANOTHER CAB TO SEE'S CAR.
psi x1000

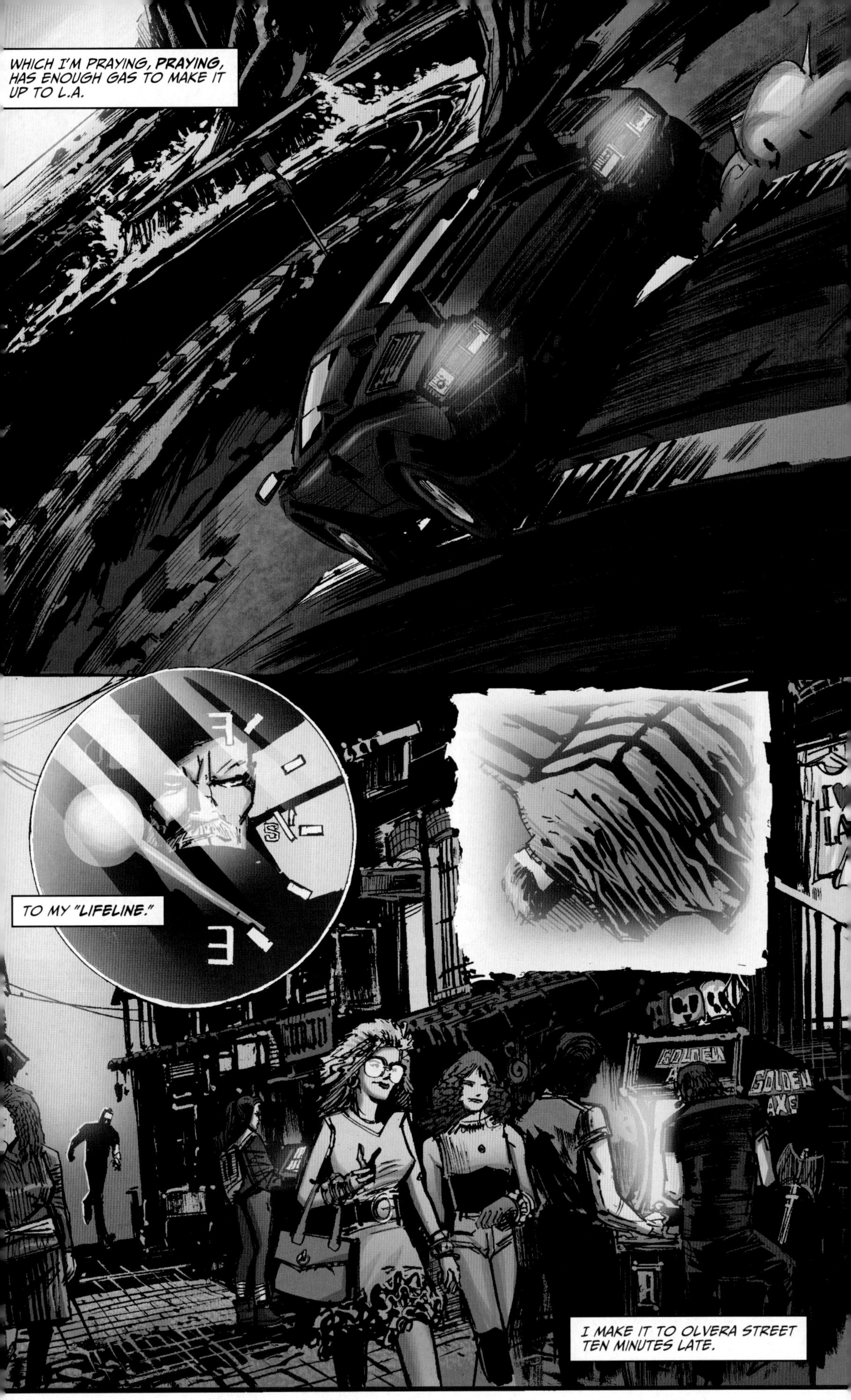

WHICH I'M PRAYING, **PRAYING**, HAS ENOUGH GAS TO MAKE IT UP TO L.A.
F
S
E
TO MY "**LIFELINE.**"
I ♥ LA
GOLDEN AXE
GOLDEN AXE
I MAKE IT TO OLVERA STREET TEN MINUTES LATE.

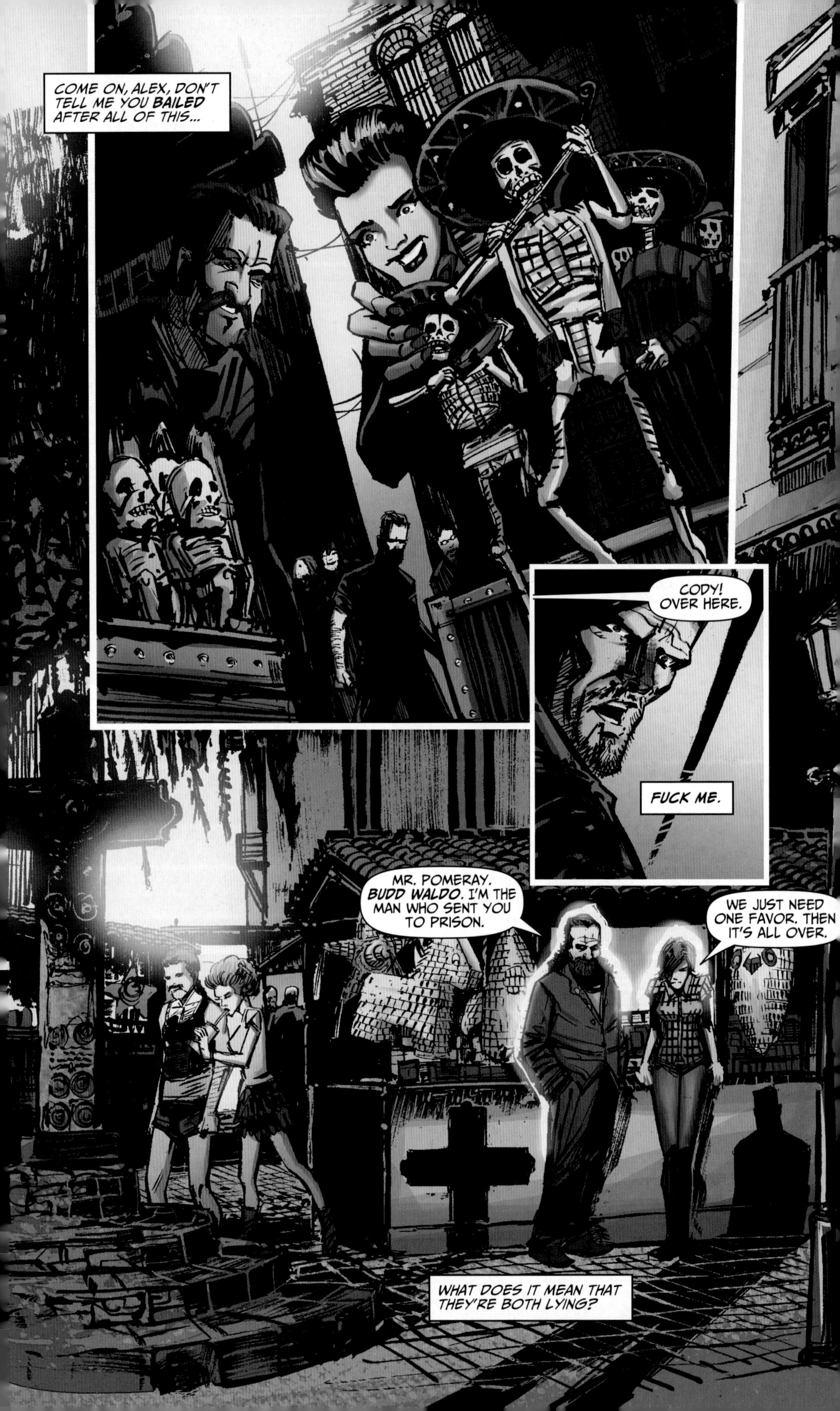

COME ON, ALEX, DON'T TELL ME YOU **BAILED** AFTER ALL OF THIS...
CODY! OVER HERE.
FUCK ME.
MR. POMERAY. **BUDD WALDO**. I'M THE MAN WHO SENT YOU TO PRISON.
WE JUST NEED ONE FAVOR. THEN IT'S ALL OVER.
WHAT DOES IT MEAN THAT THEY'RE BOTH LYING?

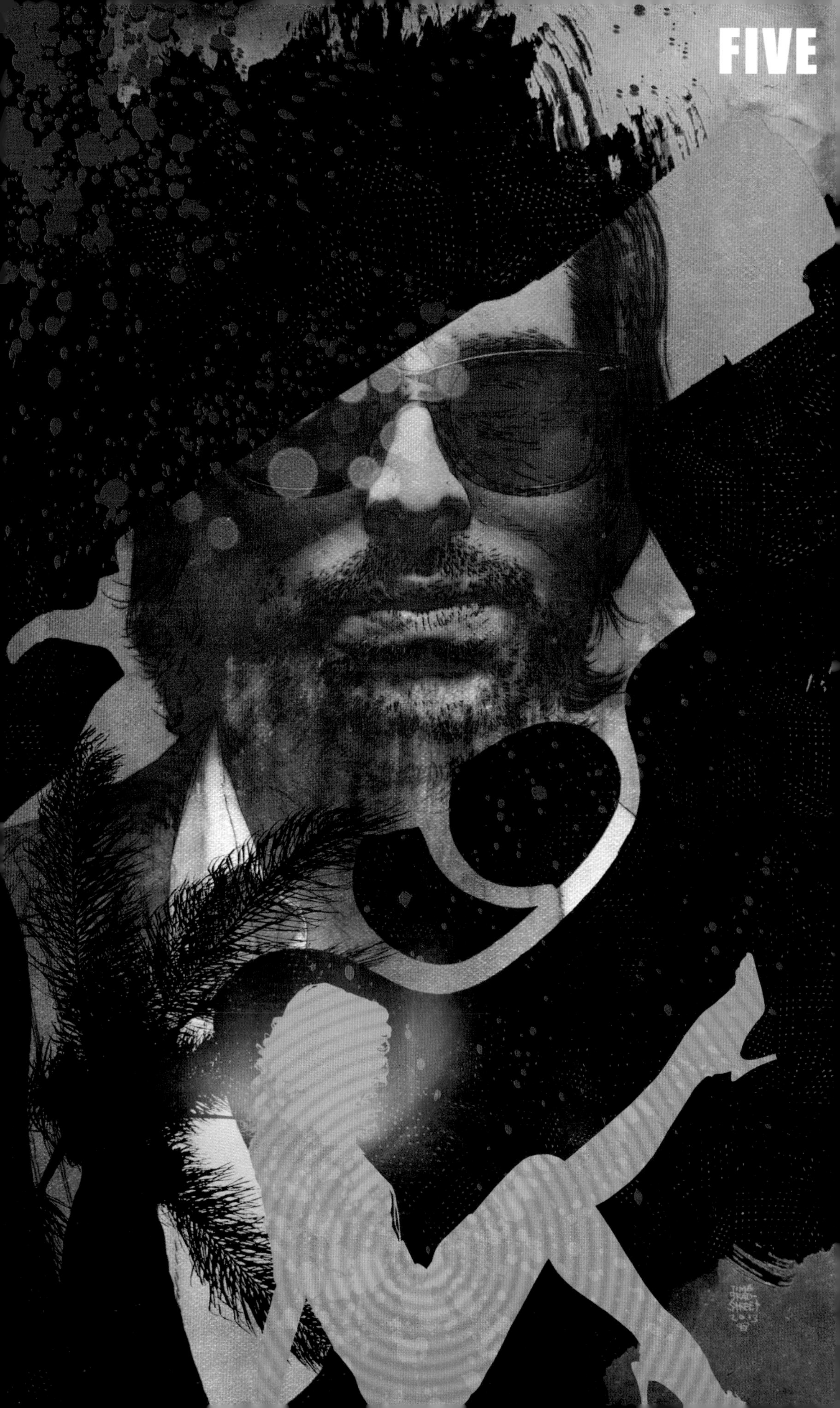
FIVE

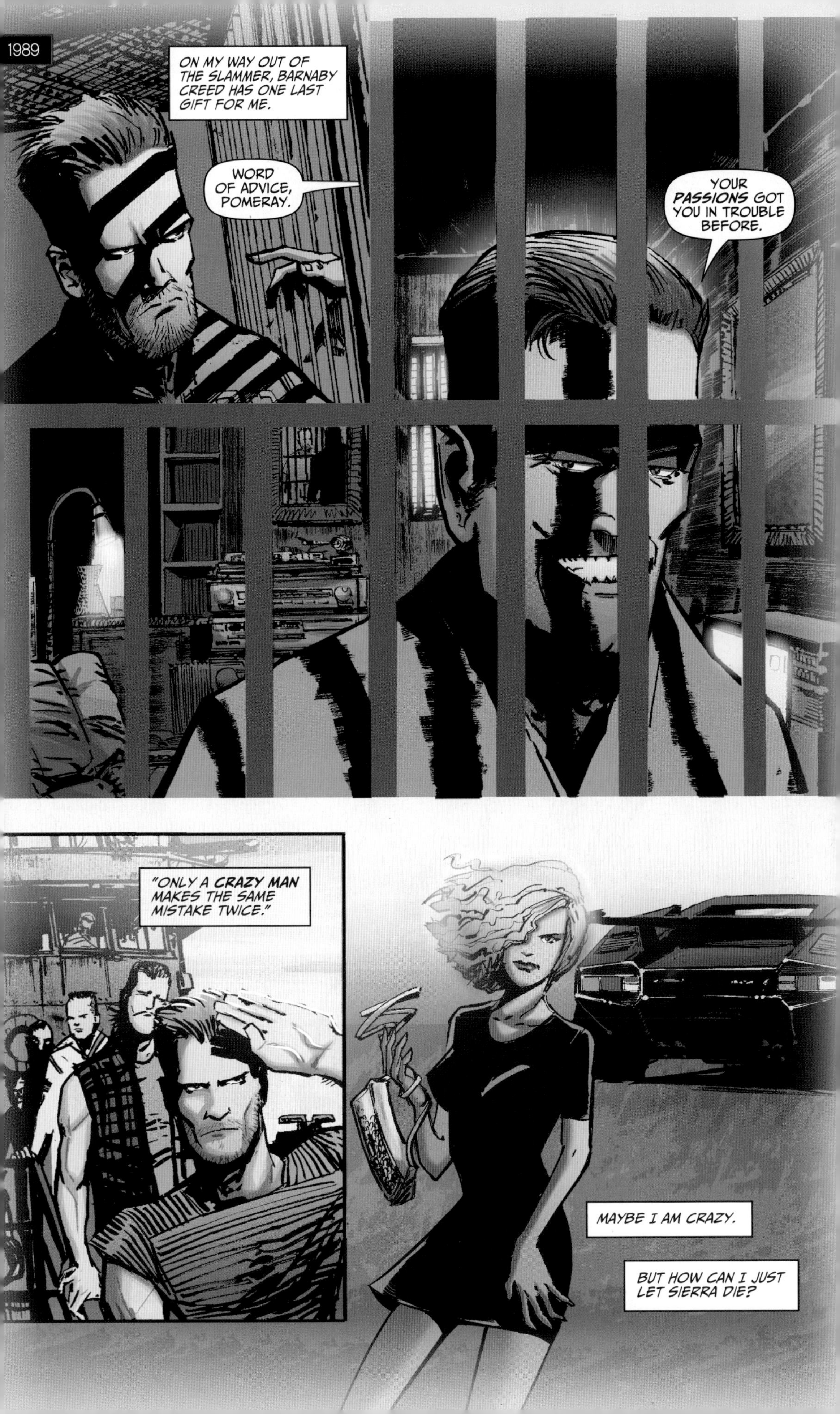
1989
ON MY WAY OUT OF THE SLAMMER, BARNABY CREED HAS ONE LAST GIFT FOR ME.
WORD OF ADVICE, POMERAY.
YOUR PASSIONS GOT YOU IN TROUBLE BEFORE.
"ONLY A CRAZY MAN MAKES THE SAME MISTAKE TWICE."
MAYBE I AM CRAZY.
BUT HOW CAN I JUST LET SIERRA DIE?

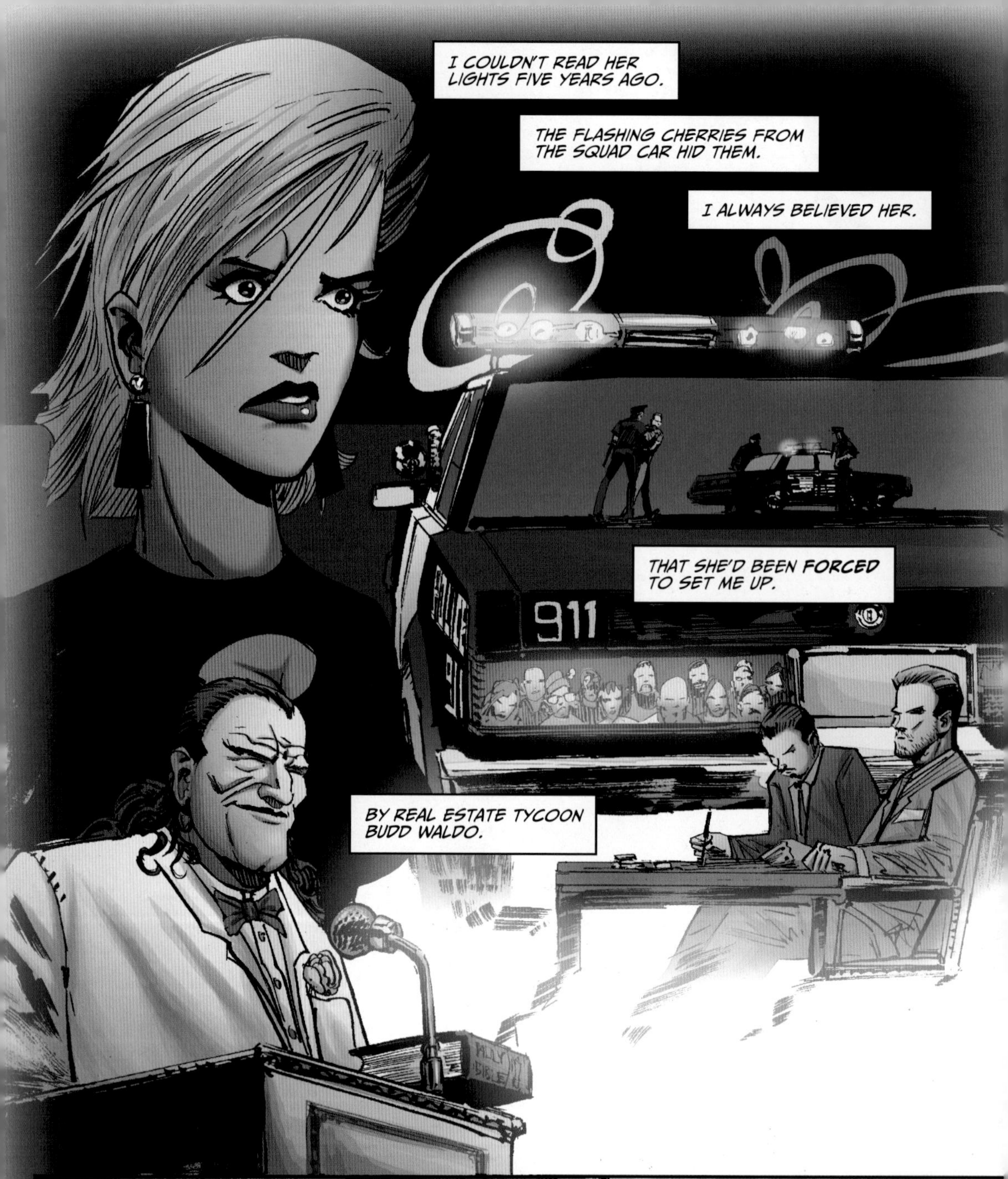
I COULDN'T READ HER LIGHTS FIVE YEARS AGO.
THE FLASHING CHERRIES FROM THE SQUAD CAR HID THEM.
I ALWAYS BELIEVED HER.
THAT SHE'D BEEN FORCED TO SET ME UP.
911
BY REAL ESTATE TYCOON BUDD WALDO.

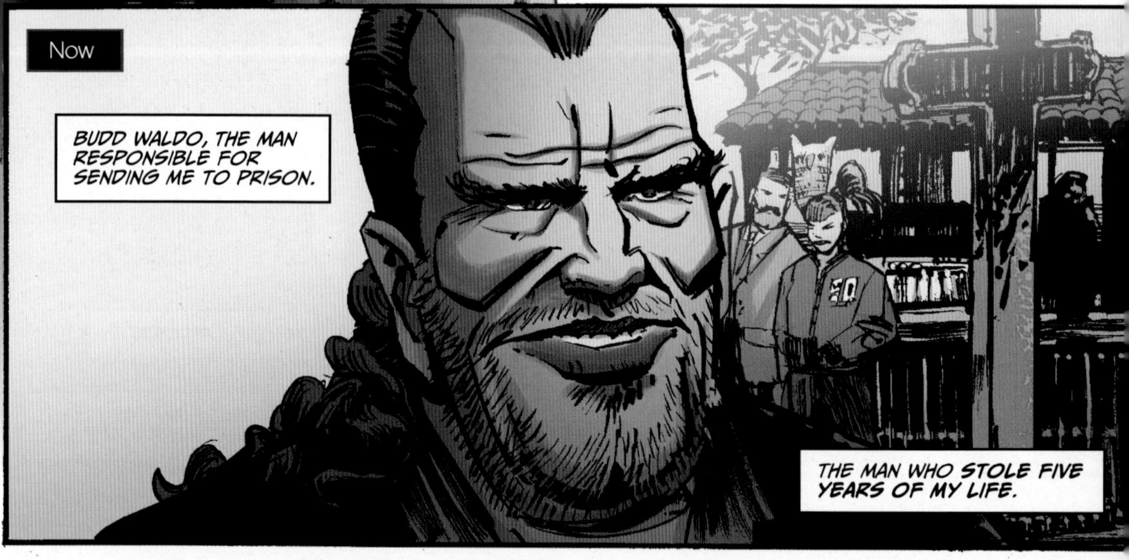
Now
BUDD WALDO, THE MAN RESPONSIBLE FOR SENDING ME TO PRISON.
THE MAN WHO STOLE FIVE YEARS OF MY LIFE.

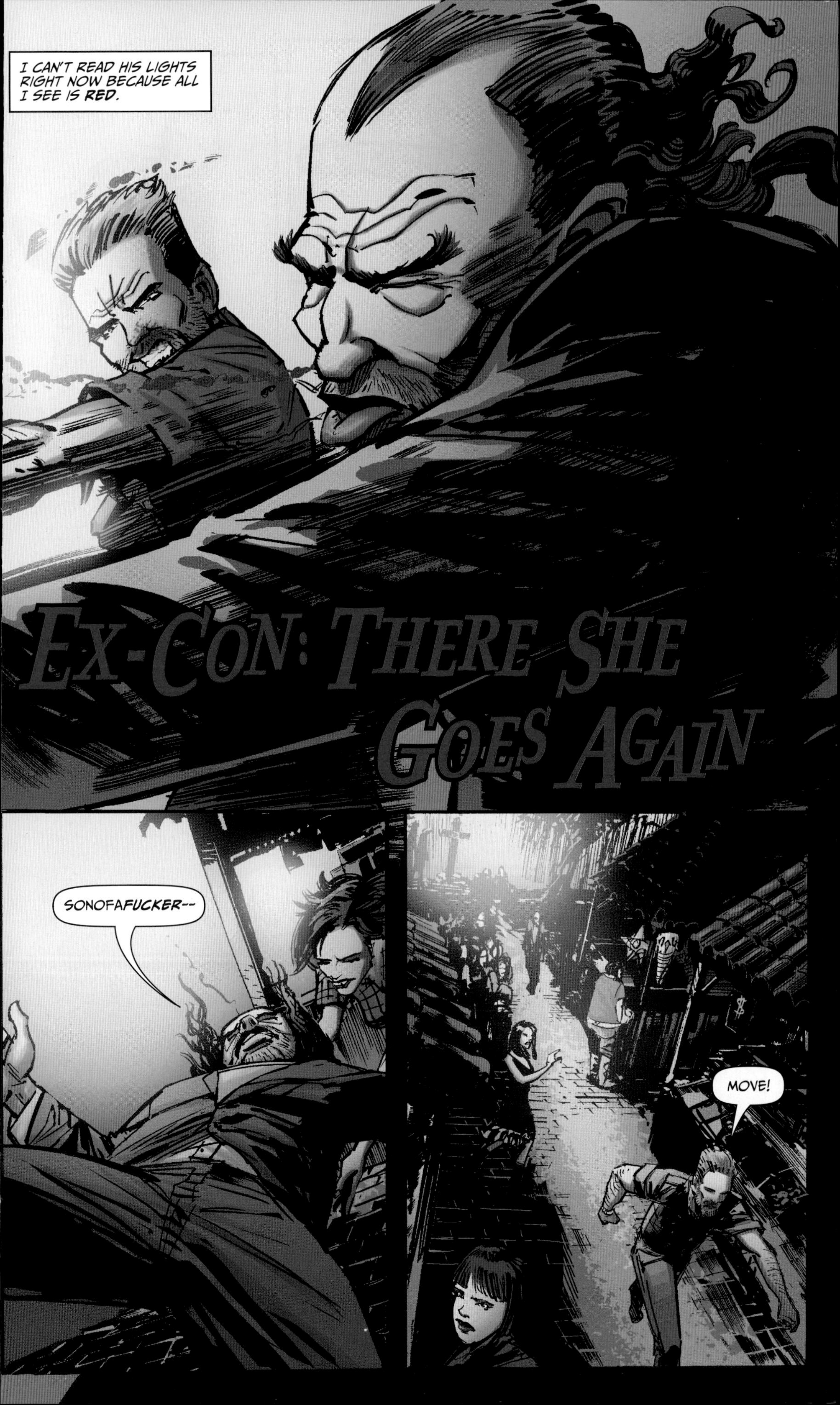

I CAN'T READ HIS LIGHTS RIGHT NOW BECAUSE ALL I SEE IS RED.
EX-CON: THERE SHE GOES AGAIN
SONOFAFUCKER--
MOVE!

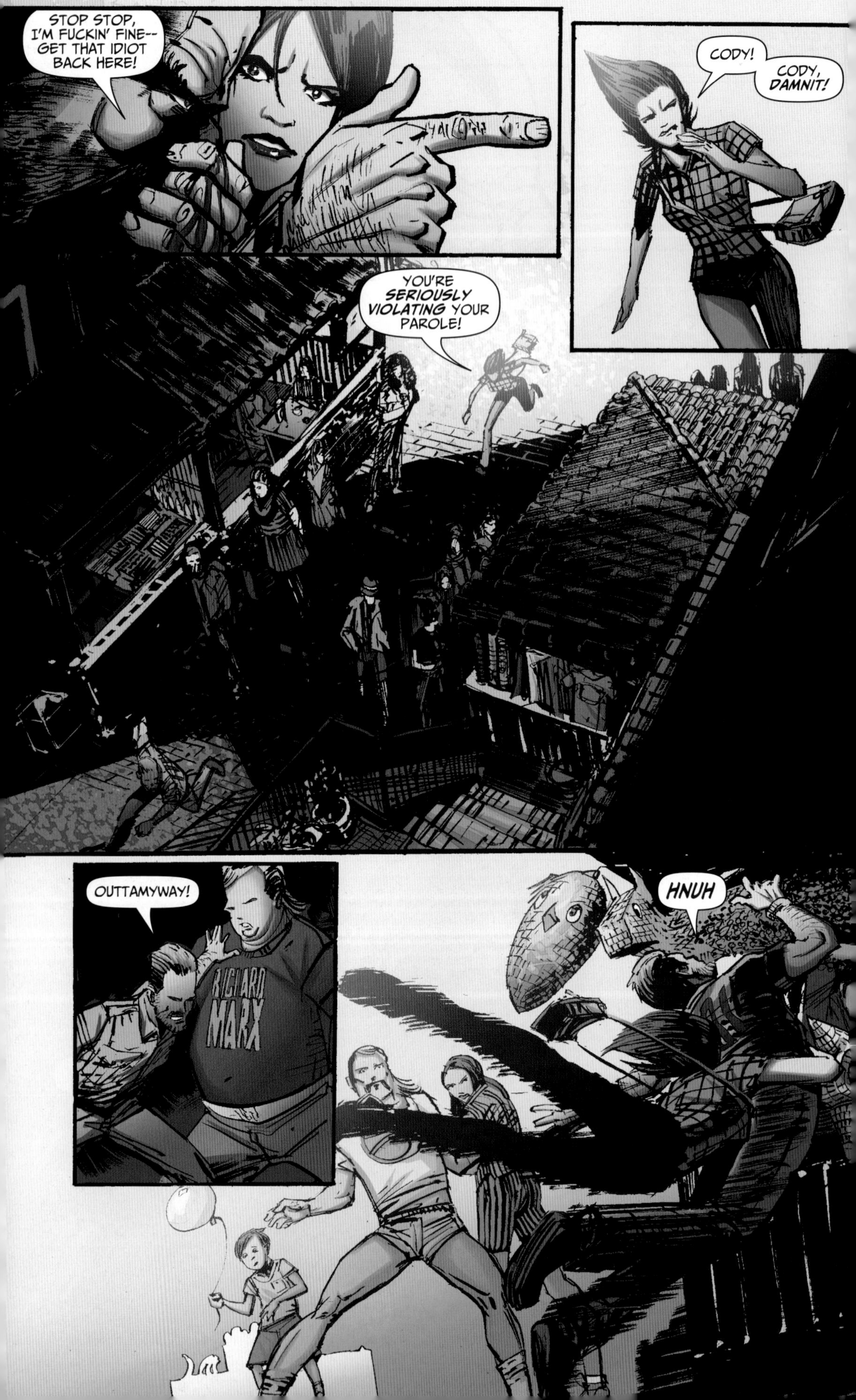
STOP STOP, I'M FUCKIN' FINE-- GET THAT IDIOT BACK HERE!
CODY!
CODY, DAMNIT!
YOU'RE SERIOUSLY VIOLATING YOUR PAROLE!
OUTTAMYWAY!
RICHARD MARX
HNUH

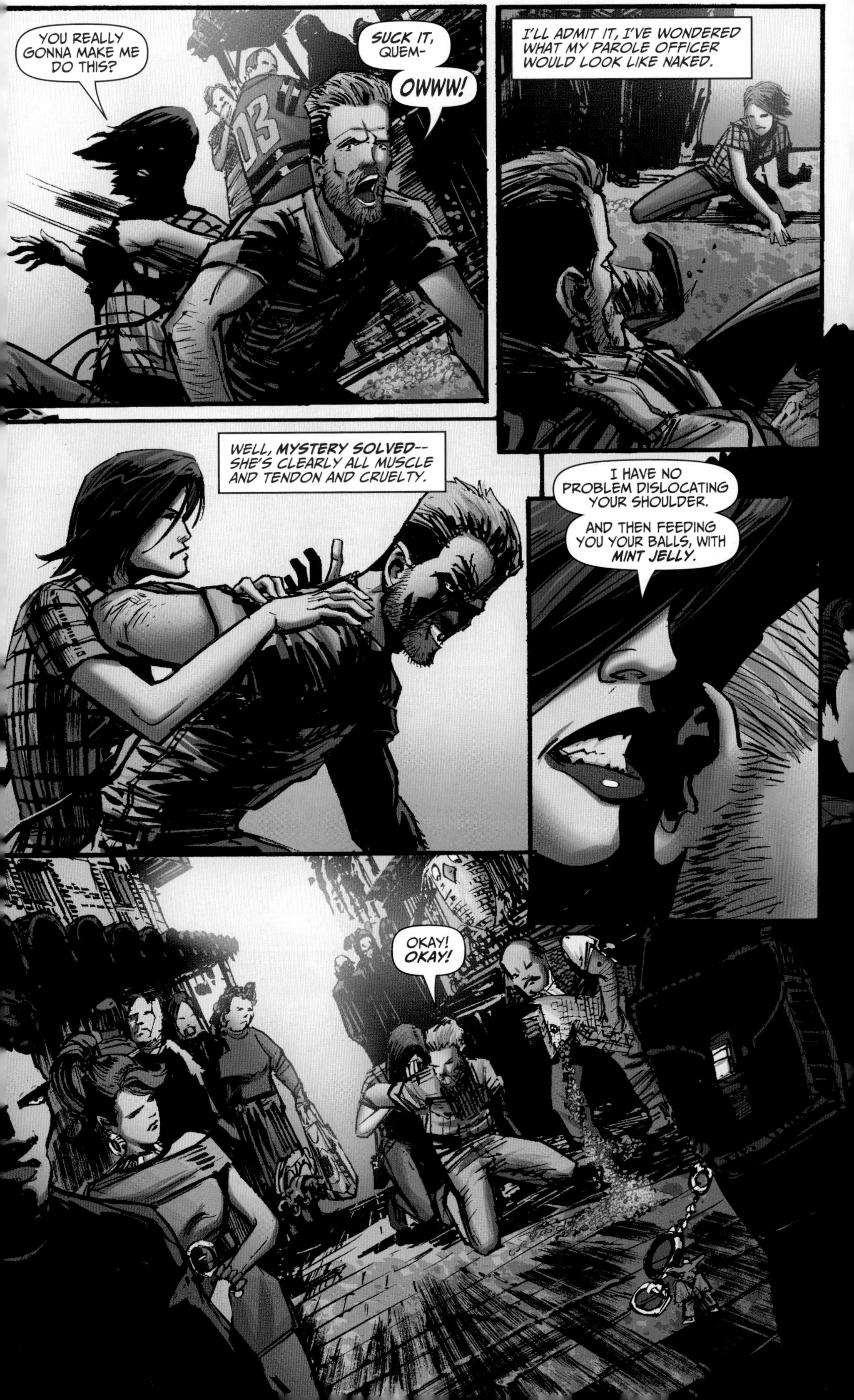
YOU REALLY GONNA MAKE ME DO THIS?
SUCK IT, QUEM-
OWWW!
I'LL ADMIT IT, I'VE WONDERED WHAT MY PAROLE OFFICER WOULD LOOK LIKE NAKED.
WELL, MYSTERY SOLVED-- SHE'S CLEARLY ALL MUSCLE AND TENDON AND CRUELTY.
I HAVE NO PROBLEM DISLOCATING YOUR SHOULDER.
AND THEN FEEDING YOU YOUR BALLS, WITH MINT JELLY.
OKAY! OKAY!

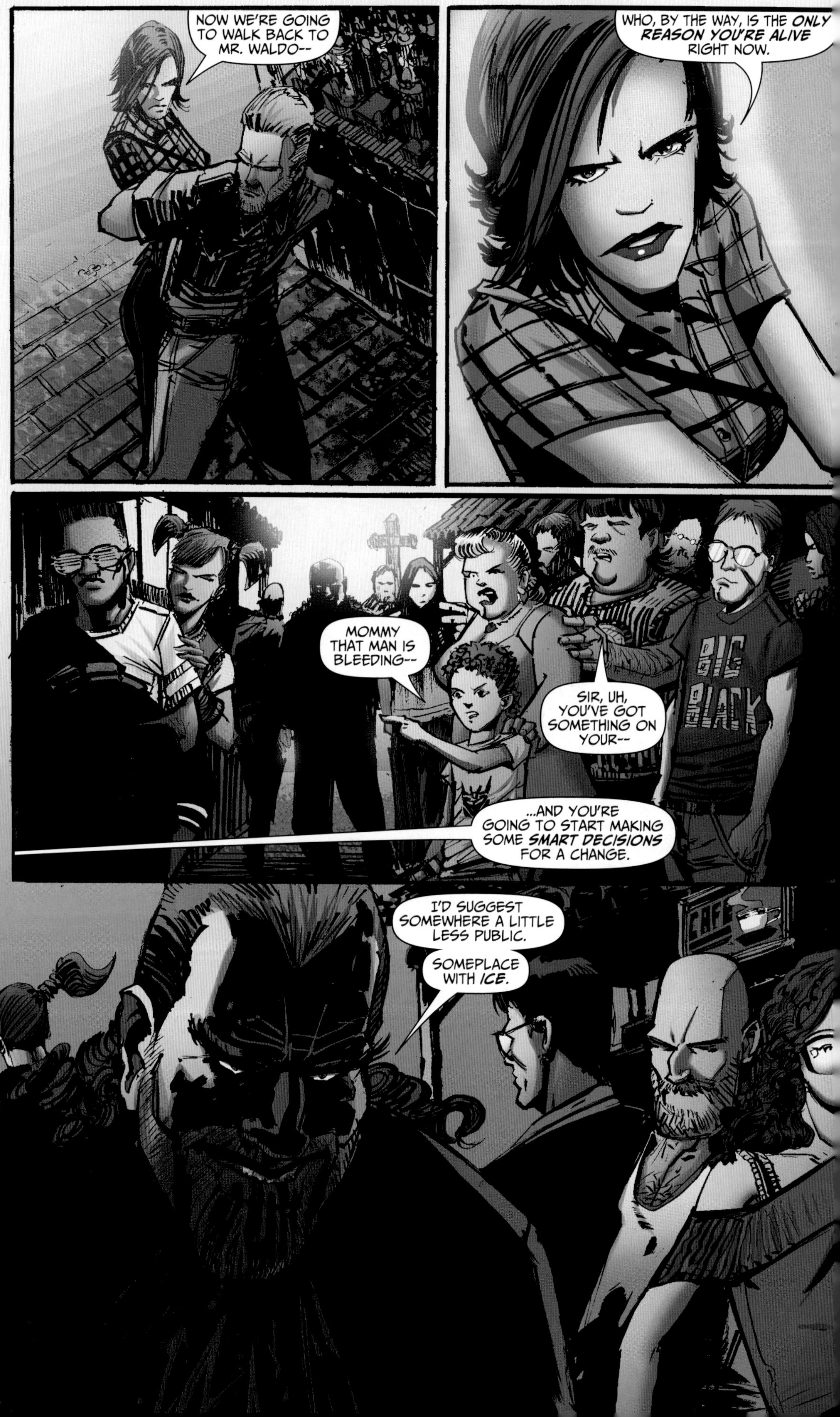
NOW WE'RE GOING TO WALK BACK TO MR. WALDO--
WHO, BY THE WAY, IS THE ONLY REASON YOU'RE ALIVE RIGHT NOW.
MOMMY THAT MAN IS BLEEDING--
SIR, UH, YOU'VE GOT SOMETHING ON YOUR--
...AND YOU'RE GOING TO START MAKING SOME SMART DECISIONS FOR A CHANGE.
BIG BLACK
I'D SUGGEST SOMEWHERE A LITTLE LESS PUBLIC.
SOMEPLACE WITH ICE.
CAFE

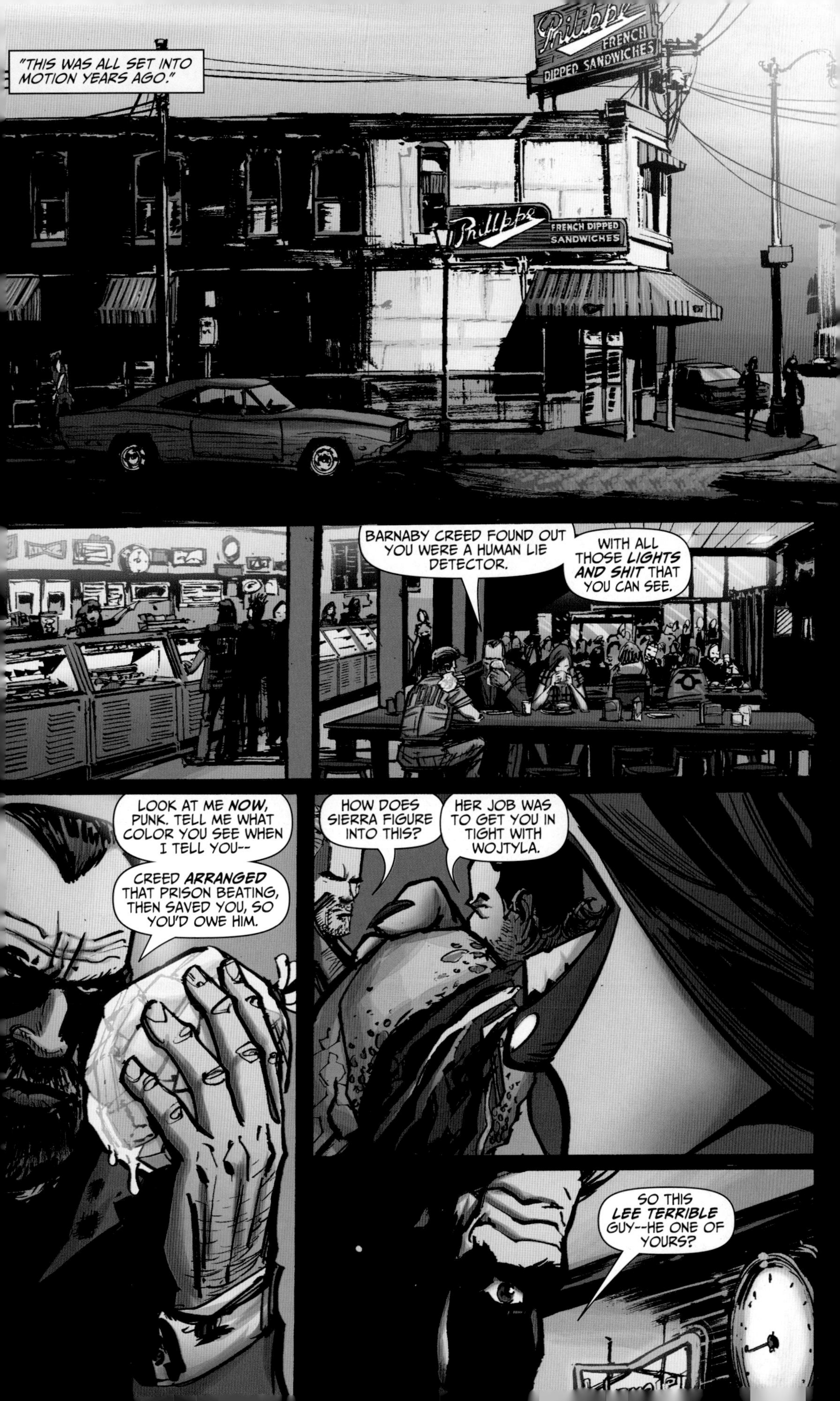
"THIS WAS ALL SET INTO MOTION YEARS AGO."
Philippe FRENCH DIPPED SANDWICHES
Philippe FRENCH DIPPED SANDWICHES
BARNABY CREED FOUND OUT YOU WERE A HUMAN LIE DETECTOR.
WITH ALL THOSE LIGHTS AND SHIT THAT YOU CAN SEE.
LOOK AT ME NOW, PUNK. TELL ME WHAT COLOR YOU SEE WHEN I TELL YOU--
CREED ARRANGED THAT PRISON BEATING, THEN SAVED YOU, SO YOU'D OWE HIM.
HOW DOES SIERRA FIGURE INTO THIS?
HER JOB WAS TO GET YOU IN TIGHT WITH WOJTYLA.
SO THIS LEE TERRIBLE GUY--HE ONE OF YOURS?

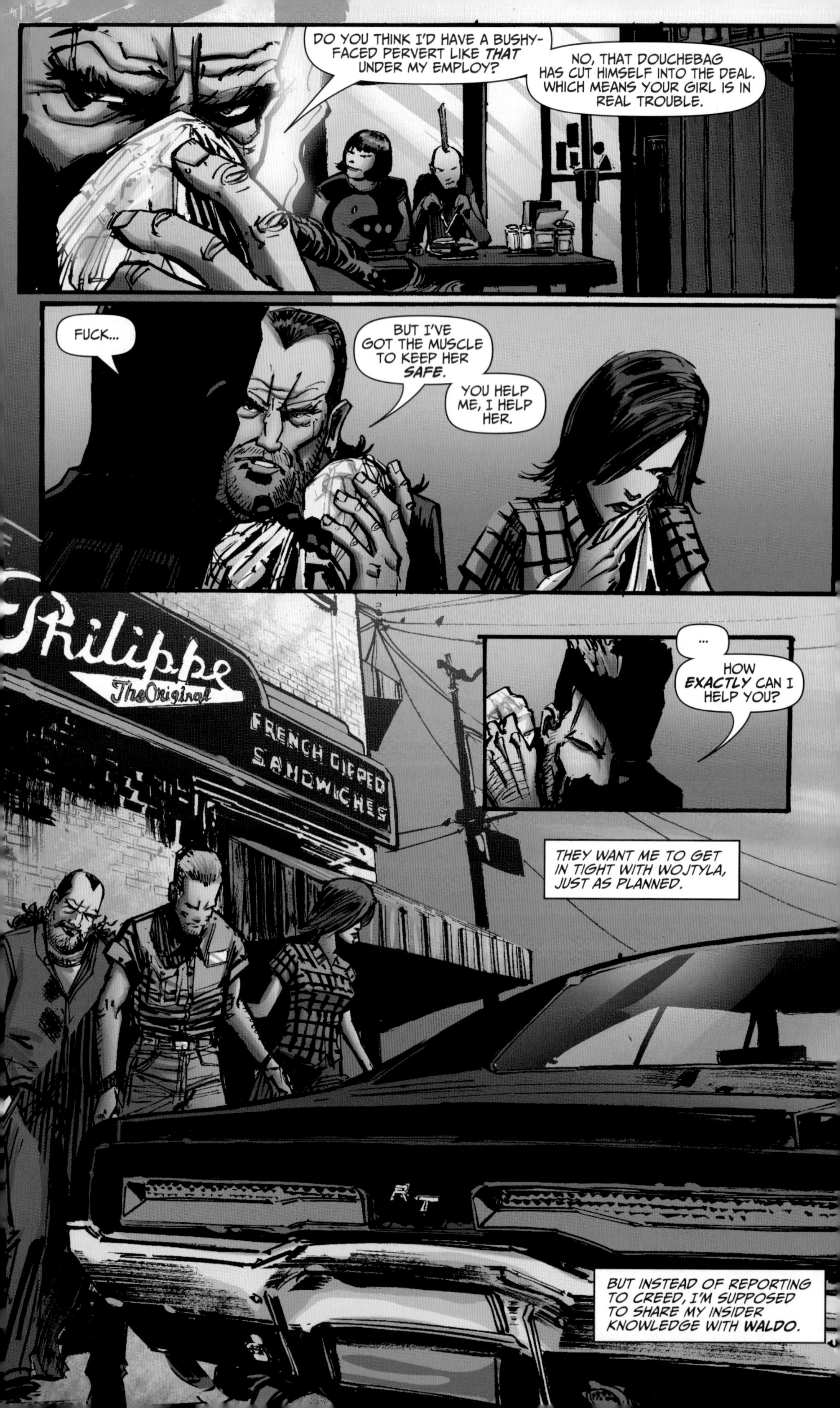
DO YOU THINK I'D HAVE A BUSHY-FACED PERVERT LIKE *THAT* UNDER MY EMPLOY?
NO, THAT DOUCHEBAG HAS CUT HIMSELF INTO THE DEAL. WHICH MEANS YOUR GIRL IS IN REAL TROUBLE.
FUCK...
BUT I'VE GOT THE MUSCLE TO KEEP HER *SAFE*.
YOU HELP ME, I HELP HER.
Philippe
The Original
FRENCH DIPPED SANDWICHES
...
HOW *EXACTLY* CAN I HELP YOU?
THEY WANT ME TO GET IN TIGHT WITH WOJTYLA, JUST AS PLANNED.
*BUT INSTEAD OF REPORTING TO CREED, I'M SUPPOSED TO SHARE MY INSIDER KNOWLEDGE WITH **WALDO**.*

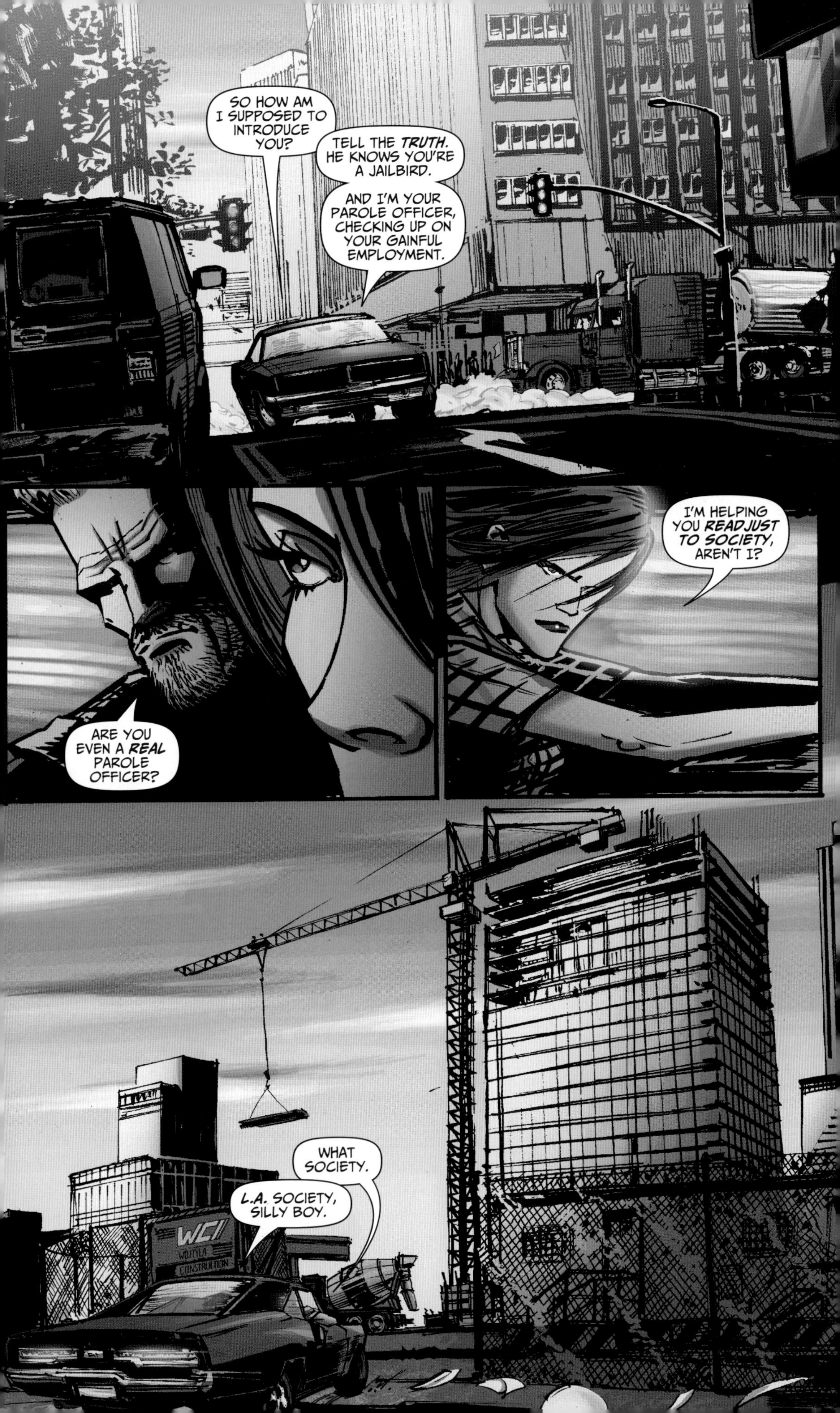
SO HOW AM I SUPPOSED TO INTRODUCE YOU?
TELL THE *TRUTH*. HE KNOWS YOU'RE A JAILBIRD.
AND I'M YOUR PAROLE OFFICER, CHECKING UP ON YOUR GAINFUL EMPLOYMENT.
ARE YOU EVEN A *REAL* PAROLE OFFICER?
I'M HELPING YOU *READJUST TO SOCIETY*, AREN'T I?
WHAT SOCIETY.
L.A. SOCIETY, SILLY BOY.
WCI
CONSTRUCTION

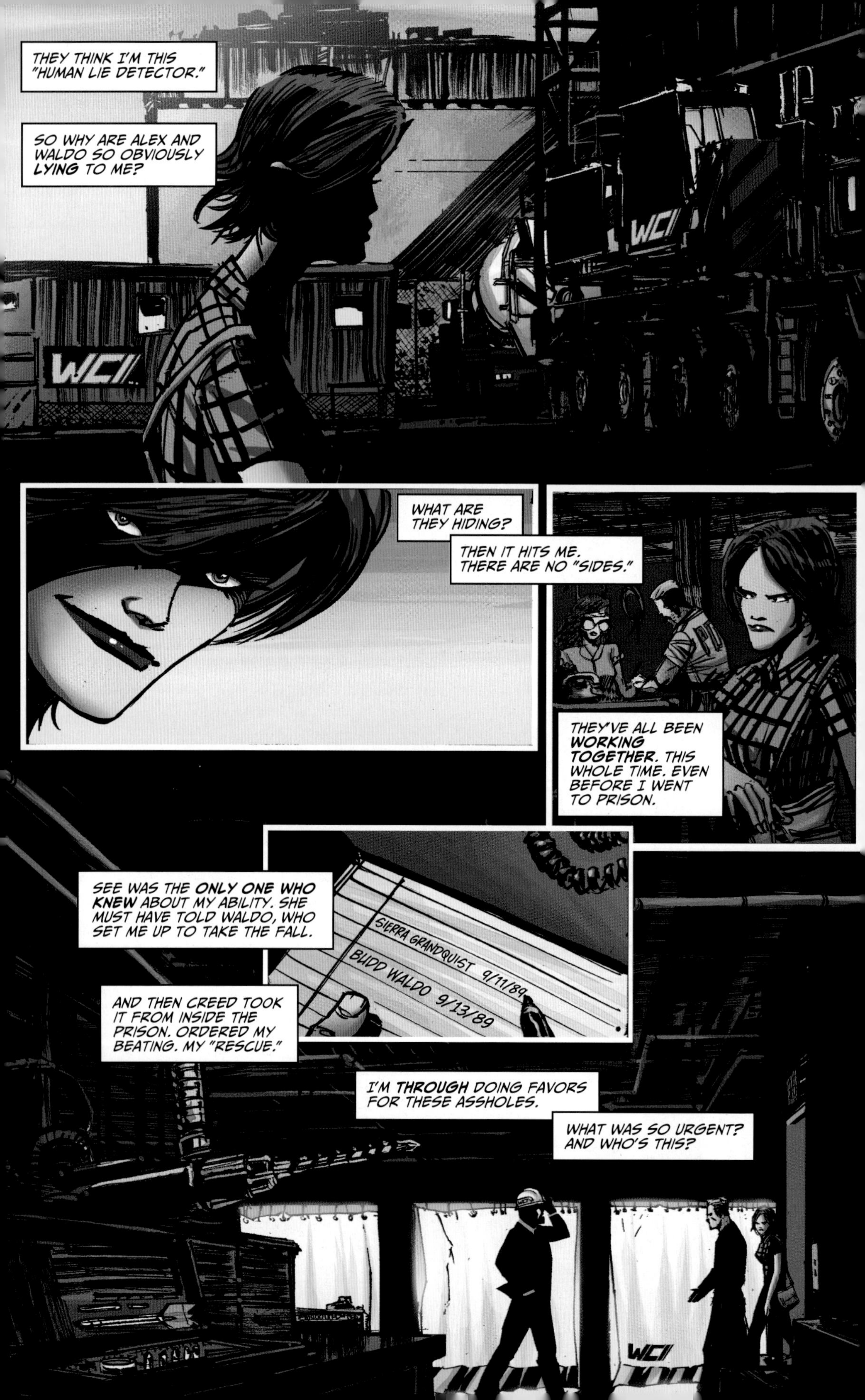
THEY THINK I'M THIS "HUMAN LIE DETECTOR."
SO WHY ARE ALEX AND WALDO SO OBVIOUSLY LYING TO ME?
WCI
WCI
WHAT ARE THEY HIDING?
THEN IT HITS ME. THERE ARE NO "SIDES."
THEY'VE ALL BEEN WORKING TOGETHER. THIS WHOLE TIME. EVEN BEFORE I WENT TO PRISON.
SEE WAS THE ONLY ONE WHO KNEW ABOUT MY ABILITY. SHE MUST HAVE TOLD WALDO, WHO SET ME UP TO TAKE THE FALL.
SIERRA GRANDQUIST 9/11/89
BUDD WALDO 9/13/89
AND THEN CREED TOOK IT FROM INSIDE THE PRISON. ORDERED MY BEATING. MY "RESCUE."
I'M THROUGH DOING FAVORS FOR THESE ASSHOLES.
WHAT WAS SO URGENT? AND WHO'S THIS?
WCI

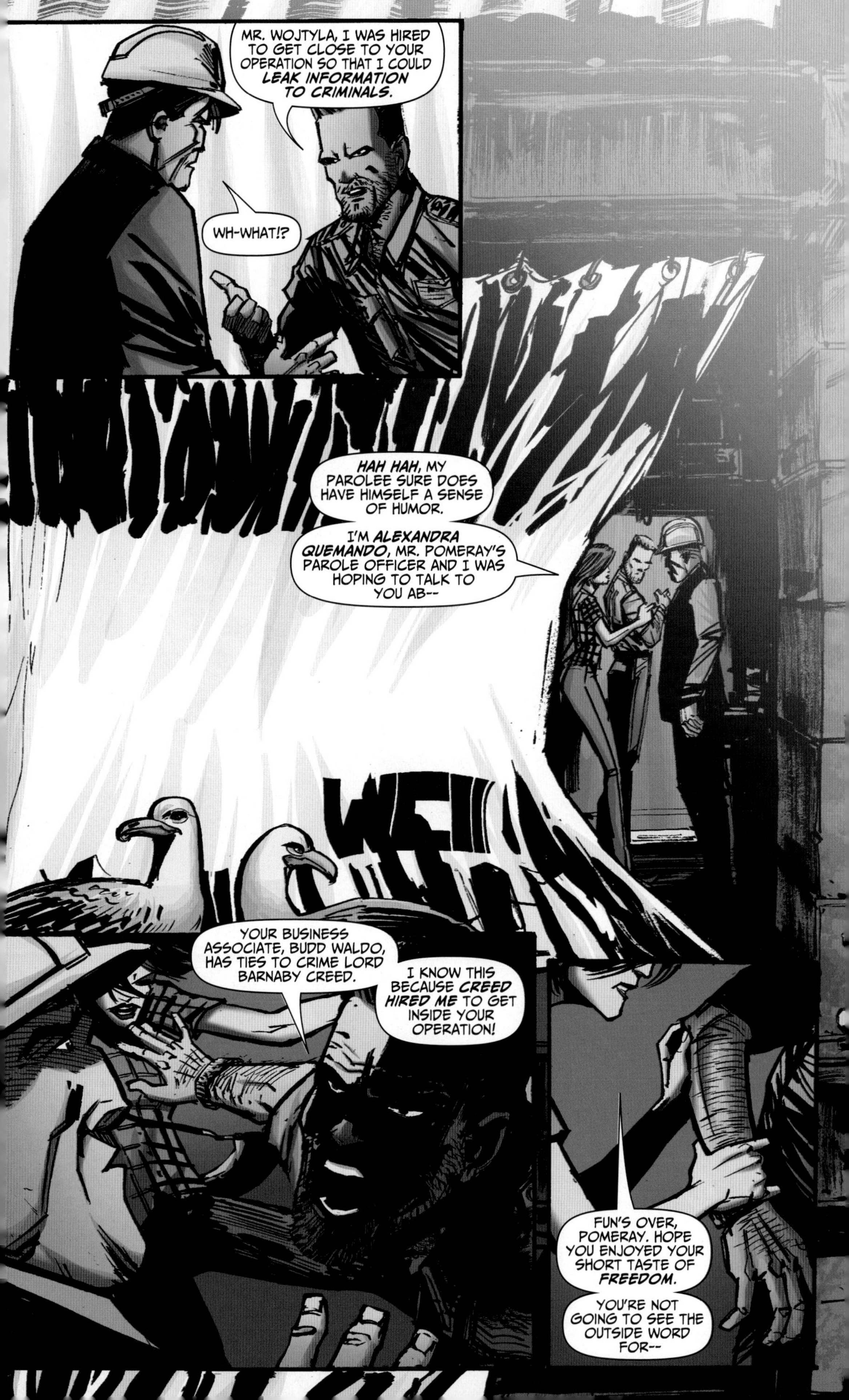

MR. WOJTYLA, I WAS HIRED TO GET CLOSE TO YOUR OPERATION SO THAT I COULD LEAK INFORMATION TO CRIMINALS.
WH-WHAT!?
HAH HAH, MY PAROLEE SURE DOES HAVE HIMSELF A SENSE OF HUMOR.
I'M ALEXANDRA QUEMANDO, MR. POMERAY'S PAROLE OFFICER AND I WAS HOPING TO TALK TO YOU AB--
YOUR BUSINESS ASSOCIATE, BUDD WALDO, HAS TIES TO CRIME LORD BARNABY CREED.
I KNOW THIS BECAUSE CREED HIRED ME TO GET INSIDE YOUR OPERATION!
FUN'S OVER, POMERAY. HOPE YOU ENJOYED YOUR SHORT TASTE OF FREEDOM.
YOU'RE NOT GOING TO SEE THE OUTSIDE WORD FOR--

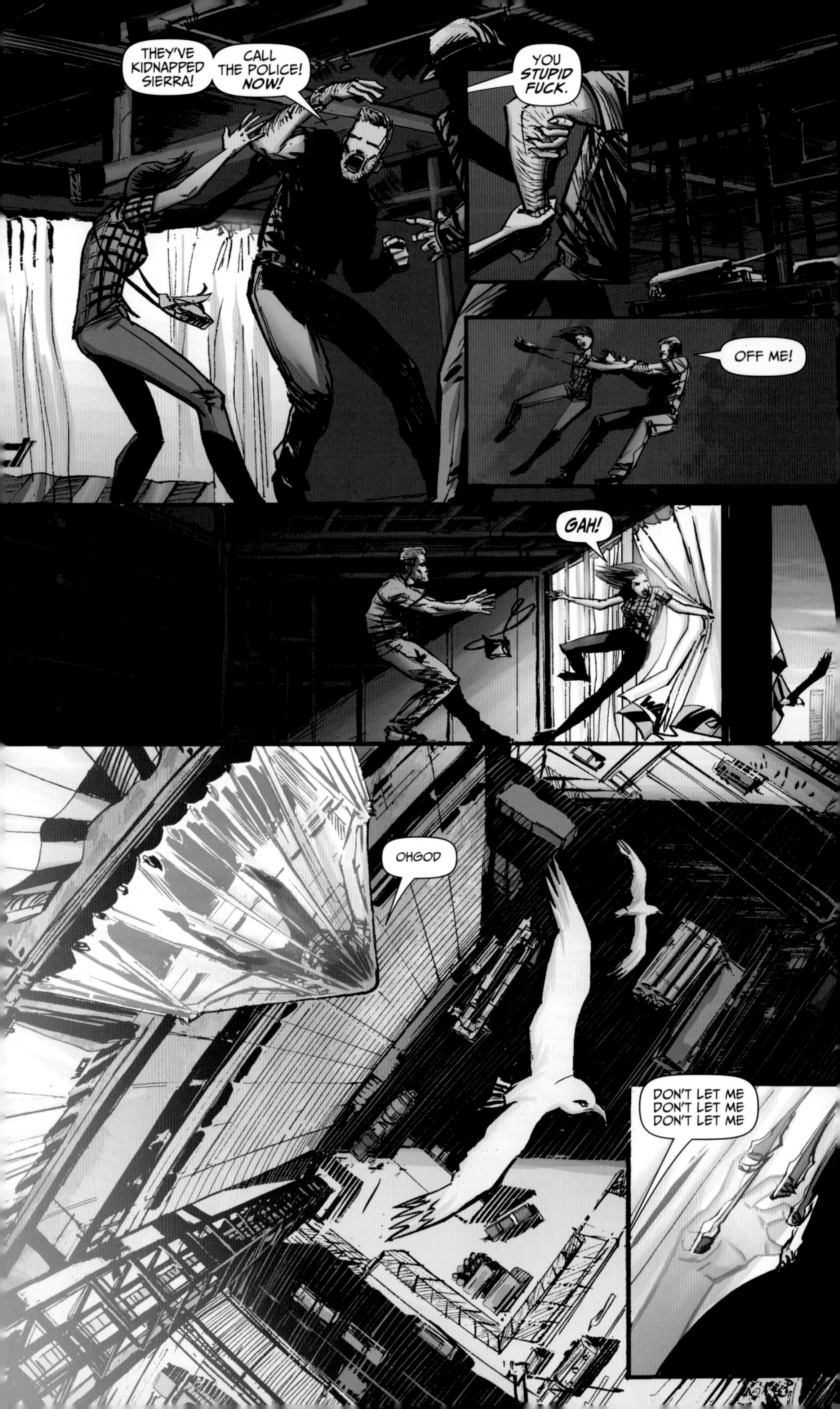
THEY'VE KIDNAPPED SIERRA!
CALL THE POLICE! NOW!
YOU STUPID FUCK.
OFF ME!
GAH!
OHGOD
DON'T LET ME
DON'T LET ME
DON'T LET ME

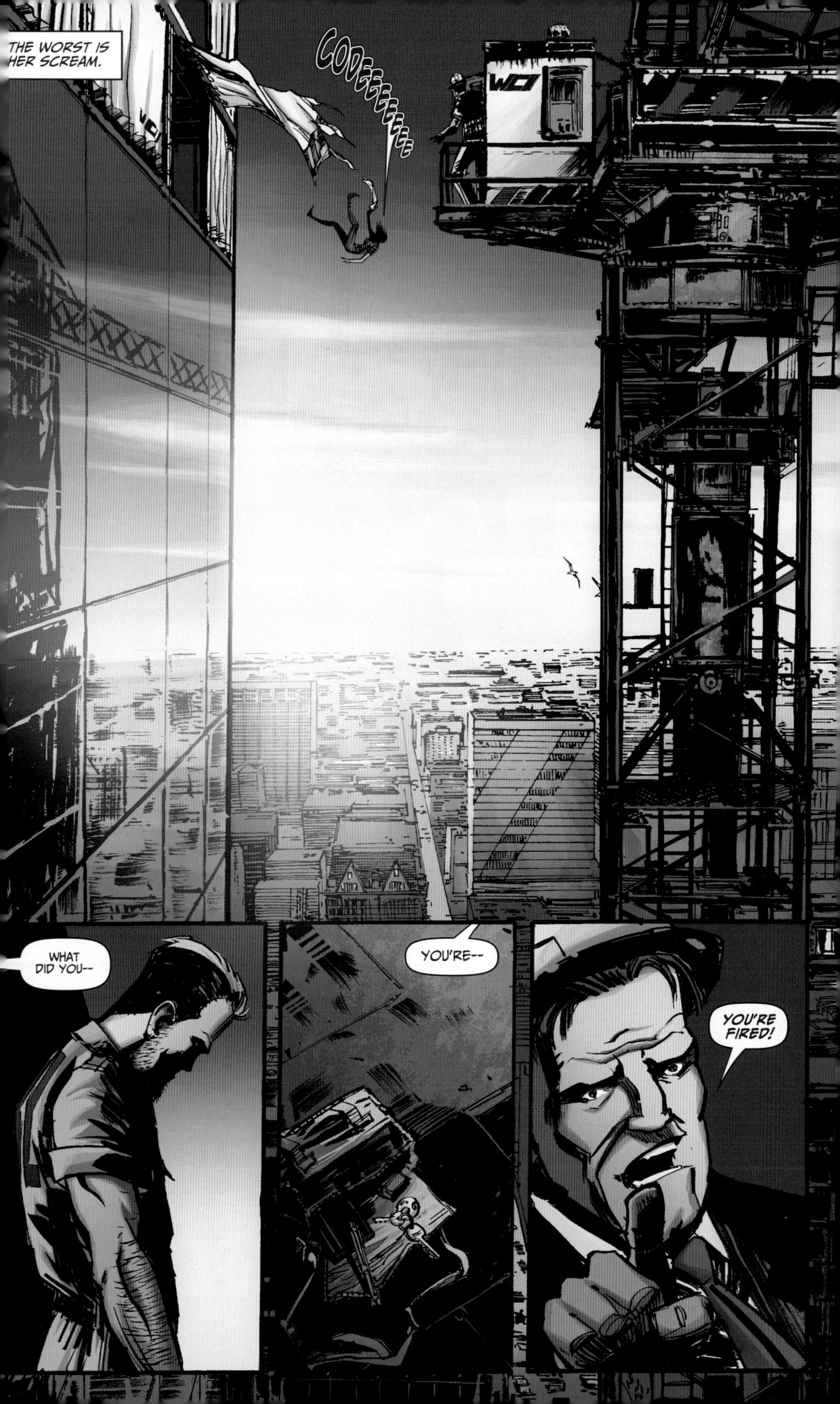
THE WORST IS HER SCREAM.
CODEEEEEEEEE
WCI
WHAT DID YOU--
YOU'RE--
YOU'RE FIRED!

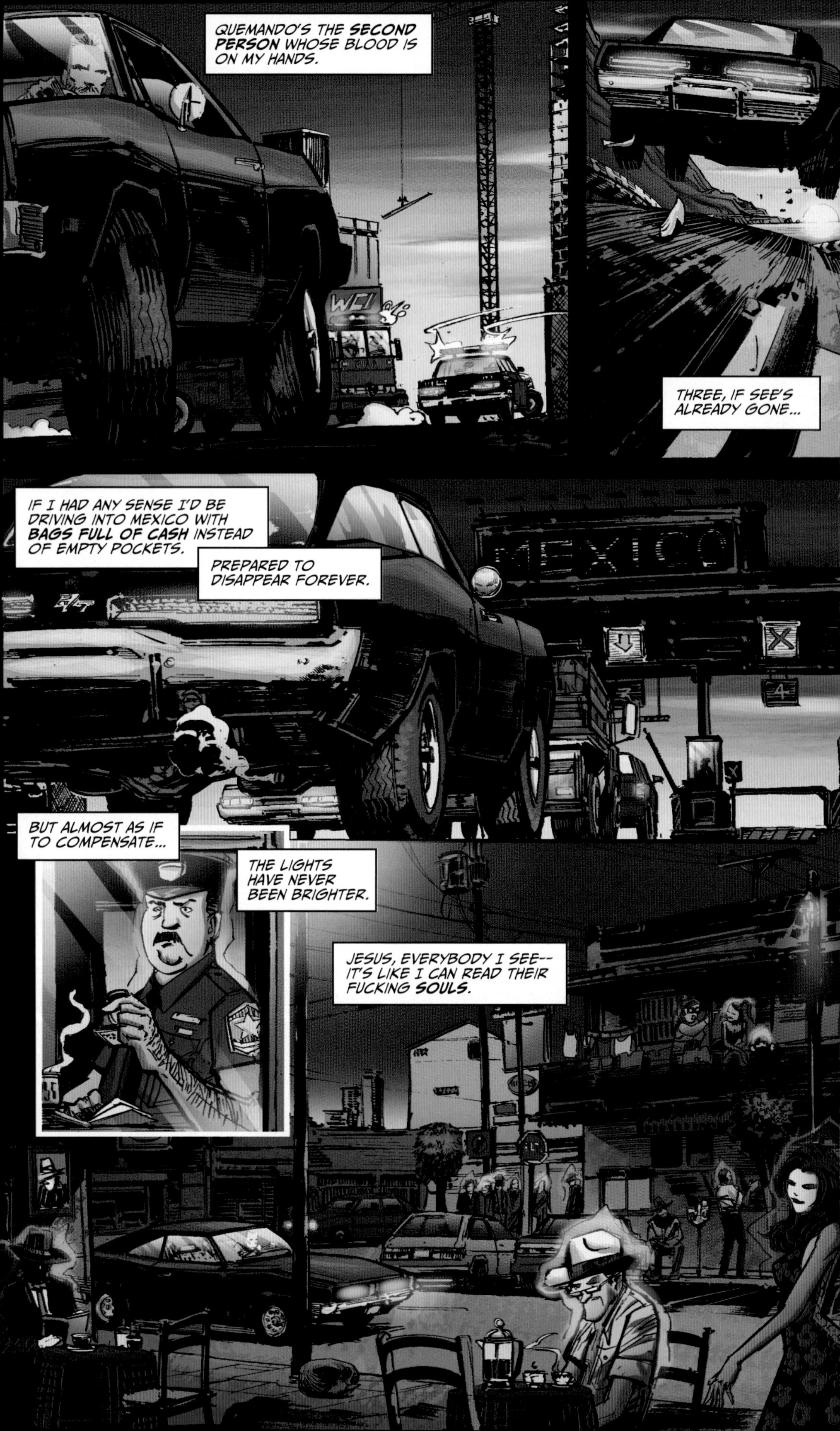
QUEMANDO'S THE **SECOND PERSON** WHOSE BLOOD IS ON MY HANDS.
THREE, IF SEE'S ALREADY GONE...
IF I HAD ANY SENSE I'D BE DRIVING INTO MEXICO WITH **BAGS FULL OF CASH** INSTEAD OF EMPTY POCKETS.
PREPARED TO DISAPPEAR FOREVER.
MEXICO
BUT ALMOST AS IF TO COMPENSATE...
THE LIGHTS HAVE NEVER BEEN BRIGHTER.
JESUS, EVERYBODY I SEE-- IT'S LIKE I CAN READ THEIR FUCKING **SOULS**.

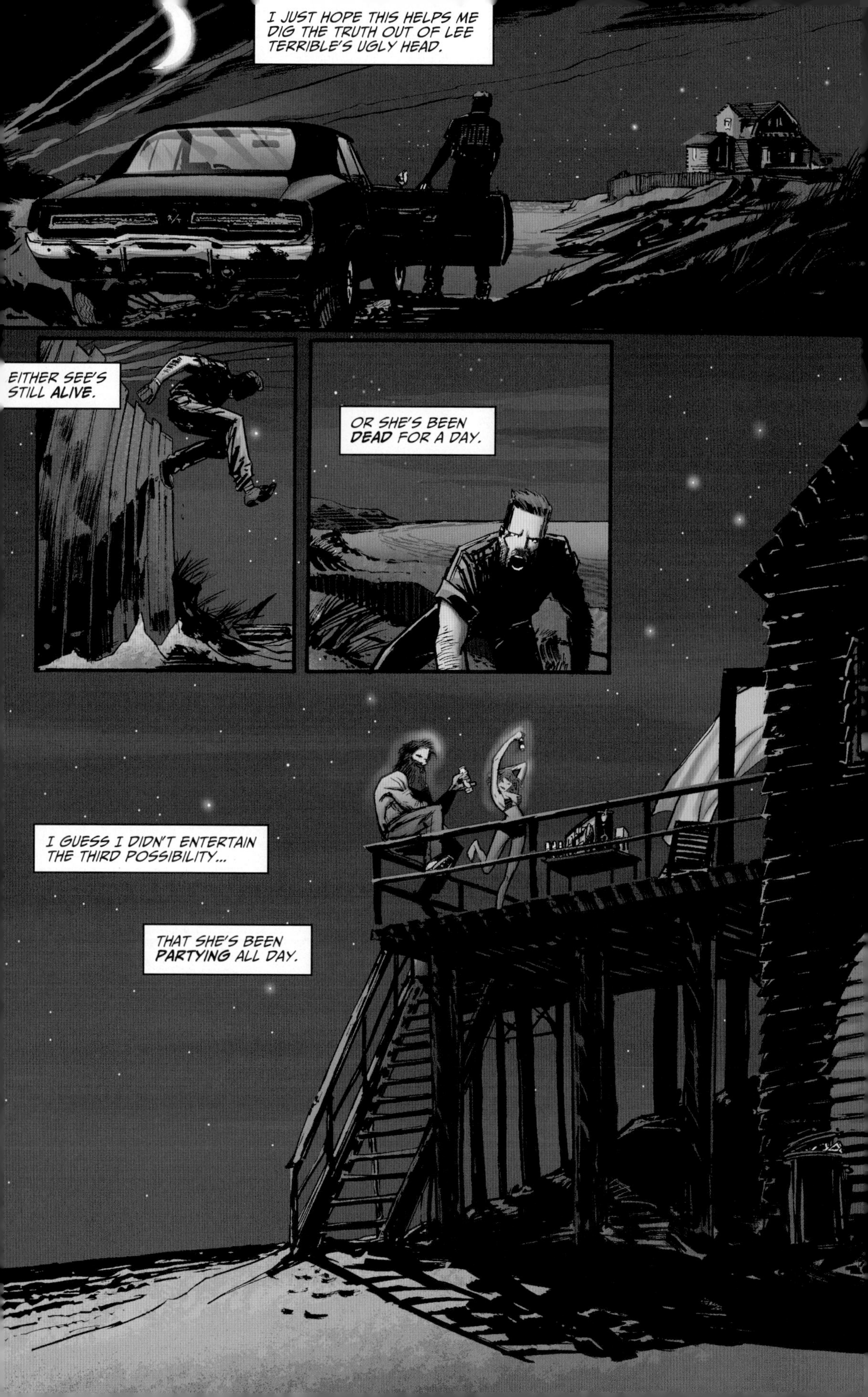
I JUST HOPE THIS HELPS ME DIG THE TRUTH OUT OF LEE TERRIBLE'S UGLY HEAD.
EITHER SEE'S STILL ALIVE.
OR SHE'S BEEN DEAD FOR A DAY.
I GUESS I DIDN'T ENTERTAIN THE THIRD POSSIBILITY...
THAT SHE'S BEEN PARTYING ALL DAY.

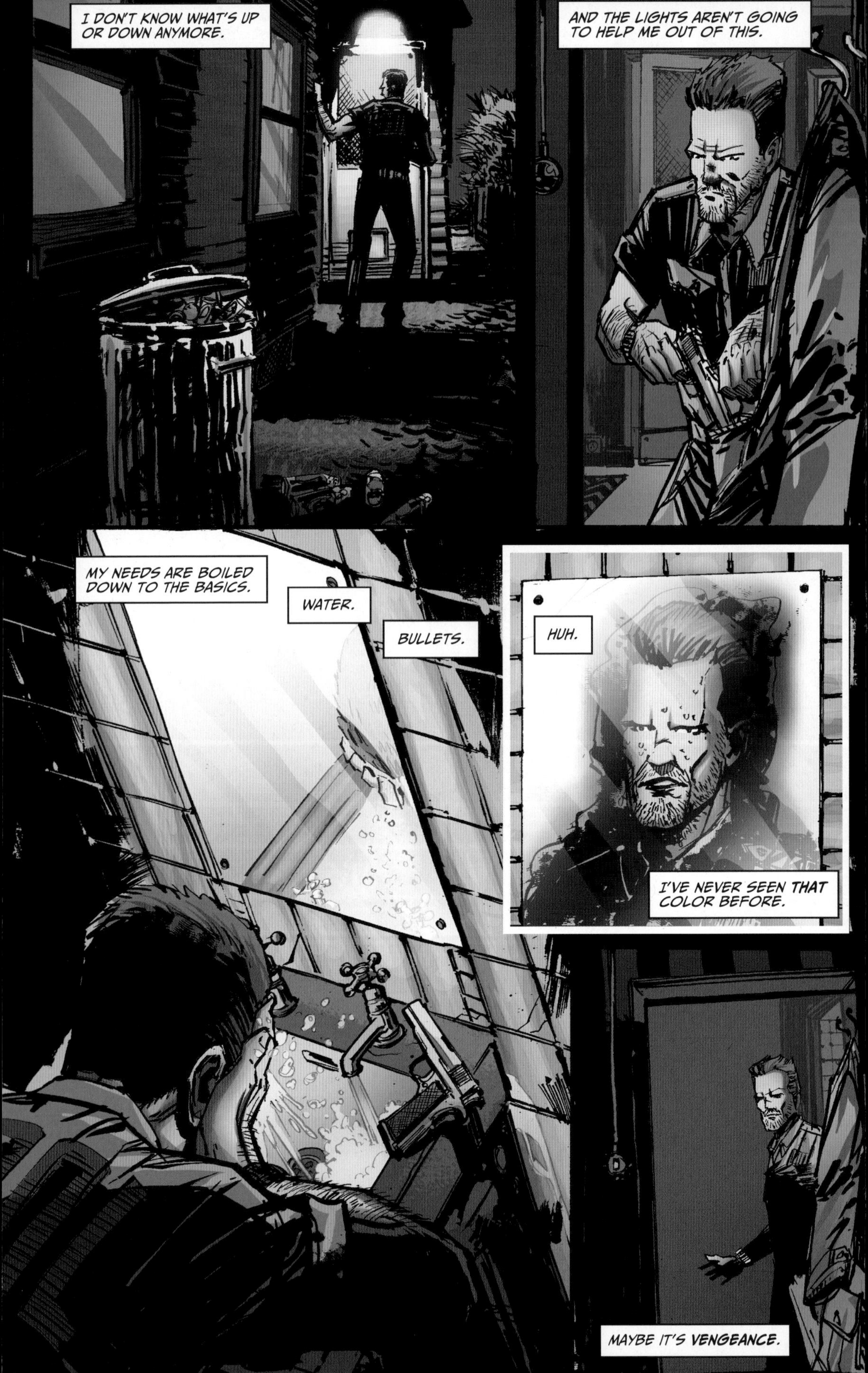
I DON'T KNOW WHAT'S UP OR DOWN ANYMORE.
AND THE LIGHTS AREN'T GOING TO HELP ME OUT OF THIS.
MY NEEDS ARE BOILED DOWN TO THE BASICS.
WATER.
BULLETS.
HUH.
I'VE NEVER SEEN THAT COLOR BEFORE.
MAYBE IT'S VENGEANCE.

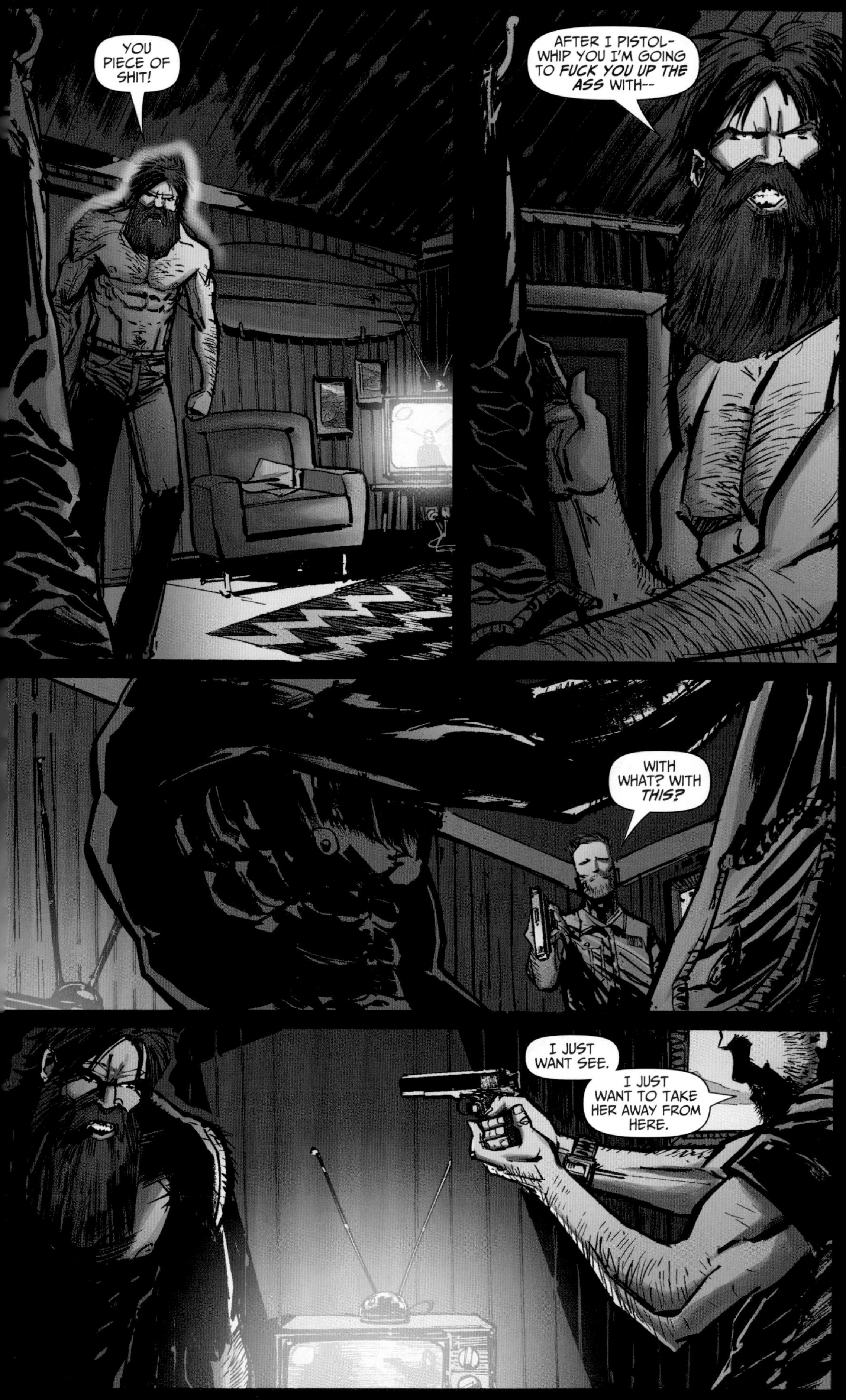
YOU PIECE OF SHIT!
AFTER I PISTOL-WHIP YOU I'M GOING TO *FUCK YOU UP THE ASS* WITH--
WITH WHAT? WITH *THIS?*
I JUST WANT SEE.
I JUST WANT TO TAKE HER AWAY FROM HERE.

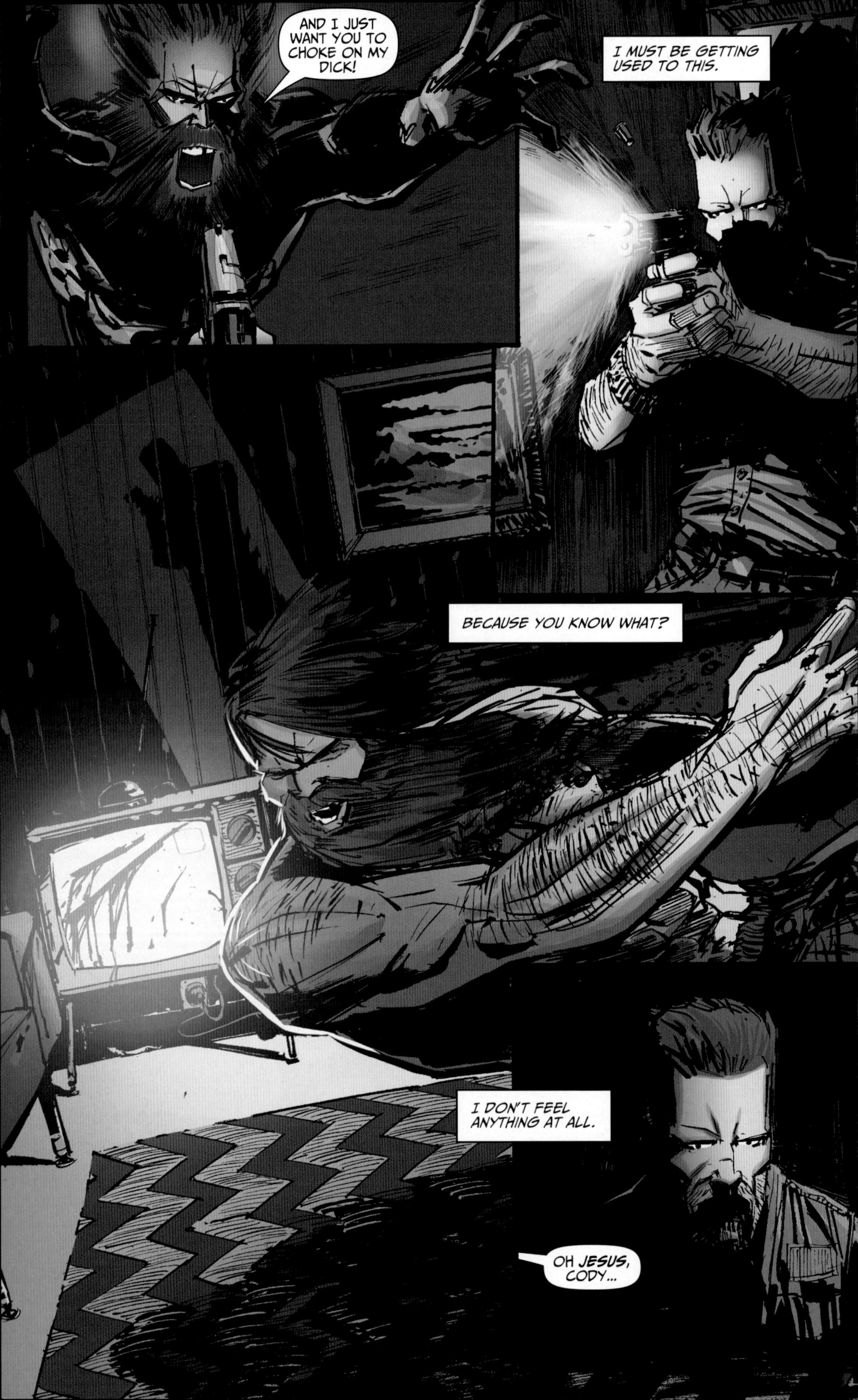
AND I JUST WANT YOU TO CHOKE ON MY DICK!
I MUST BE GETTING USED TO THIS.
BECAUSE YOU KNOW WHAT?
I DON'T FEEL ANYTHING AT ALL.
OH JESUS, CODY...

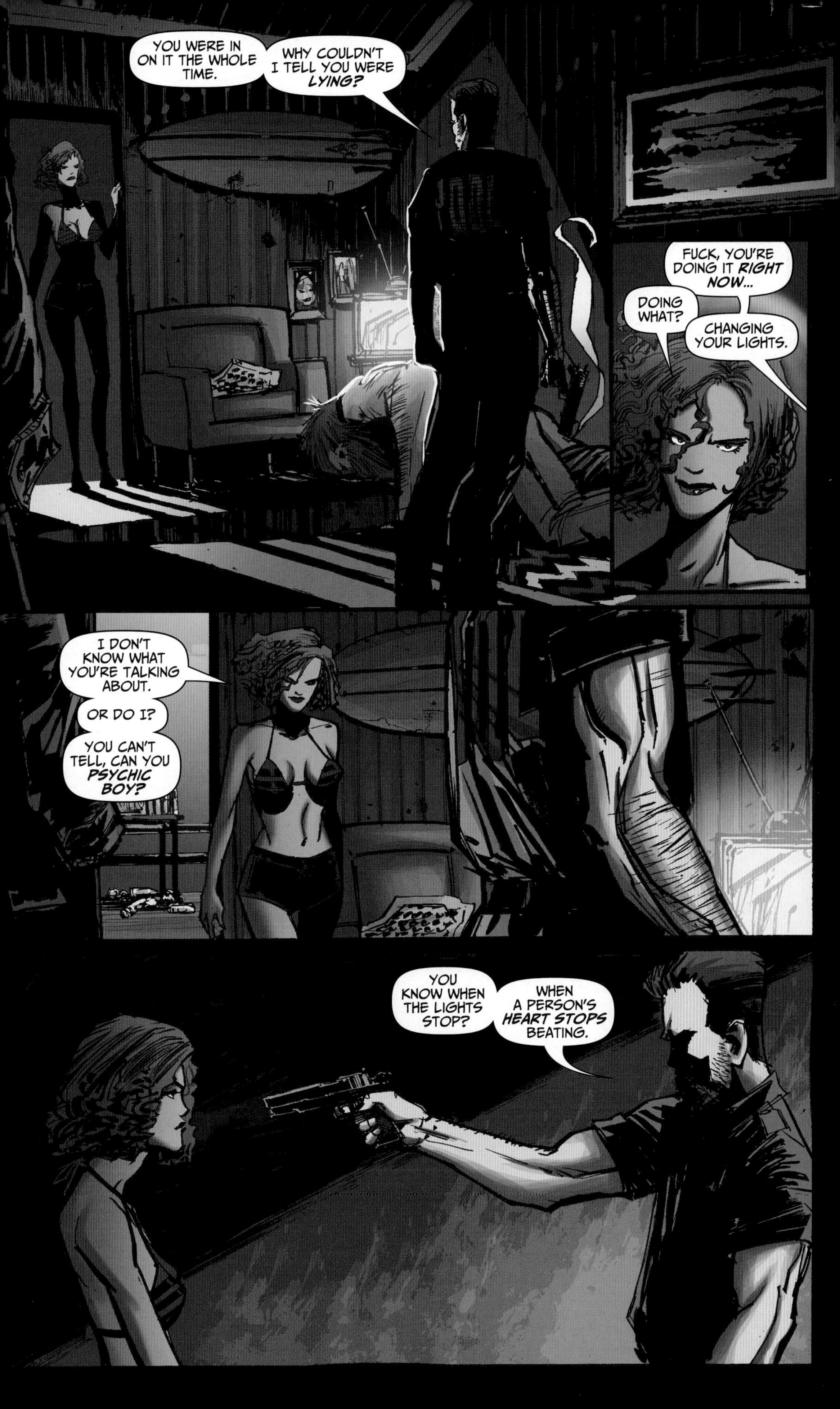
YOU WERE IN ON IT THE WHOLE TIME.
WHY COULDN'T I TELL YOU WERE LYING?
FUCK, YOU'RE DOING IT RIGHT NOW...
DOING WHAT?
CHANGING YOUR LIGHTS.
I DON'T KNOW WHAT YOU'RE TALKING ABOUT.
OR DO I?
YOU CAN'T TELL, CAN YOU PSYCHIC BOY?
YOU KNOW WHEN THE LIGHTS STOP?
WHEN A PERSON'S HEART STOPS BEATING.

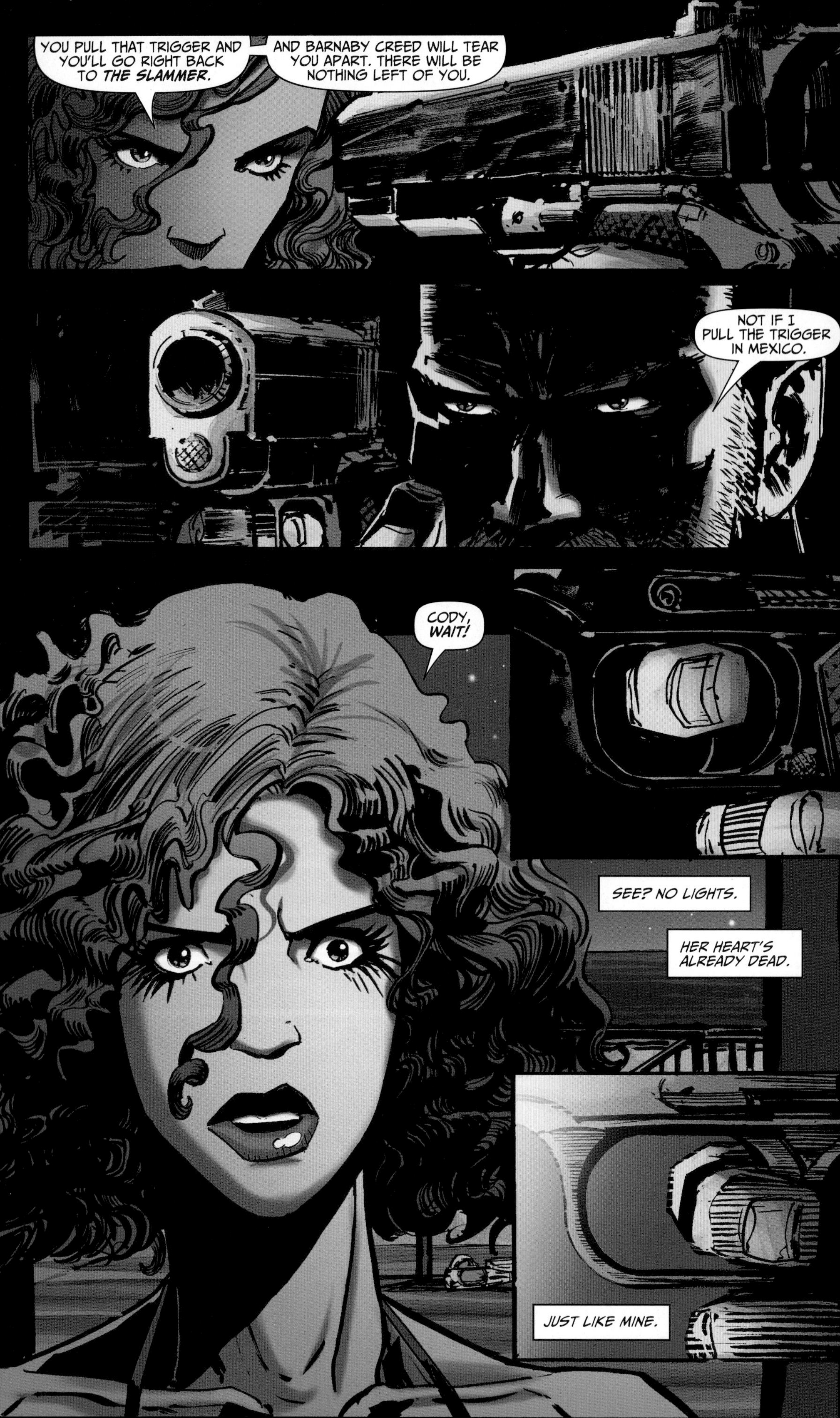
YOU PULL THAT TRIGGER AND YOU'LL GO RIGHT BACK TO *THE SLAMMER.*
AND BARNABY CREED WILL TEAR YOU APART. THERE WILL BE NOTHING LEFT OF YOU.
NOT IF I PULL THE TRIGGER IN MEXICO.
CODY, *WAIT!*
SEE? NO LIGHTS.
HER HEART'S ALREADY DEAD.
JUST LIKE MINE.

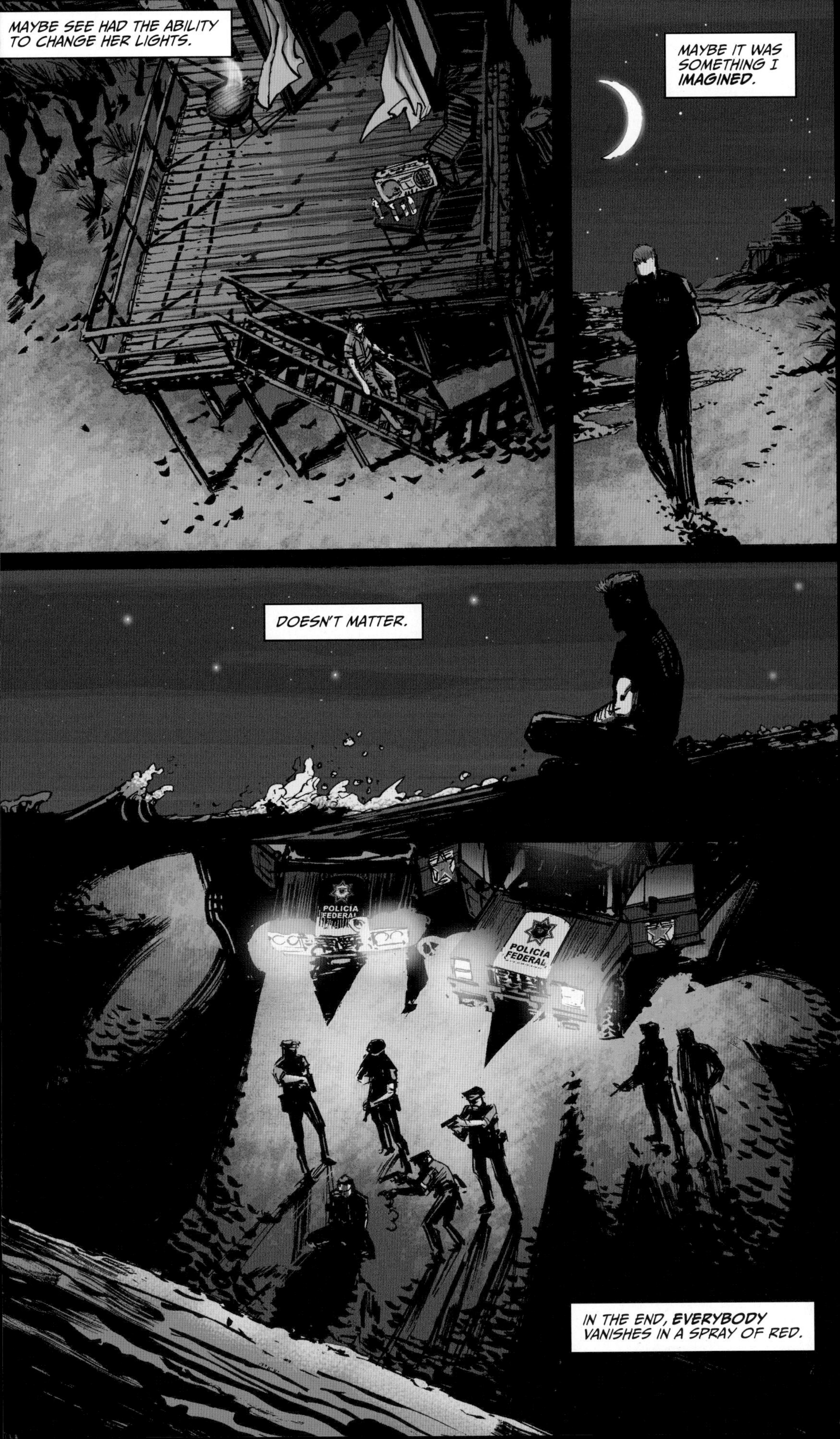
MAYBE SEE HAD THE ABILITY TO CHANGE HER LIGHTS.
MAYBE IT WAS SOMETHING I **IMAGINED.**
DOESN'T MATTER.
POLICÍA FEDERAL
POLICÍA FEDERAL
IN THE END, **EVERYBODY** VANISHES IN A SPRAY OF RED.

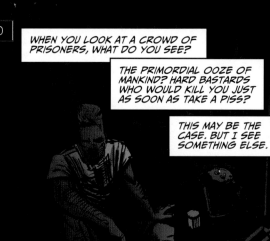

WHEN YOU LOOK AT A CROWD OF PRISONERS, WHAT DO YOU SEE?

THE PRIMORDIAL OOZE OF MANKIND? HARD BASTARDS WHO WOULD KILL YOU JUST AS SOON AS TAKE A PISS?

THIS MAY BE THE CASE. BUT I SEE SOMETHING ELSE.

I SEE THEIR *LIGHTS*.

WHICH MEANS I'M GOING TO RULE THEM ALL.

AND WHEN I GET OUT OF HERE SOMEDAY, THEY'RE GOING TO HELP ME RETURN A *CERTAIN LITTLE FAVOR*.

GO AHEAD. TELL ME I'M LYING.

The End

BONUS MATERIAL

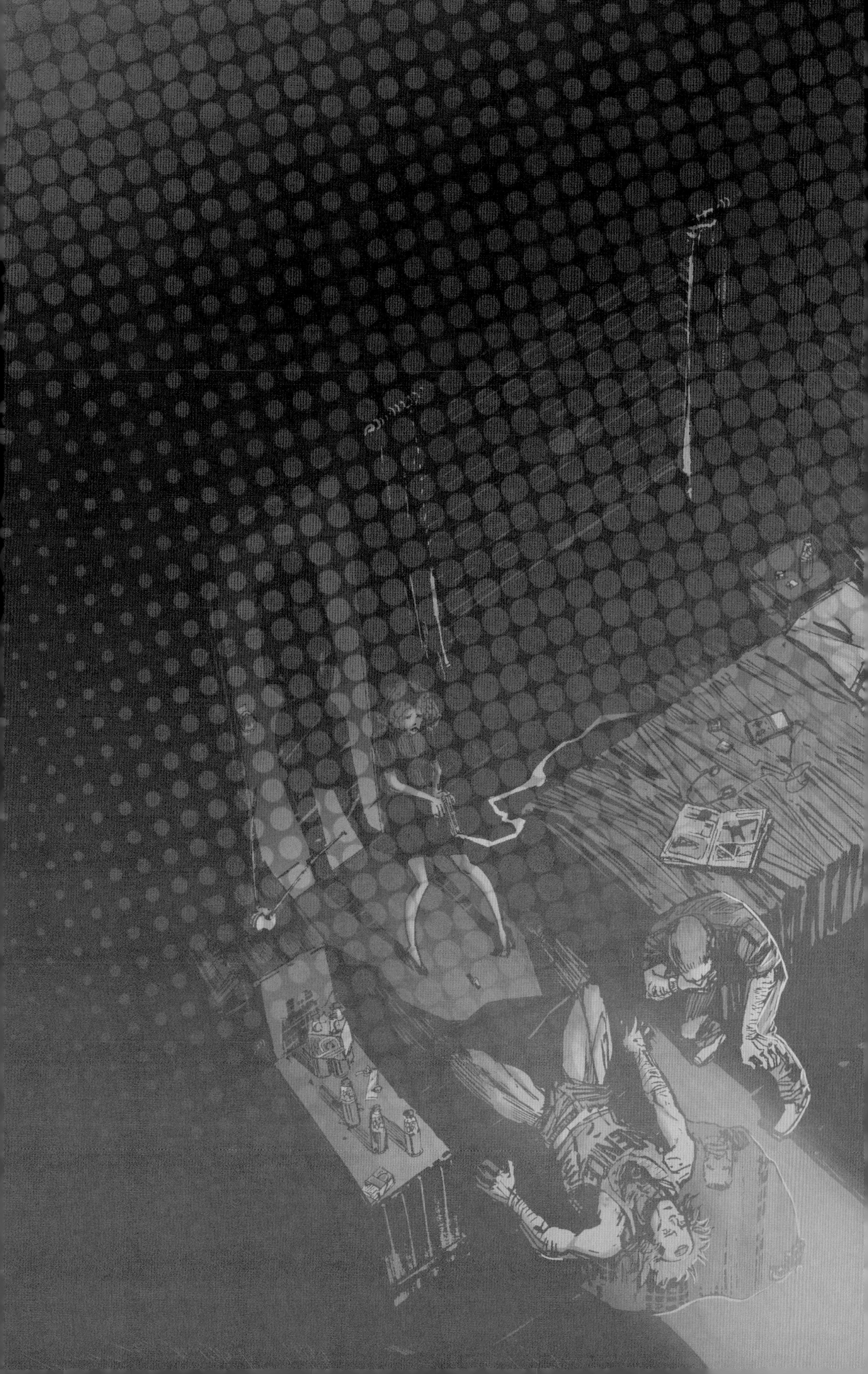

EX-CON #1

"Fading Lights"
By Duane Swierczynski
First Draft, 7-17-13

A note on the time period: This story is set in both 1984 and 1989. What I want to avoid, however, is kitschy glimpses of "Totally Awesome" 80s. No easy jokes, no lame pop culture references. Instead I want to evoke the moody L.A. noirscape of films like To Live and Die in L.A., Body Double, Repo Man, The Hidden and Less Than Zero.

PAGE ONE

1/ Establishing shot of the Malibu coastline as seen from the Pacific Ocean. Twinkling lights on the shore. The sun has just set, casting a warm red glow over everything in sight.

1 QUOTE CAP

"Psychics can see the color of time it's blue."

2 QUOTE CAP

-- Ronald Sukenick, Blown Away

2/ We push in closer to the coast, and see a mansion on a cliff with a party raging on the pool deck.

3 LOCATION CAP

Malibu

4 TIME CAP

December 1984

3/ Cut to inside that wild party, pool side, Malibu Colony. Lots of rich, beautiful types in mid-80s dress (shoulder pads, hair spray) indulging in booze, coke, music each other.

5 CAP (POMERAY)

When you look at a crowd like this, what do you see?

6 CAP (POMERAY)

The horror of unrestrained wealth? Celebrity train wrecks waiting to happen?

4/ CODY POMERAY is sipping a drink (club soda, lime) scanning the crowd. He's early 30s, rogueish, handsome. In a white linen suit, t-shirt, like he stepped out of a Michael Mann movie.

7 CAP (POMERAY)

This may be the case. But I see something else.

5/ Through his eyes, we see something strange: some of the guests have wavy, aura-like glows around their heads in varying colors: Red. Yellow. Pink. Green. Purple. Orange. Blue. (We'll learn the meanings of these colors throughout this issue.)

8 CAP (POMERAY)

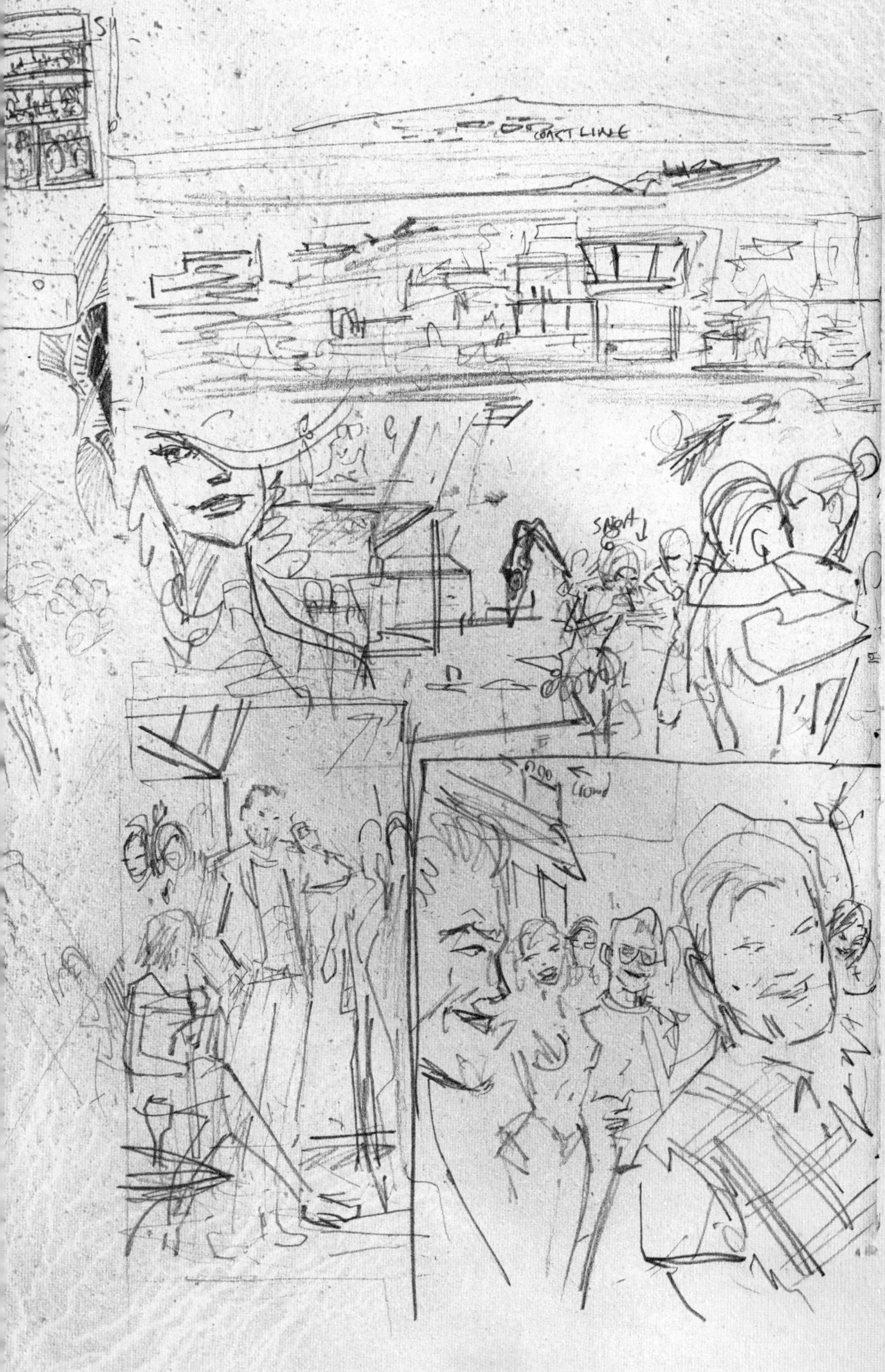
COAST LINE

Page 1 (Rough Pencils by Keith Burns)

I see their Lights.

PAGE TWO

1/ Pomeray cuts through the crowd. He's suave, handsome, with a sparkle in his eyes and just the right amount of stubble on his cheeks. Tasteful linen suit, shirt halfway buttoned. He's moving right towards a gorgeous blonde who has this soft-read aura around her head.

1 CAP (POMERAY)

It's not supernatural. I'm not psychic.

2 CAP (POMERAY)

The Lights just help me tell when a person is lying.

2/ Cut to a fat man snorting a line of coke the length and girth of a garden snake. There's a green aura around his head.

3 CAP (POMERAY)

Or greedy.

3/ Cut to a puffy-faced woman holding a martini. She smiles like she's calm and confident, but her pink aura says otherwise.

4 CAP (POMERAY)

Or jealous.

4/ Cut to a middle-aged blading producer-type who's had too much of everything. He looks strung out. Orange aura.

5 CAP (POMERAY)

Or weak.

5/ Cut to the blonde. She's gorgeous and lean, with a mischievous look in her eyes. Red aura -- blazing hot. This is SIERRA GRANDQUIST (a.k.a. "See"), Pomeray's girlfriend.

6 CAP (POMERAY)

Or wants to fuck my brains out.

6/ Sierra is smiling, taking Pomeray's hand. She starts to leads him behind the pool house. Pomeray's smiling like the devil.

7 CAP (POMERAY)

The Lights have served me well over the years.

8 POMERAY

Here? Why don't we just head home?

9 SEE

But then I wouldn't know what it's like to blow you behind a billionaire's pool house.

PAGE THREE

1/ Pomeray and See walk behind the pool house. She's still holding his hand, with Pomeray trailing behind. He's smiling, but now See has a troubled look on her face, despite what she's saying.

1 POMERAY

You already know. Two weeks ago? That TV guy's place up in Brentwood?

2 SEE

Are you actually trying to talk me out of this?

3 POMERAY

No, sweetie. Just striving for factual accur-

2/ Tight on Pomeray's face, which is now bathed in flashed red lights. This isn't his aura, though. The lights are real...

4 POMERAY

What the fuck...?

5 CAP (POMERAY)

Yeah, the Lights served me well.

3/ See steps aside, head down, ashamed to be looking at Pomeray. Pomeray puts his hands up. She's walked him right into a police sting. Flashing cherries, LAPD uniformed cops with guns drawn, the whole nine.

6 CAP (POMERAY)

Right up until the moment they didn't.

7 T&C

Ex-Con: Fading Lights

8 T&C

Writer: Swierczynski. Artist: TBD. Editor: Rybrandt.

PAGE FOUR

1/ Pomeray is cuffed perp-walked back through the party.

1 CAP (POMERAY)

My name is Cody Pomeray.

2 CAP (POMERAY)

At least that's what I've been calling myself over the past two years I've been in L.A.

3 CAP (POMERAY)

(I nicked the name from a beat novel I read while hitching my way west from Ohio.)

2/ From Pomeray's POV: the crowd of party-goers as he's marched past them. Some are gloating and have purple auras. Some are afraid, and have dark gray auras.

4 CAP (POMERAY)

Go ahead, take a good hard look, assholes.

5 CAP (POMERAY)

All of you fuckers wanted to be my best buddies just a few minutes ago.

3/ Pomeray's POV: a new set of Malibu faces. Some in purple, some in dark gray, but some in red --

some ladies still want to fuck him.

6 CAP (POMERAY)

I inhabited in your world because I knew how to act, what to say, what to wear, what to order, when to push, when to pull back.

4/ Cut to Pomeray in the back of an LAPD squad car. Staring out at us through the glass, angry look on his face. Like a hurt little boy.

7 CAP (POMERAY)

If you could only see your faces now.

PAGE FIVE

1/ Flashback: a 13-year-old Pomeray sitting in an opthamologist's chair as DR. DUNOFF uses a penlight to examine Pomeray's eyes. The office is all browns, yellows and oranges.

1 LOC/TIME CAP

Cleveland. 1974.

2 CAP (POMERAY)

I was 13 when I started seeing the Lights. My pop assumed I was jacking off so much I was going blind.

3 CAP (POMERAY)

But the eye doc had a slightly more scientific explanation.

4 DUNOFF

I want to try something.

2/ Flashback, from Pomeray's POV: On Dr. Dunoff as he leans forward into our (Pomeray's) face. Dunoff has a bold blue aura.

5 DUNOFF

My-name-is-Lance-Dunoff. I-am-an- opthamologist. I-am-married.

6 DUNOFF

Okay, what color am I?

7 POMERAY

Um... blue?

8 DUNOFF

And your father?

3/ Flashback, from Pomeray's POV: Cut to Pomeray's father. Fat. Pale. Sweaty. Bathed in a sickly yellow glow.

9 POMERAY'S FATHER

I don't have money for no surgery, doc.

10 POMERAY (O.S.)

Yellow.

11 DUNOFF (O.S.)

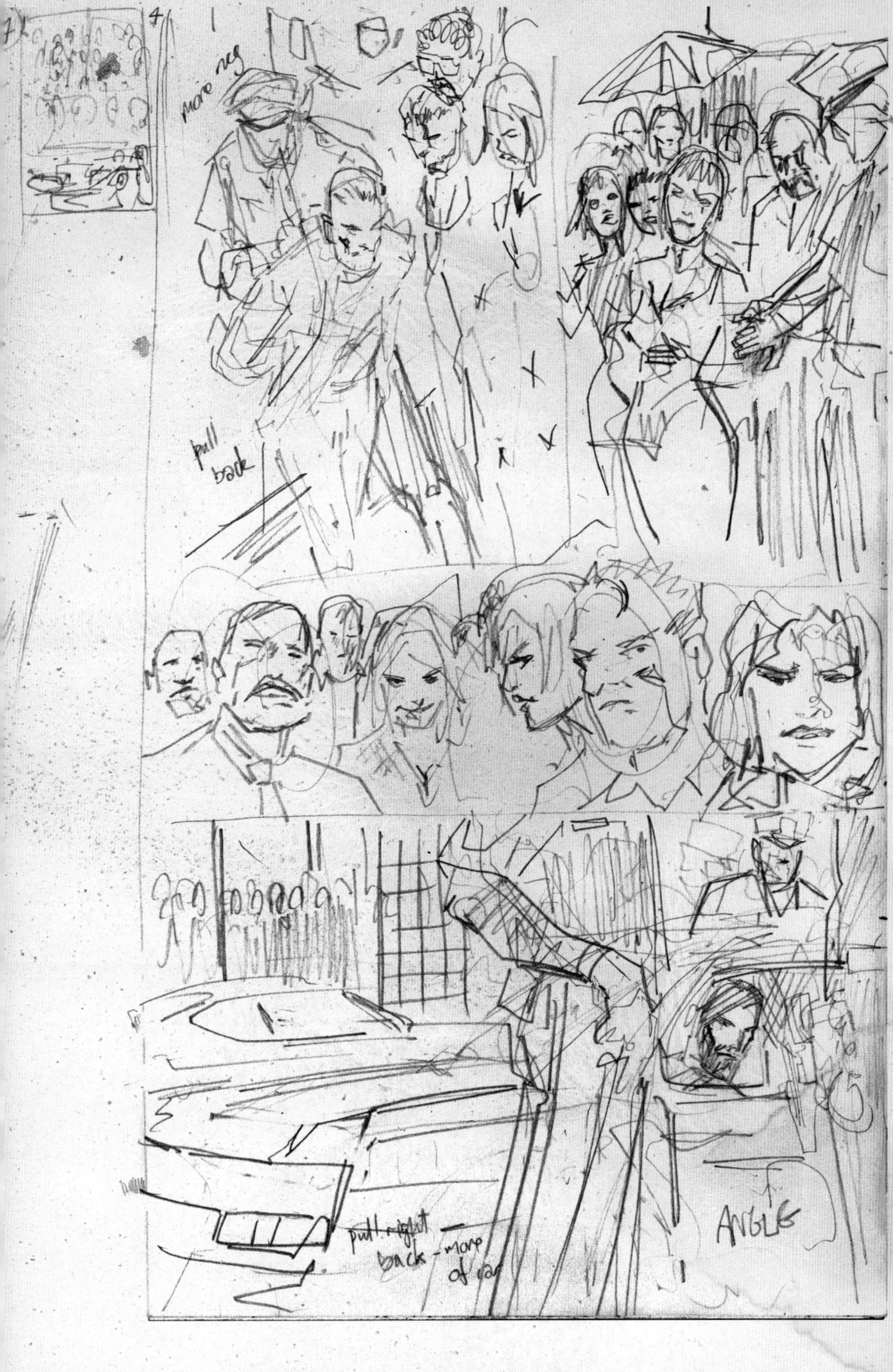
more neg
pull back
pull right back - more of car
ANGLE

Page 4 (Rough Pencils by Keith Burns)

Interesting.

4/ Flashback: A few beats later. Dunoff is in his office, explaining to Pomeray and his father.

12 DUNOFF

I believe this is a case of color synesthesia -- thought to be the result of increased grey matter in the left caudal intraparietal sulcus...

13 POMERAY'S FATHER

Whoah... what? Does he have a goddamned tumor?

5/ Flashback: Cut to the young POMERAY as a light bulb goes off in his head.

14 DUNOFF (O.S.)

No, no. There's nothing wrong with your son. His perception of human beings is involuntarily linked to colors.

15 CAP (POMERAY)

Mom, before she died, was orange.

6/ Flashback: Back to the same POV as panel 4. Now, however, the Pomeray's father has a faint orange glow.

16 CAP (POMERAY)

Orange always meant weak.

17 POMERAY'S FATHER

So he's going to be a freak all his life?

PAGE SIX

Note: All four panels on this page will be from Pomeray's POV as we flash through four key moments in his life.

1/ Pomeray's POV: We reach forward to unbutton a girl's shirt. Her body bathed in a soft, red glow.

1 CAP (POMERAY)

Red meant lust. Despite what a person was saying.

2 GIRL

No, don't... really...

2/ Pomeray's POV: We shove Pomeray's dad up against the wall. He's drunk and crying and bathed in yellow (which denotes a lie).

3 CAP (POMERAY)

Yellow was a lie.

4 POMERAY'S FATHER

The social security check didn't come yet! I swear!

3/ Pomeray's POV: We stick a pistol in a counterman's face. The counterman has a dark gray aura around him -- meaning he's terrified.

5 CAP (POMERAY)

Dark grey meant fear.

6 COUNTERMAN

Take whatever you want!

4/ Pomeray's POV: We shake the hands of a slick guy in an expensive suit -- he's bathed in a green glow (greed).

7 CAP (POMERAY)

Green was always greed, and I loved that color the most.

8 CAP (POMERAY)

I could tell who would let me into their lives because they thought they could use me.

9 CAP (POMERAY)

The Lights were a gift -- and I used the motherfucking shit out of that gift.

PAGE SEVEN

1/ Back to the present. From Pomeray's POV, looking up at a LEAD DETECTIVE and his SECOND in a dingy interrogation room in LAPD's Major Crime Unit. Both have vague, purplish glows, which means they're on the attack.

1 TIME CAP

Now

2 CAP (POMERAY)

Until they brought me here.

3 LEAD DETECTIVE

We dug up your real name, asshole.

4 SECOND DETECTIVE

Yeah, Leroy. Hell, I would have changed it, too.

5 LEAD DETECTIVE

You know what you did, Leroy? You picked the wrong mark.

2/ Surveillance cam POV to see Pomeray shackled to the table. Lead Detective paces while this second leans in, getting in Pomeray's face.

6 SECOND DETECTIVE

Only a pathetic fuck would think he could get one over on Budd Waldo.

7 LEAD DETECTIVE

You even know the kind of connections Waldo has overseas? I'm talking some serious French Connection shit, here.

3/ Tight on Pomeray and the Lead Detective.

8 LEAD DETECTIVE

You listening, Leroy?

9 POMERAY

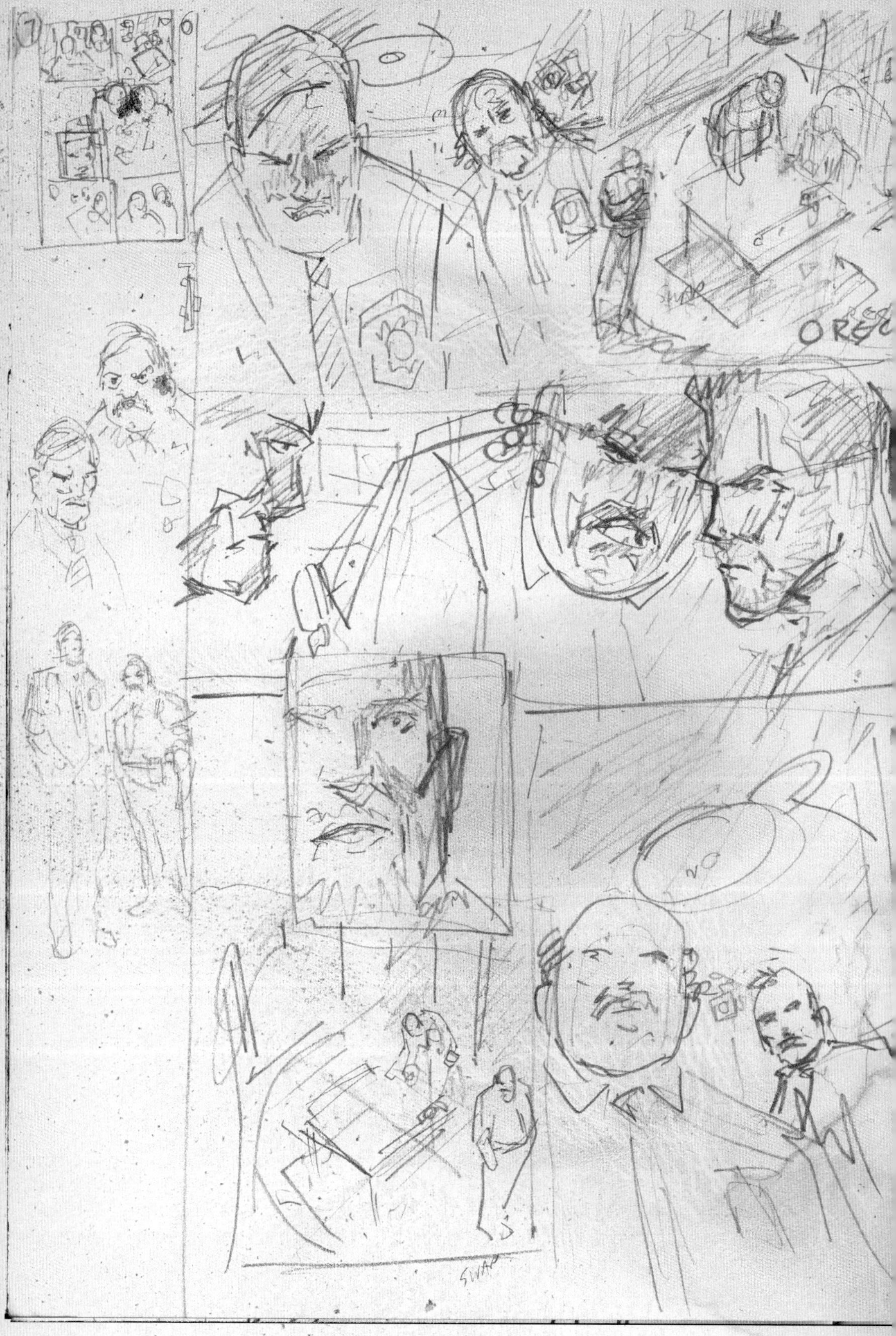

Page 7 (Rough Pencils by Keith Burns)

Again, I'd like my lawyer.

4/ Tight on Pomeray. His cool exterior is broken, and his mouth opens slightly in shock.

10 LEAD DETECTIVE (O.S.)

A lawyer ain't going to be worth shit now that Waldo's put a price on your head.

5/ Cut back to the same POV as panel 2, only now the Lead Detective is the one in Pomeray's face while his partner smirks and paces.

11 CAP (POMERAY)

The detectives gave me a choice: end up a badly-abused corpse buried the foundation of a Hollywood condo...

12 CAP (POMERAY)

Or confess now and do five in a country-club slammer.

6/ From Pomeray's POV looks at the detectives. Their auras are now bright blue.

13 CAP (POMERAY)

Bitch of it was... they were telling the truth.

PAGE EIGHT

1/ Courtroom. A stern, buzz-cut judge on the bench delivers a sentence as he smacks the gavel onto his desk.

1 CAP (POMERAY)

Up to a point.

2 JUDGE

... herby remand you to no less than five years at San Quentin...

2/ Cut to a stunned look on Pomeray's face as stands to confront his lawyer, a shifty-eye looking guy named MARC RESNICK.

3 POMERAY

San Quentin!? What the fuck, Resnick? You told me I'd be getting five years at CMC!

4 CAP (POMERAY)

CMC: the California Men's Colony, near San Luis Obispo. Known as the "Country Club of California Prisons."

5 RESNICK

I'll take of this, Cody.

3/ Cut to Pomeray, in an orange jumpsuit and shackled to other prisoners, mostly Latino, shuffling towards the intake room at San Quentin.

6 CAP (POMERAY)

Resnick did not take care of it.

7 CAP (POMERAY)

Later I learned that Waldo was tight with the sentencing judge. And the fat price on my head remained payable to any thug willing to jam a sharpened toothbrush into my spleen.

8 CAP (POMERAY)

Budd Waldo sent me to the Big Q to die.

4/ Through Pomeray's POV as he (we) walk through general population. More than half of the men in here have purple auras around them. (Purple = people with violence on their minds.) All of them predators. We notice one serial killer-looking convict, wearing thick glasses, lingering close to Pomeray, not making eye contact with him.

9 CAP (POMERAY)

I told myself the Lights would see me through this fucking nightmare. Help me spot the predators from the potential allies.

10 CAP (POMERAY)

Just like always.

5/ Cut to a non-Pomeray POV. (No auras, since we're not in his POV.)Pomeray is cold-cocked by the nerdy-looking prisoner. Blood spurts out of Pomeray's mouth.

11 CAP (POMERAY)

I was wrong about that, too.

PAGE NINE

The first three panels on this page will be shown from Pomeray's POV.

1/ Pomeray (we) look up as a crowd of snarling prisoners move forward. This is 1984, so the hairstyles should reflect that. The purple auras are strong and bright.

2/ Same POV, only now one of the prisoners has his hands around our throat and another is pulling back a bloodied fist. The purple auras as fading.

3/ Same POV, with different prisoners throwing punches at us. Our vision is hazy. The purple auras as almost gone.

4/ Cut to a non-Pomeray POV to see the same gang of prisoners pounding the crap out of Pomeray.

1 THE POPE (O.S.)

ENOUGH.

2 CAP (POMERAY)

I would have died right there, six hours into my sentence, if not for him.

PAGE TEN

1/ Cut to THE POPE, surrounded by five burly prisoners. They all look clean-cut and athletic, as if they're an 80s frat boy prison gang, in stark contrast to the grubby attackers. The Pope himself is zen and gawky, in a stoned Willem Dafoe kind of way. He doesn't wear traditional prison garb; instead, it's a pristine white robe, like he's an exiled Russian prince or something.

1 CAP (POMERAY)

His given name was Barnaby Creed.

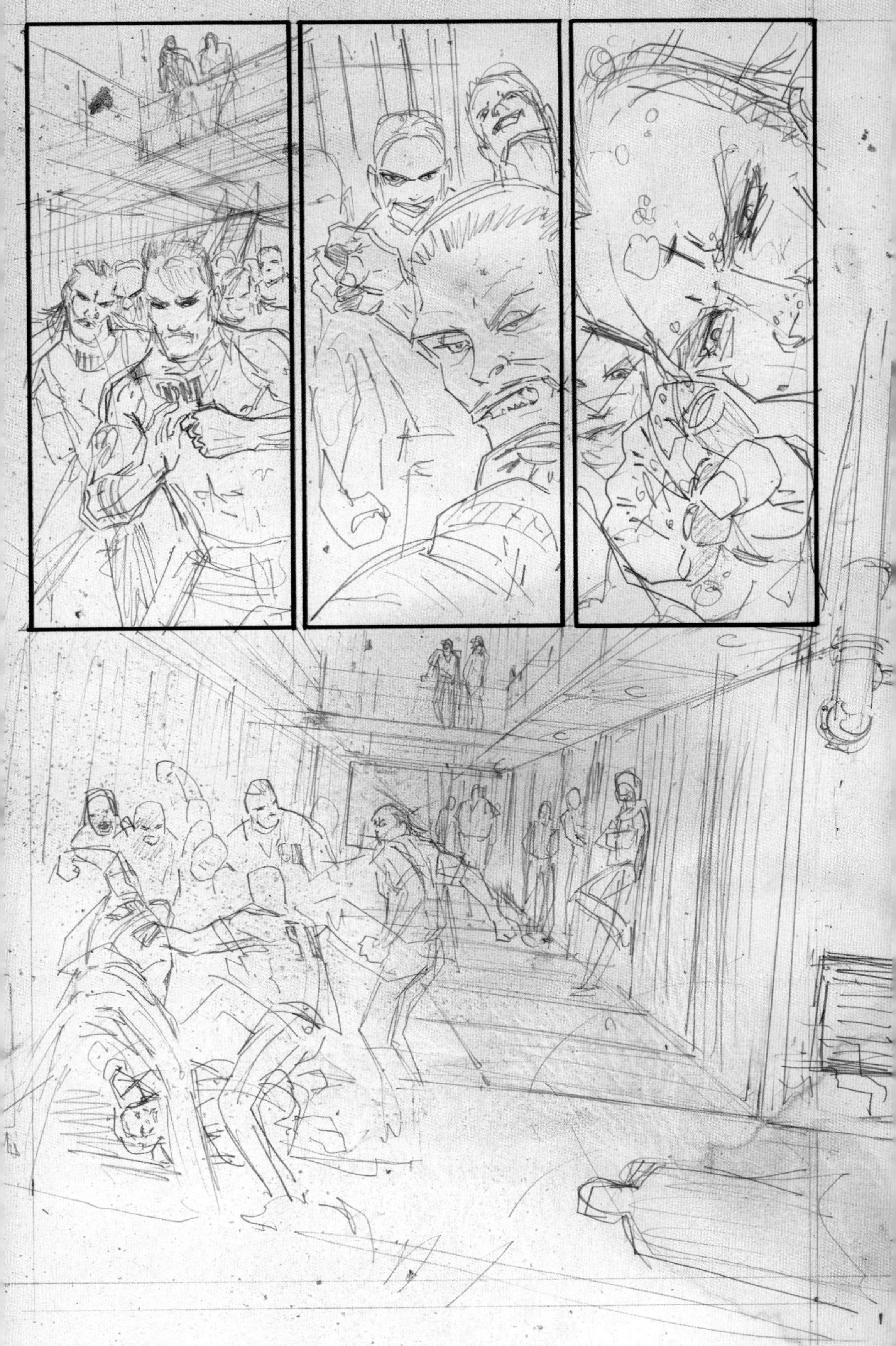

Page 9 (Tight Pencils by Keith Burns)

2 THE POPE

We'll take it from here, vatos.

2/ On the gang of attackers. A VATOS LEADER steps forward.

3 VATOS LEADER

This ain't none of your fuckin' business, Barnaby.

4 VATOS LEADER

Pretty boy's ours!

3/ On the Pope. Smirking.

5 CAP (POMERAY)

But here in Big Q, everyone knew him as The Pope.

6 THE POPE

Heh heh. You're actually defying me.

7 THE POPE

Gentlemen, please cave in their fucking heads.

4/ A frozen, silent moment of a brutal jail fight as The Pope's men attack the Latino assassins with shivs, lengths of pipe and even brass knucks.

No text--I don't want to do any SFX in this series.

5/ A few beats later. The assassins are dead or dying on the floor. The Pope steps through the bodies, the hem of his robe brushing up against the blood-splattered men.

8 THE POPE

Take him to the infirmary. And set up a meeting with the warden.

PAGE ELEVEN

1/ Cut to the infirmary. It's night. Pomeray's eyes open in a sudden panic.

1 THE POPE (O.S.)

Finally awake?

2 POMERAY

Stay the f-fuck away from m-me!

2/ On the Pope and Pomeray, shrouded in darkness. The Pope is standing in the doorway.

3 THE POPE

Relax. I'm a fan, Mr. Pomeray. Especially when I heard how you set up poor Budd Waldo.

3/ On the Pope. Smiling.

4 THE POPE

Anyone who takes a shot at that porcine prick is okay with me.

5 THE POPE

So I'm willing to grant you protection within these walls in exchange for one thing...

4/ On Pomeray. Wary.

6 POMERAY

I'm not like that.

5/ From Pomeray's POV as he looks at Pope, trying to read his Lights. There's nothing. Not even the faintest glimmer of an aura.

7 THE POPE

Heh heh.

8 THE POPE

No. I want a simple favor, of a non-sexual nature, upon your release in five years' time.

9 CAP (POMERAY)

My mind skips over the word favor. I don't even hear the words five years' time.

10 CAP (POMERAY)

Instead I wonder why I can't see this man's Lights.

6/ On the Pope. Growing impatient.

11 THE POPE

Well?

12 THE POPE

This offer expires the moment I leave this room. You can take your chances back out on the yard.

7/ Pomeray looks utterly defeated.

13 CAP (POMERAY)

What could I say?

14 CAP (POMERAY)

Was this even a choice?

PAGE TWELVE

1/ Establishing shot of a prisoner transport ferry headed away from San Quentin.

1 TIME CAP

Five years later

2/ An older, rougher-looking Cody Pomeray steps off the prisoner transport ferry. He's squinting in the sun, as if the world's too bright for him now.

2 CAP (POMERAY)

The eighties are almost over. I'm sprung just in time to catch the last of it.

3/ From a POV over Pomeray's shoulder as he sees a 1989 Lincoln Town Car waiting for him, complete with uniformed DRIVER holding a cardboard sign with Pomeray's name on it.

3 CAP (POMERAY)

And already, the outside world confuses me.

4 DRIVER

Mr. Pomeray?

5 DRIVER

We've got a six-hour drive ahead of us. There's some vodka, gin and mixers in the back.

4/ The Driver holds open a door for Pomeray. Pomeray hesitates before stepping inside.

6 POMERAY

Hold on. Who sent you?

7 DRIVER

Make yourself comfortable.

8 CAP (POMERAY)

All I can think is that this is Barnaby Creed. Cashing in that favor right away.

PAGE THIRTEEN

1/ Cut to Pomeray in the back of the Town Car, nervously sipping a gin and tonic. He still has that prison body language -- drinking as if he's afraid someone's going to snatch away his drink at any moment. In stark contrast to the confident man we saw on page one.

1 CAP (POMERAY)

I've been obsessing over this favor every day for the past five years.

2 POMERAY

Come on, man. I got to know who sent me.

2/ Tight on the driver's eyes in the rear-view mirror.

3 DRIVER

Name on the invoice is Grandquist. Mean anything to you?

3/ Flashback 1984: a glimpse of the blonde we saw at the Malibu party five years ago: SIERRA GRANDQUIST. She's looking at us (Pomeray) with a slightly guilty look on her face. Still, that red aura of lust surrounds her body.

4 CAP (POMERAY)

It means a fuck of a lot.

5 CAP (POMERAY)

Sierra Grandquist. The woman who set me up.

4/ Flashback 1984: Pomeray and Sierra exchanging one last look at each other as a cop puts a hand on Pomeray's head, easing him into the backseat of the squad car.

6 CAP (POMERAY)

She liked to be called "See" instead of Sierra. Oh, if only I could have seen...

5/ Flashback 1984: Pomeray snorting coke off Sierra's taut belly.

7 CAP (POMERAY)

We were together for one high-flying booze-and-blow-fueled summer.

8 CAP (POMERAY)

She'd introduce me to targets. We'd pick them clean and move on to the next.

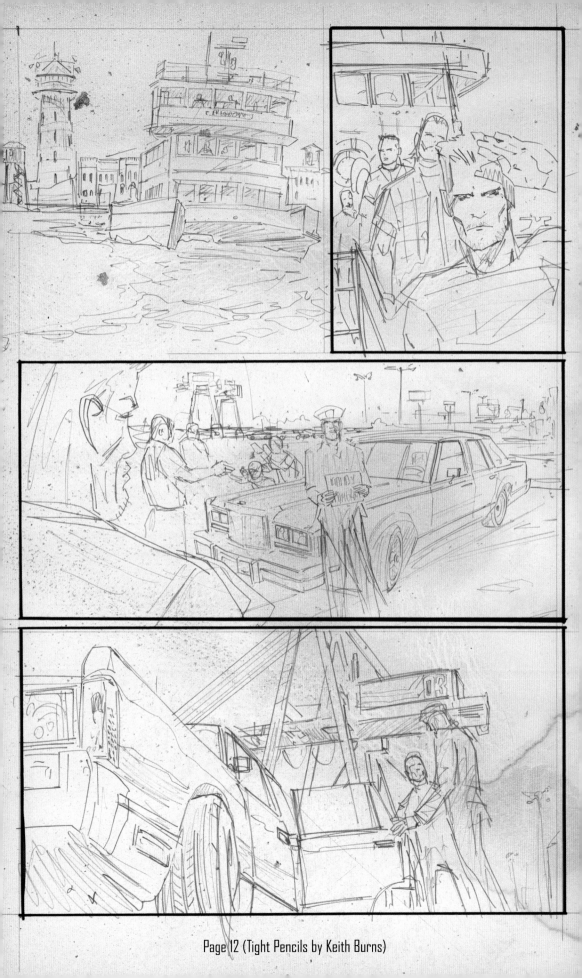

Page 12 (Tight Pencils by Keith Burns)

9 CAP (POMERAY)
Until I became her target.

PAGE FOURTEEN
1/ Back to the present. The Town Car zooms down the Hollywood Freeway. In the background we can see the skyline of downtown Los Angeles. Big panel.
Here's a shot of downtown L.A. is it appeared in 1989: http://www.panoramio.com/photo/19050700
1 CAP (DRIVER)
"Welcome back to L.A., Mr. Pomeray."
2/ Cut to Pomeray is in the backseat, sipping a gin and tonic. His fourth or fifth. He's not drunk, though!
He's brooding. In a dark place in his own head.
2 DRIVER
We'll be at the place in a few minutes.
3 POMERAY
Okay.
3/ Through Pomeray's window, we have a glimpse Sierra, five years older and even more glamorous-looking, standing outside lobby of a downtown L.A. skyscraper that's still under construction.
4 CAP (POMERAY)
Fuck, it really is her.
5 CAP (POMERAY)
For the record: 1989 is making no sense to me at all.

PAGE FIFTEEN
1/ See holds out her hand to shake it. Pomeray just stares at it.
1 SEE
I wasn't sure if you were going to show.
2 SEE
I know you have your first meeting with your P.O., but don't worry -- we'll get you there on time.
2/ See leads him through the unfinished lobby towards the elevator bank.
3 SEE
You're not even going to ask me where we're going?
4 POMERAY
Does it even matter?
3/ They step into the elevator.
5 CAP (POMERAY)
I'm not talking because I'm too busy trying to read her.

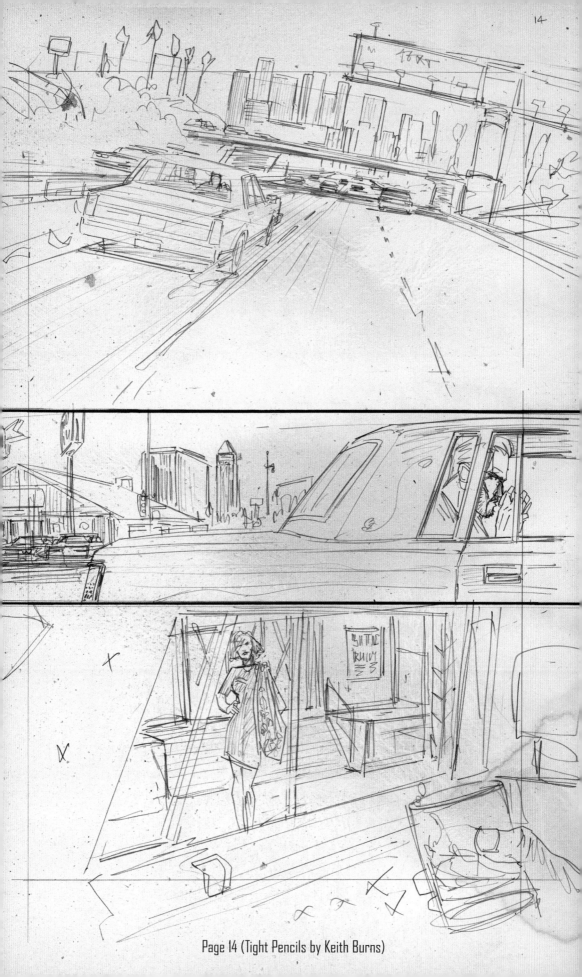

Page 14 (Tight Pencils by Keith Burns)

6 CAP (POMERAY)

But nothing. Just like it's been nothing for the past five years. Thought with See it would have been different. Maybe kick-start something...

4/ In the elevator. Sierra looks over at Pomeray. Pomeray stares at a wall.

7 CAP

Which is the only reason I climbed into the back of that car.

8 SEE

Look, Cody, I'm glad you came. I was a different person back then, really messed up and the cops had me in a corner and-

9 POMERAY

And I really don't give a shit, See.

5/ Same POV. Sierra goes cold.

10 SEE

I can smell the Seagram's oozing out of your pores.

11 SEE

You need to be more careful with that. Peter won't like it.

12 POMERAY

Fuck Peter. Whoever he is.

PAGE SIXTEEN

1/ Cut to a ceiling fire sprinkler POV oft the half-finished office of high-rolling investor PETER WOJTYLA. 50s. Fit but not handsome. His massive oak desk sits in the middle of a virtual construction site, with missing walls, exposed beams, work buckets on the bare floor. There's an electric typewriter on his desk along with a land line phone and lots of manila folders and pencils. There are no chairs, forcing everyone to stand around the desk.

1 CAP (POMERAY)

That would be Peter Wojtyla, real estate developer.

2 CAP (POMERAY)

At least that's what it said on the business card I nicked from his desk.

2/ Pomeray's POV: on Wojtyla. No aura around him at all. He's not even making eye contact with us. See looks at him, nervous body language, like an assistant.

3 WOJTYLA

Did you brief him, Sierra?

4 SEE

No, I thought you wanted to be the one wh-

5 WOJTYLA

Go ahead, go ahead.

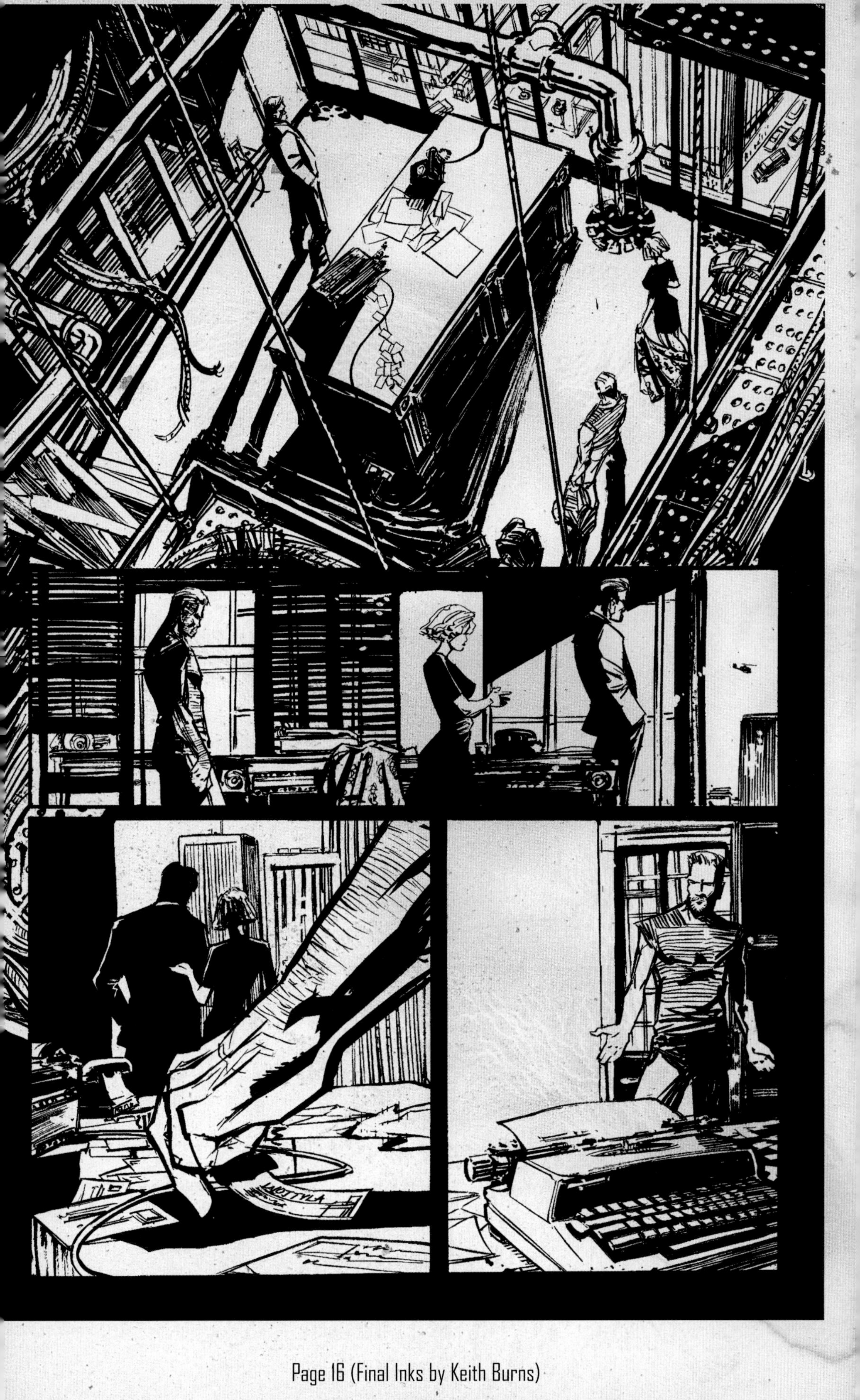

Page 16 (Final Inks by Keith Burns)

3/ As See explains the job, Pomeray nicks a business card from Wojtyla's desk while the man himself has his back turned.

6 SEE

Peter is in the process of acquiring several properties in the Venice Beach area.

7 SEE

Someone's been setting them on fire right after he finalizes the deal.

8 WOJTYLA

And your job is to find out who.

4/ Pomeray takes a step back, perplexed.

9 POMERAY

My job?

10 POMERAY Do I look like a private detective to you?

PAGE SEVENTEEN

1/ On Wojtyla as he turns back around. Distasteful look on his face.

1 WOJTYLA

I don't care what you are. I need you to find this-

2 SEE (O.S.)

Hang on Peter, let me-

2/ New angle as Wojtyla glances over at See.

3 WOJTYLA

I thought you said he could do this.

4 SEE

Of course he can. Like I told you, Cody is skilled at traveling in any social circle.

3/ Pomeray smirks a little as listens to See.

5 SEE

The fact that he survived five years at San Quentin means he was able to do the same with the criminal element.

6 CAP (POMERAY)

I listen to See as she spins her bullshit.

7 CAP (POMERAY)

I wonder if that cocktail lounge on wheels is still parked outside. I'm going to need a ride to my halfway house.

4/ On Wojtyla. Impatient.

8 WOJTYLA

Fine, fine. I'm sure your contacts will help you uncover this little prick and his matchbook.

9 WOJTYLA

You'll report to Sierra. She'll make the arrangements.

5/ See escorts Pomeray out to the hallway, towards the elevator bank.

10 POMERAY

Nice catching up with you, See.

11 POMERAY

Please tell Peter to go fuck himself.

PAGE EIGHTEEN

1/ Pomeray walks away from See. Finally, she loses her composure. Starts screaming at him.

1 SEE

This is my way of making things up to you, you stupid prick!

2/ From Pomeray's POV: See, staring back at us. But something disturbing now: her face is blurred to the point of being almost blank. We can't see any features at all.

2 SEE

Can't you see that?

3 CAP (POMERAY)

Honestly? I can't see much of anything.

3/ Cut to Pomeray at a pay phone in downtown L.A.

4 CAP (POMERAY)

I call in, like I'm supposed to. I have to explain that a friend gave me a ride and it took a little longer than I thought.

5 CAP (POMERAY)

(I omit the fact that I've had three more G and Ts.)

4/ Cut to Pomeray walking up the front steps to his crummy halfway house in Boyle Heights. Siding is falling off the sides of the hosue; the front lawn is overgrown and trash-strewn.

6 LOCATION CAP

Boyle Heights

7 CAP (POMERAY)

They tell me my P.O. is already waiting for me at the halfway house.

8 CAP (POMERAY) Some dude named Alex Quemando. Probably a hard-ass.

PAGE NINETEEN

1/ Cut to inside as Pomeray steps into a shitty studio apartment. ALEX QUEMANDO -- late 20s, Latino, tomboyish and pretty -- is sitting in an ancient easy chair, legs crossed, smoking a cigarette.

1 QUEMANDO

You Pomeray?

2 QUEMANDO

Of course you are. You've got that twitchy, squinty look of freshly-sprung meat.

3 POMERAY

You're Quemando?

2/ Quemando crosses the room to shake Pomeray's hand.

4 QUEMANDO

I am. And considering we've got a date every day for the next 120, pretty boy...

5 QUEMANDO

You can call me Alex.

3/ Pomeray steps back and watches as Quemando looks around the room, as if looking for hidden con-
traband, despite the fact that Pomeray has never set foot in the place.

6 POMERAY

I didn't expect... you here so soon.

7 QUEMANDO

Two of my other ex-cons are your housemates. But don't be jealous.

4/ New angle as Quemando puts a hand on Pomeray's forearm.

8 QUEMANDO

We start looking for jobs tomorrow.

9 CAP (POMERAY)

I don't tell my new pal "Alex" that I've already been offered a gig.

5/ On Quemando. Smiling, with a little tenderness in her eyes.

10 QUEMANDO

Hey, don't worry. I've got a lot of people willing to give an ex-con a shot.

PAGE TWENTY

1/ That night, Pomeray sits in the same busted easy chair, drinking, pondering his sad-ass situation.

1 CAP (POMERAY)

"Ex-con."

2 CAP (POMERAY)

The word didn't sink in until just this moment.

3 CAP (POMERAY)

Truth is I'm an ex-everything. I spent my life struggling to expand my options, and now they're all collapsing around me.

2/ New angle as Pomeray hears a noise, snaps his head to the right.

4 CAP (POMERAY)

Never mind that favor I owe to a killer..

3/ Pomeray's POV: A faceless woman peering through the screen door at him. We can see every other detail expect the facial features.

5 FACELESS WOMAN

... Cody?

4/ Cut back to Pomeray drops his drink and stands up, ready to fight. Body tense.

6 POMERAY

Who are you? You can't be here!

5/ Pomeray creeps towards the screen door we see that it's Sierra.

7 SEE

What the fuck is wrong with you?

6/ Pomeray's POV: on Sierra. We can see her features again.

8 SEE

You going to let me in or what?

PAGE TWENTY-ONE

1/ Pomeray and Sierra sit nex to each other on his busted-ass houndstooth couch.

1 POMERAY

Look, I really can't do anything for you. I've got this seriously over-enthusiastic P-

2/ Same POV, only now Sierra turns and smashes her lips into Pomeray's.

2 POMERAY

Oh.

3/ Cut to a few beats later. Pomeray and Sierra are on the floor, fucking.

4/ Pomeray's POV: a flash as we look up to see See's face has disappeared.

5/ Reverse angle to see Pomeray's slightly frightened reaction.

6/ Afterward, on the floor, in the afterglow of white-hot fucking, Pomeray and See stare up at us on the ceiling.

3 SEE

I can help you with that parole officer.

4 POMERAY

I don't know the first thing about finding an arsonist.

7/ On Pomeray.

5 POMERAY

So I'm going to tell your boss or whatever I can't do it.

6 POMERAY

My P.O.'s taking me to find a straight job, and after that-

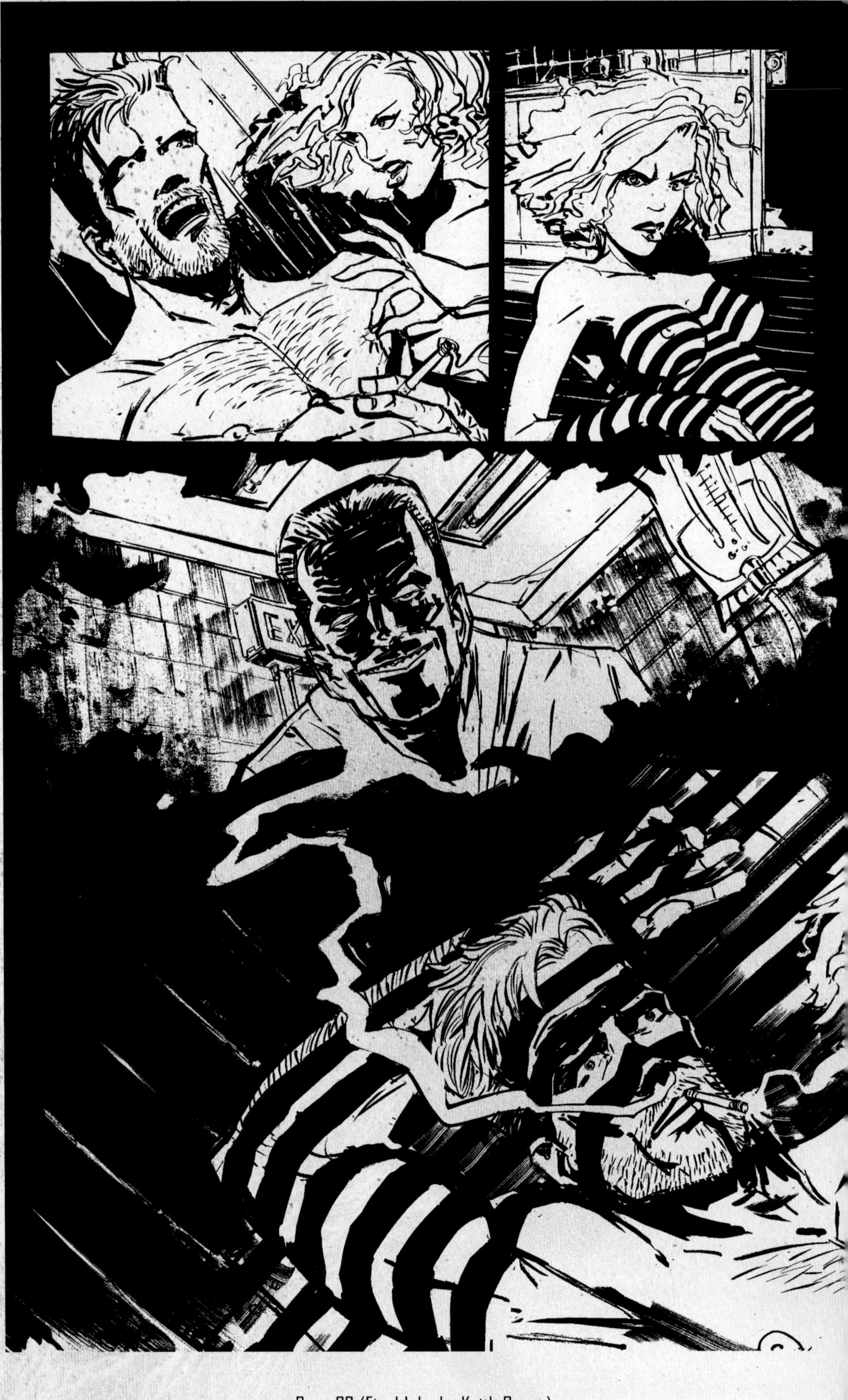
EX

Page 22 (Final Inks by Keith Burns)

PAGE TWENTY-TWO

1/ New angle as See pinches one of Pomeray's nipples -- hard.

1 SEE

Cody, you have to take the job.

2 POMERAY

Ow!

3 POMERAY

No, I fucking don't.

2/ On See as she leans up on one elbow. Serious as a heart attack.

4 SEE

Yes, you do. Otherwise, the Pope won't be very happy with you.

3/ Flashback: the Pope. Five years ago. Grinning down at us (Pomeray) looking up from our infirmary bed.

5 CAP (POMERAY)

Though my ability seems to be gone for good...

4/ Ceiling POV as we go back to Pomeray, lying on teh floor, staring up at us, smoke curling from his nostrils and mouth, a look of utter resignation on his face.

6 CAP (POMERAY)

... finally, I see the light.

7 CAP

To be continued...

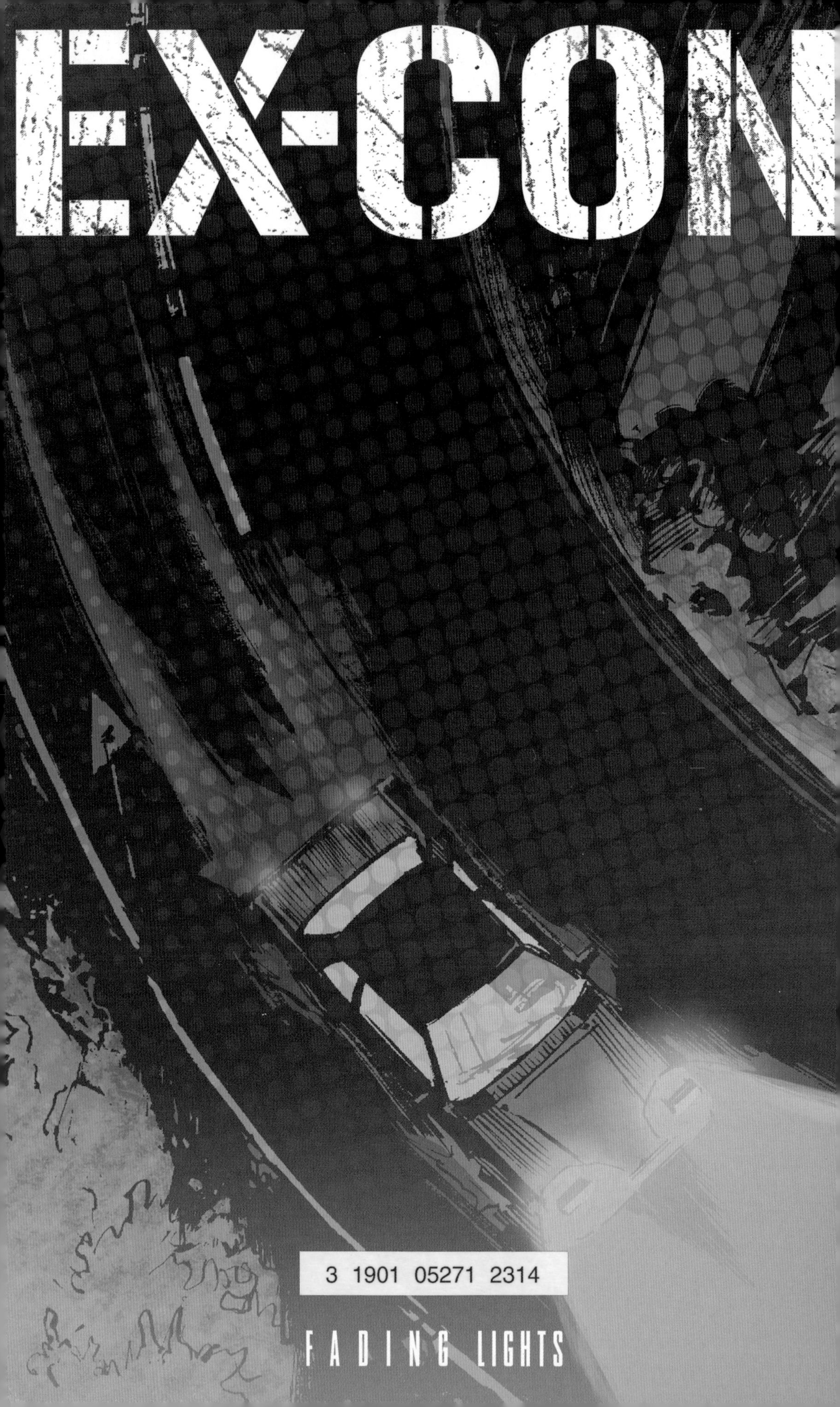
EX-CON
FADING LIGHTS